Windows Speech Recognition Programming

Speech Software Technical Professionals Series

Windows Speech Recognition Programming

With Visual Basic and ActiveX Voice Controls

Exploring Speech API (SAPI) & Software Developer Kit (SDK) for Voice Input & Output Enabling of Windows Applications

by
Keith A. Jones, Ph.D.

iUniverse, Inc.
New York   Lincoln   Shanghai

Windows Speech Recognition Programming
With Visual Basic and ActiveX Voice Controls

iUniverse, Inc.

For information address:
iUniverse, Inc.
2021 Pine Lake Road, Suite 100
Lincoln, NE 68512
www.iuniverse.com

ISBN: 0-595-30843-0

Printed in the United States of America

To my wife Elena and baby daughter Emelena,
who first made it impossible for me to finish this book;
then later made it impossible not to.

Contents

List of Figures

Sample Code Listings

Introduction

This is an unusual little computer book that meets an unusual technology information need. It is written to address several audiences, and it should serve both as a solid introduction to speech recognition programming for beginning Windows Visual Basic and Speech API (SAPI) programmers, as well as a detailed reference for advanced Windows speech application programmers. It is even more unique because it is written almost entirely based on coding examples from Microsoft SAPI 4.0, yet published at a time shortly after the new version of SAPI 5.0 was released.

Although it may sound very unusual indeed to publish a book with examples for a previous version, in this case it is appropriate to include coding samples from both SAPI version 4.0 and 5.0 SDKs. The "Version" number is a bit misleading, since SAPI 5.0 is not really a new version as much as "Extensions" to SAPI 4.0, and as such it probably could just as easily have been released as "SAPI 4.1".

This latest new release of SAPI in 2003 was long awaited, since SAPI 4.0 dates all the way back to 1998, and 5 years is a long time to wait for a new release of a critical emerging technology. But Microsoft had 2 major Windows operating systems (ME and XP) within this span of time, so Microsoft apparently decided Version 5.0 was a good way to make the point a lot happened in that time.

But aside from the fact a lot went on at Microsoft in those 5 long years (and 5 years is a virtual lifetime in the computer technology industry!), a lot also happened in the speech software world. From IBM *ViaVoice*™ to Dragon Systems *NaturallySpeaking*™ to Lernout and Hauspie to ScanSoft, and back again to a "new" revived Microsoft, it was a long hard road for everyone in the speech technology industry. By the time SAPI 5.0 was finally released, the landscape was a diverse and multi-colored tapestry with a dozen new speech technology vendors and SDK toolsets.

In almost every case, speech vendor tools are based on SAPI 4.0, just as SAPI 5.0 is basically 4.0 add-ons. In fact, SAPI 5.0 is mostly automation and platform architecture enhancements to accommodate new Microsoft Visual Suite speech platforms and development standards for Microsoft SALT (Speech Application Language Tag) extensions to HTML and XML for dynamic web speech applications.

All high level functions from SAPI 4.0 are essentially unchanged, and can be used with SAPI 5.0. So the new SAPI 5.0 is not only upwardly compatible with SAPI 4.0, but is more efficient to leverage high level speech with same ActiveX voice controls and links to low level COM. But best news for Windows programmers is SAPI 5.0, just like 4.0, it *is still a free download.*

Yet as you can probably guess, even though SAPI 5.0 also may be freely downloaded, and is also provided with a wealth of free documentation—as with most freely downloaded Microsoft software libraries and documentation, it may be voluminous. But it is also not very easy to understand or follow—which is the main reason for this book. The official documentation from Microsoft for both versions of SAPI are extremely technical and difficult for any beginning programmer, or even for most advanced Windows speech application programmers, to easily understand and use to link high to low level functions.

Yet, there is a lot of gold in the nearly 50 Megabytes of SAPI 4.0 downloadable libraries, and this book seeks to help both beginning and advanced Windows programmer to quickly locate, review, and understand the very best SAPI 4.0 nuggets. Notably, the best nuggets of easily learned and adapted SAPI Visual Basic ActiveX speech controls are all located in the SAPI Version 4.0 downloads, and without this book, might be easily overlooked entirely.

This book is based on a revisions to materials explaining SAPI 4.0 using simple exercises from two earlier books by this author, the *Official Dragon NaturallySpeaking Programmer Guide* and *SAM's Teach-Yourself VB6 Speech Programming in 21 Days* not previous published in those books. Many programmers have contacted the author since those books went out of print requesting updated editions to those books.

Since many Windows speech programmers also have observed that SAPI 4.0 was easier to learn and apply than to start by jumping into SAPI 5.0—instead, an entirely new book spanning from SAPI 4.0 to 5.0 is written here by combining unused materials from both earlier books not previously published.

The author is currently working on a several new companion books in this series that will build upon foundations in this book in order to teach advanced SAPI 5.1 usage in Windows Virtual Suite speech programming for the web and for foreign language localization translations, and several other hot topics.

Thus, the author welcomes comments and suggestions from like-minded speech programming professionals with interesting applications, and can be contacted by visiting www.qualimatic.com.

Chapter One

Welcome to Windows Speech Recognition Programming

Speech software has been one of the hottest topics in the computer industry for as long as there have been computers. Computer speech is actually a technology that has been around in one form or another for over 30 years, but for the first 3 decades of computing, most speech software of the past has been possible to run only on very big, fast, and expensive computers hardware.

But thanks to Microsoft, the size or speed of your computer is no longer a major limitation to computer speech. Just like with so many other computer technologies, it took Microsoft to make speech software easy to program, and even easier for PC users to run speech software along with their other Windows applications. And with Windows Visual Basic ActiveX Voice Control Automation Services, complex computer speech synthesis, and even speech recognition, has become more accessible to all programmers for Rapid Speech Application Development (RSAD), regardless of whether the programmers skills are Basic, Intermediate, or Advanced.

Since 1996, the Microsoft Speech API (Application Programmer Interface) has made it possible for programmers to create powerful speech software using Visual C++, Visual J++, or Visual Basic.

But with the release of the Microsoft Speech SDK (Software Developer Kit) Version 4.0 in 1999, it is now also possible for even non-programmers and advanced Windows users to program speech. By writing simple Java scripts, HTML scripts, or Windows Office Suite macros for Word or Excel to develop powerful voice aware functions and add-ons for speech programs using ActiveX controls.

These new capabilities and functionality of Windows Speech Automation Services (WSAS) were enhanced in SAPI Versions 5.0 and 5.1 in 2002, and

1

expanded further with the introduction of Microsoft Speech Server dotNet platform in 2003.

This book will provide the reader with a detailed exploration of the underlying Windows Speech Automation Services via Visual Basic ActiveX and Voice Controls available in Microsoft Speech API Versions 4.0 to 5.1+. It will provide a good introduction to Microsoft Windows Speech Recognition Programming for beginning as well as advanced programmers.

In this chapter, you will learn about the following:

- A short introduction into the history of computer speech technology
- Your first look 'under the hood' of some Windows speech apps
- How Microsoft technology supports speech software technology on Windows
- Some basic information about the Microsoft Windows Speech API and Speech SDK Suite for rapid speech application development
- How to create and run your first simple Windows Speech API programs using Visual Basic with ActiveX and HTML web scripts

1.1   A Brief History of Computer Speech

Computer generated speech and speech recognition are concepts that were first introduced to the public as science fiction, on such TV shows as *Star Trek* and movies like *2001: Space Odyssey*. Computer speech was a concept that was understood long before the first real attempts to launch a human being into outer space. For a long time it was regarded as even more of a *'holy grail'* for scientists than even landing a spacecraft on the moon. But in fact the history of computer speech has always been closely related to the history of spaceflight.

The actual origins of modern computer speech technology originally began as part of NASA and Russian space race projects, yet were also focus of a lot of commercial 'think-tank' lab activity at places like AT&T Bell Labs, IBM Watson Labs, and Xerox Palo Alto Labs. These were all part of the original basis for some of the first talking computer games and related video games that introduced speech software to an entire generation of programmers, both on classroom computers and PCs sold by Apple.

It is impossible to confirm, or deny for that matter, but in all probability by far, the lion's share of all the first computer speech research was conducted in military labs. In fact, many dozens of secret military labs in both U.S. and former Soviet Union ('Russia', for the really young speech programmers among us).

This was a very different image of speech recognition programming that was far more ominous than the out-of-control speaking 'HAL' computer on the spaceship in the movie *2001*. For more than a decade the most vivid image of computer speech was an out-of-control talking military computer in the movie *War Games*, which tried to destroy the world with a pre-emptive all-out nuclear attack. And then there was the supposedly fictional voice-controlled Russian MIG fighter jet stolen by an American pilot in the movie *Foxfire*— which could easily mis-fire missiles at the wrong targets if voice commands were not spoken clearly or were even ill-conceived. Fortunately the world has changed a great deal since then, and both personal computers and the Internet have been a big part of making the world better for us all.

1.2   Microsoft Impact on the History of Computer Speech

Microsoft and Windows programming have been especially critical in making both the personal computer and access to the Internet more affordable and reliable, with the greatest number of computer users of any software platform in the world.

Speech programs generally involve either computer generated speech synthesis, or human speech with computer voice response, or both.

By the mid 1990's, the number of users of Microsoft Windows and Microsoft Internet browser standards had passed 100 million people worldwide. That number is still steadily growing, despite a lot of efforts by Microsoft competitors to slow the growth of Microsoft. But Windows is clearly here to stay.

After Microsoft had solidly established MS Windows as the dominant graphical user interface (GUI) operating system, and MS Internet Explorer as the world's leading web browser, one of the top priority projects of Microsoft R&D labs was speech software technology.

By 1995 Microsoft had already spent several years secretly developing its own speech technology that rivaled anything that the secret military and space labs had developed. In 1996, Microsoft began to release information to the press and public explaining its technical initiative and announcing each major new computer speech development.

1.3   Early Open Systems Speech Program Standards

It should not be a surprise that Microsoft was not the only major computer company that was working on speech software technology and speech programming standards from the early 1990's. Actually almost every major computer hardware company as well as most of the major software and database companies across all major platforms was working on speech software technology.

Back in 1991, the *Open Systems Architecture Speech Recognition Committee (OSASRC)* was founded by Novell, IBM, Intel, Panasonic, 3Com, and Philips, and smaller companies that were to become major players in speech software, such as Kurzweil Tech, Dragon, and Lernout & Hauspie (now ScanSoft).

Microsoft was invited to join the Open Systems Architecture Speech Recognition Committee the next year, and quickly joined in the major activities of the OSASRC. The top priority for OSASRC, as well as Microsoft, was to develop a standard specification for a Speech Recognition API (SRAPI) and speech programmer developer tools library, which was first released unofficially in 1993. The platform architecture layers for SRAPI standard are shown in Figure 1.1.

Even though the SRAPI standard and tools also supported Microsoft Windows, the main focus from the beginning was more focused at UNIX and the IBM OS/2 operating platforms, and it even attempted to integrate Netware and OpenDoc. So even though OSASRC really was trying to be everything to all people, as we all know, you can not please all of the people all the time.

But in 1996, when SRAPI Version 2.0 was officially released, it was a cumbersome and confusing speech standard. SRAPI suffered from the usual problems with open systems support. Arguments broke out among the various vendors as they tried to get everyone else using the same standard they developed to do things their way, and only their way.

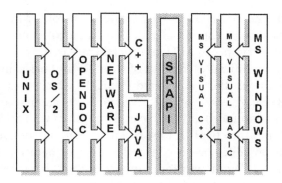

Figure 1.1.

The first major standard to support Windows programming was SRAPI, the Speech Recognition API, which is used mostly on UNIX platforms running X-Windows.

1.4 Microsoft Does Speech Its Own Way

It should not be any surprise to learn that by 1995 or so Microsoft had lost patience with the OSASRC, and began to be openly critical of the limitations of SRAPI.

So in 1996 Microsoft announced that it was developing its own speech recognition programming standard and speech API library which it code-named 'USAPI' (very simply, the 'Universal' Speech API). The new Microsoft API was designed not only for speech recognition, but to completely re-engineer and revolutionize both speech recognition and computer speech generation technology.

The frustration of Microsoft with OSASRC was exemplified by stories reported in the computer industry trade press about unconfirmed rumors that the original production name for the Microsoft speech API was originally to have been called 'SLAPI', for the 'Speech Linguistics API'. This had some credence because Microsoft based their new API even more upon the science of linguistics than the SRAPI specification that preceded it. But it was widely felt that Microsoft intended its own speech API as a "slap in the face" of the often counter-productive SRAPI committee.

However, regardless of how serious Microsoft was about the early leaks of the name for their own speech API, the official name was simply 'Speech API (SAPI)'. So although there were reports in the computer industry press and web news groups that Big Blue and some of the other OSASRC founders may have regarded the name SLAPI as some kind of affront, Microsoft officially took the high road. And the upper hand, as Microsoft went "simply SAPI" when their proprietary speech API was officially released.

Microsoft did not officially back-out of OSASRC but basically stopped their active participation as they developed 'USAPI', which was first officially released in very early 1997, as SAPI Version 2.0, its first official release. Microsoft simply announced did not have any problem with SRAPI as an open system standard. But they felt that they had to remain independent in order to develop the best possible speech API and speech recognition programming toolsets for Microsoft Windows programmers, without having to wait on out-side reviewers to approve their designs (as Microsoft contended that they had with Java standards).

Microsoft did not criticize SRAPI as an open speech standard or any other way. There were a some criticisms and hard feelings from a few other computer companies in OSASRC. But Microsoft just ignored the talk, and went on about their business of developing the very best possible Windows platform speech recognition programming standard.

In retrospect, it was a situation not a whole lot different from several other open standards committee back-outs that Microsoft did during that same time period, which initially got Microsoft into a bit of hot water for a few years. But in the end they were vindicated since it was a good strategic business decision for Microsoft, and with even greater benefit for Windows speech program-mers, and the result began an unprecedented new era in speech recognition programming that was accessible, easy, and fast.

1.5   Microsoft SAPI Out-classes the Open System World

The SAPI standard and API that Microsoft had developed quickly became the speech API and standard of choice for all programmers, not only Windows programmers. It has also sometimes been said that SAPI was one more nail in the coffin of more than a few Microsoft opposition operating systems, includ-ing IBM's open platform competitor OS/2.

By the end of 1997, all of the major computer vendors, including IBM and Phillips, as well as the emerging leaders in speech engine software, Kurzweil Technologies, Dragon Systems (now ScanSoft), and Lernout &Hauspie (also now ScanSoft), were all dropping SRAPI and converting everything to SAPI.

You should not expect that just because SAPI is now the major speech API standard that it will be the only speech standard that you need to know about, or that you can even forget about learning about SRAPI or any of the open systems speech standards.

As you can expect, just like with everything else that was left behind when the smoke cleared after the open standards revolution, most speech programmers often have to deal with legacy speech API code. This includes SRAPI, which is especially common in legacy speech software anywhere that was loyal to OS/2 all the way to the very end, and some early ViaVoice or Dragon software that was created before SAPI became the standard.

You should be much more seriously aware of all forward looking speech standards as they relate to SAPI, since you are much more likely to need to interface your own SAPI speech software applications to emerging speech standard specifications and API libraries.

This included both IBM ViaVoice, which was converted to SAPI, and the L&H realtime automated foreign language translation software, which was originally dependent on OS/2 ViaVoice, and when IBM switched, L&H (and Dragon NaturallySpeaking) did too. This also included the more advanced wireless handheld and palmtop speech technology that was being developed by Phillips and 3Com, which converted into a technology development strategy that is now based on MS Windows/CE.

The result was that SAPI has become the most important speech recognition programming standard and speech software developer environment not only for Windows programmers but all programmers. In the next section we will take a little closer look at how Microsoft supports speech recognition programming with its Windows Speech API. This SAPI standard is shown in Figure 1.2.

1.6 Microsoft SAPI Gets Its Own Speech SDK

Although some of the concepts first introduced in this section may be expanded upon later in this book, from now on, the focus will be on the specifics of how to write speech programs using Microsoft SAPI. Since this is a book about how to program speech software for Microsoft Windows environments, the tools that will be used to demonstrate how to program Windows speech software will be based upon the official standards for Windows speech programming. These are now MS Windows Speech API, Windows Speech Developer Kit (SDK), and Windows Speech SDK Suite. These standards and tools will provide the platform environments which you will build from for all Windows speech programming now and in the future, and can be used to create any speech application, ranging from very simple to very complex.

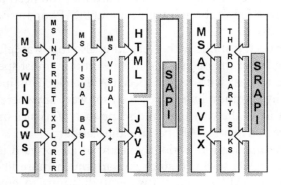

Figure 1.2.

By far the most popular and widely used Windows speech recognition programming standard is SAPI, the Speech API, which was designed specifically for use within MS Windows Open Systems Architecture (WOSA) environments.

The Microsoft *Speech API* (also known as 'SAPI') is a special Windows API and standard that support Windows compliant speech processing for Windows Open System Architectures (WOSA). Although the term SAPI should by now sound familiar to you, you need to know that it is fully integrated into the WOSA standard and Windows object model!

The significance of Windows Open System Architecture (*WOSA*) is most important to SAPI with regard to both quality and extensibility benefits. It not only assures that all speech application object management and messaging will be effective as well as efficient, but also makes it possible to easily integrate SAPI functions with other important WOSA standard library functions, including the Microsoft Windows web e-Mail API (*MAPI*) and the Telephony API (*TAPI*).

Used together, Microsoft SAPI and other WOSA compliant object libraries such as Microsoft MAPI and TAPI provide a very powerful and strategic set of tools. Windows programmers and information technology development organizations who want to be leaders on the cutting edge of all the most exciting and fast-paced advances in intelligent Windows multi-media, accessibility, phone, Internet and automated language translation technology have everything they need by combining SAPI, MAPI and TAPI!

1.7   Your First Listen at Some Windows Speech Software

You are very likely most interested to get a 'first listen at' is the Windows Speech simple program samples that are bundled by Microsoft in SAPI. You will be looking first, and then modifying, the sample code and working application examples, as well as Microsoft MSDN speech recognition programming best practices and coding guidelines, before you move on to more complicated speech recognition programming projects throughout the rest of this book. All of the speech programs first introduced in this section can be found in the directory folder where you first load your Microsoft Speech API Version 4.0 and Visual Speech SDK Suite, in Folder 'SAMPLES', and all of the programs are also in the Sub-Folder 'ACTIVEX'.

If you have already installed and loaded your Microsoft SAPI 4.0 and Microsoft Speech SDK Suite software, you can use Windows Explorer to go to either your CD media or hard disk Windows directory with the SAPI 4.0 sample program code. You might take some time to explore the executables and project files for SAPI 4.0 speech application programs that will be discussed on the next few pages.

SAPI 4.0 normally assumes that you will be both developing and running your speech applications on Windows 95 or greater, so all examples and references in this book will be directed to Explorer rather than the Windows 3.1 File Manager. You should be aware that all code, controls and voice files in SAPI 4.0 are also supported with SAPI 5+. However, SAPI 4.0 will still run on Windows 95, but SAPI 5+ will not (which is another reason to start with SAPI 4.0 to learn speech programming using MS Speech API).

Before you get your first look at the sample speech applications that you will be working with (or if you already have the SAPI 4.0 software loaded), you can 'listen along' as they are identified and reviewed in this section.

1.8   Checking Out the Visual Basic TTS Animation Sample

The first SAPI 4.0 speech application program sample that we will look at can be found in your 'ACTIVEX' folder in a sub-folder named 'VB5'. This is the folder with Visual Basic speech program samples, which should be especially exciting to programmers, since we are now looking at real executable speech programs, not just add-ins. You may be wondering why the folder is named 'VB5', and not 'VB6', since when SAPI 4.0 was first released in early 1999, Visual Basic 6 had already been released over a year.

The reason is that SAPI 4.0 is only fully compatible with Visual Basic 5.0, and there are some compatibility issues that were not resolved in time to test SAPI 4.0 for Visual Basic 6.0 before the SAPI suite was first released. This issue will be discussed more later, since there are some potential warnings and errors you could receive because of this problem and you need to know what to do about them.

However, you are unlikely to need these VB5-only functions for learning basic SAPI speech recognition programming, and all examples in this book should work with either VB5 or VB6 on your PC.

So for now, do not be too concerned, since fully 99% of your SAPI speech program functions can be coded with Visual Basic 6.0, and fully 100% of the SAPI suite sample programs can be run and changed from within the Visual Basic 6.0 developer environment. This folder should contain one file and 8 folders. The folder that you should open next is named 'BASICTTS'. You should see 5 files, 4 which are Visual Basic 5 form objects and one executable, 'BASICTTS.EXE'.

You can either click on the icon for 'BASICTTS' in Explorer, or find the executable speech program 'BASICTTS.EXE' from your Start menu and Run from there, which ever you prefer.

You should be aware that even though the underlying speech engine methods for both this sample program and the last one are the same. It is actually in this next case mostly just the speech mode that will be changed, with some additional dynamic program changes to the speech control tags. When the BASICTTS application finishes loading, you should see a screen something like Figure 1.3.

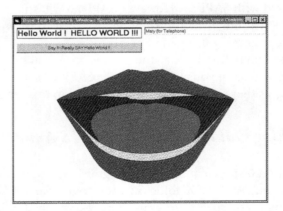

Figure 1.3.

The Windows SAPI Visual Basic standalone executable "Talking Mouth" animation program moves its lips as it speaks the phrase "Hello World", or anything else that you enter as keyboard text, in the female gender of selected voice "Mary (for Telephone)".

This application is known as the "Talking Mouth", for reasons which should be obvious to see.

You should notice three form controls on this screen which set session specific runtime attributes:

- A text entry box
- A drop-down list box
- An event click button

Later we will look more closely at the details behind the drop-down list box, but for now lets just simply make this fun little program say "HELLO WORLD". Simply type the words 'HELLO WORLD' into the text entry box and click on the button 'Say It'. If all of the necessary speech engine files are installed, and your sound system speakers are configured properly, you should hear the words "HELLO WORLD" in a female voice. Each time you click on the 'Say It' button, the words will be repeated, and the lips should move as animation in sync with the words.

You can change the words to be spoken simply by typing new words in the text box. You can also change the voice to something other than female by selecting from the options in the drop-down combo list box. If you click on the drop-down box you will see a list of other voices that are selectable by type according to characteristic names. Just for fun, try changing the voice to the selection for "Mike in Hall" and click "Say It! Really SAY Hello World just to see and hear what happens. You can ignore the new button caption, since as you can probably guess as a Windows Visual Basic programmer how this was changed. You should see an immediate change in the color and thickness of the lips, as they become more masculine than with the "Mary" voice, as shown in Figure 1.4, and the tone should drop an octave or two.

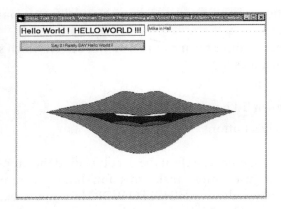

Figure 1.4.

When you change the drop-down voice selection to "Mike in the Hall", not only does the voice become more masculine, but the animated lips become more masculine as well!

Feel free to play with this fun little program for a few minutes, but do not take too long, as we still have a lot of ground to cover.

You can rest assured that this is not the last you will see of this fun little program, and we will never get to the really serious speech recognition programming!

1.9   Checking Out the Web Browser TTS Animation Sample

The next SAPI 4.0 speech application program sample that we will look at for now can be found in your 'ACTIVEX' folder in a sub-folder named 'WEB'. This is the folder with Internet and HTML scripting speech program samples, which should be of interest both to seasoned programmers as well as any Internet power user who knows how to define web pages using basic HTML.

Open the sub-folder 'LADY', which should contain 5 files, including 4 HTML files and one JPG image file. The HTML file that you want to open first is 'LADY.HTM'. You can use Microsoft Explorer to run the HTML by clicking on MSIE icon next to it (if you have MSIE defined as the Explorer runtype for the.HTM extension). Or you can open and run the web page 'LADY.HTM' from within Microsoft Internet Explorer as a local web browser. When your MSIE 4+-compliant web browser finishes loading the 'LADY.HTM' web page, you should see a screen something like Figure 1.5.

This application is also known as the "Talking Lady"—though many SAPI programmers say it looks more like a very famous (or more often "in-famous") notorious male rock super-star. You know the one—who reportedly underwent a lot of facial surgery—and also for that matter, many say the SAPI "female" voice sounds strangely like his real voice as well! (This may be yet another example to demonstrate the original Microsoft developers had a very clever tongue-in-cheek sense of humor and really enjoyed their work—as do all Windows programmers—as well as some Windows computer book authors!).

Figure 1.5.

Windows SAPI HTML Script based web browser "Talking Lady" animation program moves lips and changes facial expressions as it speaks any other text phrase you enter.

You should notice that there are 2 web form controls on this screen:

- A text entry box
- A submit form button

Simply type the words 'HELLO WORLD' into the text entry box and click on the button 'Say It'.

If all of the necessary speech engine files are installed, and your sound system speakers are configured properly (and if you have a compatible version of a Microsoft Internet Explorer browser), you should hear the words "HELLO WORLD" in a female voice.

Each time you click on the 'Say It' button, the words will be repeated, and the lips should move as animation in sync with the words. Actually, very much like the previous example in many ways, yet still very different in other ways, as we shall see later.

You can change the words to be spoken simply by typing new words in the text box. You can not change the voice however, on this particular speech application, as you could on the last one (sorry).

Feel free to play with this fun little web page a few minutes, but just like before, do not take too long, as this is not the last you will see of this fun little program either.

But first we will review some fundamental concepts that you should know about before we start to take apart the sample SAPI speech programs we have just seen, and really get a look under the hood!

1.10   How Microsoft Windows Does Speech

You already know that no one does Windows better than Microsoft, and nothing makes Windows speech software better than Microsoft SAPI. Also, as you have learned, there are a lot of other speech standards and speech related API's that you may need to understand in order to make other software work with your Windows software made with SAPI.

Just so you can start being aware of some of these standards, a select few of them are:

- SAPI: The Microsoft Speech API
- MAPI: The Microsoft e-Mail API
- TAPI: The Microsoft Telephony API
- SRAPI: Open Systems Committee Speech Recognition API
- SVAPI: Open Systems Committee Speech Verification API
- HAPI: Open Systems Committee Handwriting API
- STAPI: Speech Technology API (U.S. Air Force)
- VPAPI: Voice Pilot API (palmtops)
- CARAPI: Courtesy Account Recognition API (voiceprint)

Don't worry too much about the many other speech software standards and API libraries, since all of them conform to the same basic technology that Microsoft uses in SAPI. The concepts that are first reviewed here will be expanded upon greatly later in this book.

1.11   Some Basic Speech Recognition Programming Concepts

You should not be too concerned if some of the new concepts that are introduced in this section seem at first to be just a little bit overwhelming. For now we just need to quickly review some basic principles and new terms that you should be at least a little bit acquainted with before you learn more about the internals of Microsoft Speech API and Windows Speech SDK tools.

First of all, you should be aware that all speech technology is based on over a century (that's right, over 100 years) of research in the field of *computational linguistics*. This research had nothing to do with computers, but instead primarily involved statistical computations related to analysis of speech in human beings.

This included lots of diverse topics, such as measurements of human voice box and tongue, frequency of speaking particular words, speed of speech, accents and dialects, and relationship of sounds for similar words in different geographic areas and across foreign languages.

All of this research, which probably seemed very esoteric and strange at the time (and probably would seem even stranger today) was all in fact useful, and often critical, when Microsoft designed SAPI.

The main reason why this is important to you should be quite obvious once you think about it. Be happy you have SAPI, because it does a lot of tedious boring things you do not really want to do!

And you should be able to guess that a big part of that has to do with all the esoteric and befuddling little details about the way people talk and understand speech that were programmed at a very low level into SAPI, so that you should never have to worry about them. But if you enjoy things like that and feel like enough of an expert on linguistics and related topics that you believe you can do a better job than Microsoft SAPI does (which is known as writing your own speech engine), those topics will also be covered briefly later in this book.

1.12   What Microsoft Used in SAPI from Linguistics

There are however, some basic things that you need to know about how SAPI uses basic linguistics principles. One of the first is that you need to know about a strange coding convention that linguists have always used to very specifically describe speech sounds as they are put together in conversational speech.

This coding scheme is known as IPA Unicode. You do not normally need to specify speech Unicode yourself. But you do need to know that you should regard it as a very special character set. You may need to be able to understand

IPA Unicode in order to be able to quickly debug speech string buffers, among other things, or just to make a very specific and precise match parameter, or delimiter, so it can be quickly processed by a SAPI-compliant speech engine.

IPA stands for International Phonetic Alphabet. These are the contemporary basis for speech *Unicodes*, and are a standard system for specifying and recording specific sounds involved in all human speech, in any human language, which was first originated over a century ago back in 1886.

Unicode is the 16-bit character set that replaces ASCII and allows any phoneme to be represented as a text string that can be processed much more quickly than ASCII text. Unicode was adapted in 1986 to be able to directly specify the International Phonetic Alphabet (IPA). This has the additional benefit of more quickly translating IPA from text to speech, or vice versa. It is the standard character set used in all Windows speech recognition, as well as speech synthesis, for all Windows COM speech engines.

There was a major update to the IPA over a decade ago, at the first century anniversary of IPA back in 1986. Every major speech technology, including Microsoft Windows speech, has assumed its elemental speech functions should be based on IPA phonemes, regardless of whether the language to be recognized and spoken is English, or any other past or future human language to be localized.

The next thing that you need to know is how linguists put the IPA and Unicode character sets together to make speech. The lowest level of element of speech is a phoneme, which is probably a term that you already know or can guess, since it is similar to phonetics or phonics, which a lot of people have encountered in their early childhood education.

You should understand that a phoneme is not a word, a phoneme is just a sound, or sub-word, that is concatenated as a string to make a word. But you do not have a word as far as SAPI is concerned unless the phonemes have a specific meaning.

A *word* is (right we all know what a 'word' is, but linguists have a more specific definition...) the smallest possible unit of sound that has a particular unique meaning. A word may be built based on one or more vocalization sounds or word-part phoneme elements, but the critical distinction is that phonemes never have any meaning but a word has only one meaning. Thus, a *word list* is a file or string buffer with unique meanings.

Of course you also know that a phrase is a series of words. But as far as SAPI is concerned, it is not a phrase unless it is a series of SAPI words (which can be one or more logical words) that have a particular context that should be treated as a logical word by SAPI.

Sometimes there may be a space between parts of a word, as in the word *"New York"*. But *"New York"* really is only one word, not two, even though there are also other words *"new"* and *"York"*, which are both different than *"New York"*, and also different than the words *"New York City"* and *"New York City Museum"*. According to the SAPI specification, *"New York City Museum"* would be one word. But *"New York City Museum event"* would be two words (*"New York City Museum"* and *"event"*).

This may seem like nit-picking right now, but later in this book, you will hopefully begin to appreciate the difference as a speech programmer. Be prepared that understanding that difference, and providing for it in your programs, will be the most important factor in whether your programs are sluggish and dull, or fast and smart!

Although this sounds complicated, it really is not and you will get used to it after you get more deeply into the technical details. So for now, just be aware that there is a progression in SAPI, that follows a prescribed path:

```
1) phoneme -> 2) diphone -> 3) word -> {4a) phrase /
4b) wordlist}
```

A *phoneme* is the smallest part of a word that can be vocalized as a unique sustained sound all by itself. A phoneme is a spoken word creation element, and most often defined via IPA Unicode.

You should be aware that you can not simply make up your own phonemes! Even if you think you can create a sound no human being has ever made before, you should hopefully understand that it has either already been isolated, and specified as a phoneme to the IPA and Unicode. Or else it is already a combination of phonemes already defined to IPA and Unicode.

That does not necessarily hold true with 'robot' or 'alien' voice sounds, but if you are able to create a robot or alien voice sound not yet on IPA and Unicode—but then it can still not be regarded as a new phoneme, it is just simply a new *noise*!

Diphone is a sound input that consists of two phonemes, one of which starts with a particular sound and the other ends with a particular sound. For example, the word *Hello* involves two phonemes, which can be said slowly as *Hell-oh*.

The importance of *diphones* is that they make it possible to split words up into elemental parts. It should be easy for any programmer to understand that the more you can break up and reuse the parts of anything the way that you reuse program objects, you will use less space and run faster on any computer environment.

There are a lot less elemental phonemes, as well as diphones from two-part phoneme combinations, than there are words in a full-scale unabridged English dictionary. So it is faster for PC's to put phonemes together than lookup and retrieve words from large files that contain 99% of all the words that you will probably never use.

Just think about it for a second, how many words do you use on a daily basis out of a 200,000 word unabridged dictionary? Most research indicates that most people use only 200 words or less each day. How would you like to have to look up each word you say in a big dictionary each time you say it, or would you rather just make a 200 word 'short-list' and not carry around the other 199,800?

1.13   What Microsoft Used in SAPI from Electronics

Once you understand the hierarchy and progression of elemental speech objects, as they were first defined by linguists and then used to design SAPI, the next thing that you need to be aware of is the first really great speech technology innovations of the last half century.

There are two major technologies which are the basis for all of the computer hardware advances which are needed in order to make speech software possible. These two electronic technologies that are assumed to be the basis of all input to SAPI and other speech software technologies.

The first critical speech technology is known as Pulse Code Modulation (PCM). This sounds a lot more complicated than it is (or is actually a lot more complicated than you need to know, thanks to SAPI). But basically PCM is simply a very specialized type of analog to digital conversion that is needed to code speech signal inputs.

The Pulse Code Modulation (PCM) technology is the most common way of encoding an analog voice into a digital bit stream. First the amplitude dimension of the voice input signal is sampled, then the sample values are recoded into binary data according to some threshold or range rule logic so that the resulting binary data can be switched, transmitted or stored for processing by a computer.

The second critical speech technology is known as a Digital Signal Processor (DSP). This can actually be a lot of things, from hardware line filters to special electronics to damp or adjust line sinks so that the signal is not too loud, not too quiet, and the intelligence to know the difference. Sometimes the DSP can be all electronics and sometimes it is some combination of electronics and a microprocessor.

But the whole purpose of a DSP is to very simply to help 'clean' or 'pre-process' the incoming speech data, and is usually either designed specifically for a particular application, group, or individual, or else generally to be able to handle speech inputs from the greatest common range of people.

The computer speech Digital Signal Processor (DSP) is usually a micro-chip or complete microprocessor board that is designed to electronically receive and pre-process audio inputs from a microphone or data communications line. It can usually both convert an analog or continuous signal into discrete or time-sliced digital values. It also has some level of capability to filter or ignore audio inputs that are clearly not voice inputs or speech patterns, such as the barking of a dog or sound of a shutting door.

Another important development in computer speech that was made possible by DSP is that they could not only filter out unwanted signals. Also, most DSP's can also join together diphones, or parts of words, to create a single pseudo-phoneme or entire words, in a process known as diphonic concatenation. This process was used in some of the large computer speech labs mentioned earlier, but Microsoft was the first to make this a reliable technique that could be ported to a personal computer using SAPI.

Diphonic concatenation is the process that Microsoft Speech API uses in all of its Text-To-Speech (TTS) engines to string together short digital audio segment as parts of words and phrases to be spoken over the sound system speakers. The diphonic concatenation method used by SAPI also performs automatic 'smoothing' of the sounds and frequencies as controlled by intelligent statistical functions in order to produce a continuous sound that is a very good emulation of human speech.

1.14   *Windows Does Speech Better and Faster*

Most early computer speech synthesis and talking computer applications were in fact all hardware based. But computer recognition of human speech is a different kind of animal and for a number of efficiency reasons that should be obvious, this is a task that can only be done by software.

The earliest speech recognition software could only handle what is known as discrete speech. This involves specific responses to a very small number of words to be recognized, so computer resources required can actually be quite modest. This type of speech recognition application is also known as speech command control, since it is the most common type of voice command software.

Discrete speech requires that the speaker stop-and-pause between words, usually for a time interval that is expected by the software, or taught to the user as part of some training exercise which provides feedback and coaching until there is some human user learning of the expected pauses and delays.

Because of their inherent resource demand limitations, discrete speech systems are normally only practical if there is a very small number of words, or commands, that the software must be designed to recognize and respond to. Such discrete speech systems require very modest computer resources, and are thus very effective on small computers such as laptops or palmtops.

This includes Windows CE and embedded microprocessor chip software, such as talking appliances or talking vehicles. But these systems are also prone to misrecognition and inappropriate response errors, and until there are more advances in hardware technology in the small footprint platforms, these systems should not yet be used in any application that involves human health or safety!

The demands of continuous speech, on the other hand, can be very overwhelming, and for that reason it was not generally possible in the past except on very large computers. However, within the last half of the 1990's, the incredible advances made in hardware, including both microprocessor and storage speeds and lower costs, have made it more feasible to put continuous speech, natural language and dictation or transcription software on personal computers.

Continuous speech refers to an uninterrupted speech vocalization without any need for pausing between words. Only very advanced, and normally very big, speech recognition engines can handle continuous or natural speech. All continuous natural speech engines have to be intelligent enough to make breaks between words, or at the ends of phrases, based on some combination of phoneme timing and speech delay criteria, often as well as word or phoneme audio matching criteria.

Regardless of whether a speech application is for speech generation or speech recognition, and whether it involves discrete or continuous speech, the next big hurdle that faced early speech software standard architects was the challenge of how to control just how the speech engine software will speak. And also to recognize words, and what words to speak or recognize, as well as how to speak or recognize them.

The conventional methods that are used in speech software technology, including the Microsoft Speech API, are known as grammars and rules. These can be as simple as a string of words known as a wordlist, or as complicated as a lot of nested and branching conditional logic.

Although the concept of grammars had been used in even the earliest speech software, in SAPI Microsoft was able to far surpass anything that had ever been done with speech technology grammars.

Part of this was due to some very creative Microsoft SAPI innovations in standardizing types of grammars and rules, and making them easier to specify, which was especially easy with regard to the way Windows handles object events.

This was especially important to the way that Windows SAPI implements word spotting which is a technique for filtering out words with special meaning for special handling. Word spotting was a technique that had also been around a long time, but Microsoft and Windows made it faster and easier to implement.

A speech software grammar is a set or list of words or phrases that should be recognized by a particular Windows speech engine. All Microsoft Windows speech grammars are usually external OLE or COM objects that an application has been instructed to look to in order to compare incoming speech or word matching processes, so it will know what to listen for, and what to selectively ignore.

You should be aware that more than half of all the work that you need to do as a speech programmer will not involve simply writing code. You will also need to spend at least half of your speech recognition programming efforts and time in the creation, management and maintenance of speech grammars and their related files!

As you will see later in this book, there are many alternative strategies for defining the speech grammars and rules that will control the speech engines used in your speech applications. Regardless of whether you program in Visual Basic, or Java, or C++, you will use the same basic methods and processes across all speech environments in order to define your speech control grammars and rules. You should always start out with default or standard grammars the same way that you start with the standard voices, but if you want to be a real power programmer in the speech software domain, most of your success will depend on grammars!

The term word-spotting relates to the strategy of using very small active vocabulary files which are referenced from within your Visual Basic or other Visual programming code in order to control condition Windows software event actions for particular speech recognitions.

Usually word spotting is used only in discrete command control speech applications. A word spotter file is a small grammar file that only lists the word that you want your speech application program to listen for, or to respond to in particular specific ways.

Word-spotting is also increasingly used in continuous natural speech applications, where a very small list of words is continuously 'listened' for with a higher priority than all other active speech recognizer engine events and functions.

You should also be aware that there are several methods of matching audio digital speech waveform patterns to words with meaning. But they all depend upon the same database and file management programming methods and design efficiency considerations that you may have already used in your Visual Basic or Office Suite database and spreadsheet applications.

1.15   Localizing for Advanced Windows Speech Applications

There have been many practical applications of the word-spotting technique, some of which you may have heard of already, but many of which you might never have even guessed.

Because of increased emphasis on security issues in public places as a result of numerous violent tragedies in the past decade, this has come into high demand. Many intelligent speech recognition systems have just been implemented based on speech software interfaces to existing security systems in public schools, court houses, offices, casinos, fast food restaurants, airports, and even onboard flying aircraft.

These speech software systems are continuously monitoring microphones that do not always record, but are instead constantly analyzing audio from multiple sources to pick up human spoken keywords that may indicate it might be a good idea to start recording to videotape, and alert security staff.

If you are a good citizen, like 99.999% of the civilized world is, you should not be intimidated by this. But be aware you can no longer 'joke around' at public places and say sensitive words with potential dangerous meanings, because just saying those words near a hidden microphone may be recognized by a speech program, and some people may watch you for awhile to determine if you are a bad guy or not.

This is really not anything new, and you may already be aware that most speech recognition technology we have today was originally based on phone speech recognition software systems that were first developed in the early 1980's by the U.S. government. This technique was first used in order to automatically monitor telephone conversations of suspected international spies and drug dealers. Despite what you always see in the movies, most legal wiretaps are not normally done by guys with headphones out at the street in vans, they were usually done from the phone center using software!

Another very critical and leading edge application of Windows speech by Microsoft involves a concept known as localization. This is a topic that has become especially important due to the growth of the Internet and the need to be able to quickly or even automatically change the content of web pages from English to any other language.

Because of the way Microsoft had integrated Internet Explorer into Windows, this made MSIE the browser of choice for web localization applications. For the same reasons, Microsoft had another good reason for foreign language localization experts like Dragon Systems and Lernout & Hauspie to switch from SRAPI to SAPI so quickly.

A localization is a specialized lexicon or grammar rules that define how a particular word equates to a series of phonemes, or vice-versa, across human languages such as English-to-French, Spanish-to-English, as well as specialized technical or professional localizations, such as lexicon or grammar rules for the legal or medical professions.

Localization files can also include specialized speech file templates for a particular linguistic dialect or alphabet convention subset, which can be particularly important for Asian, or Russian and other CIS languages, as well as some Romance languages, like Spanish and French, that have special characters and complex pronunciation rules.

This is one of the very hottest and most exciting areas of speech programming. The Internet is becoming more and more popular around the world in countries that do not read (or speak) English, and especially as the next generation Internet involves more API speech generation and web phone options.

1.16 *Creating Your First Simple Speech Program*

You are now ready to create your first speech program. You have learned about the foundations of speech technology, you have seen (and hopefully heard) some typical kinds of speech programs written in Visual Basic, macros and web scripts, and you have been exposed to the Microsoft Speech API and its related ActiveX and object model foundations.

So you should be ready to learn how to code the same tradition first program "*Hello World*" message as a simple speech output code ActiveX object in Visual Basic and as an HTML reference.

Get ready. And try to prepare yourself that after all you have learned already, this will probably also seem incredibly simple!

It is assumed that if you have made it this far, you are either already a fairly well experienced Visual Basic or other Windows application programmer, or else a very advanced Windows or Internet power user who at least knows the ins and outs of macro scripts or HTML.

If so, the following code samples should in fact seem very simple. If not, the following code samples will probably seem very cryptic. But even if you do not understand them now, rest assured that we will explain them in much more detail for the rest of this book, and by the time you get to the end you will probably be able to recite them in your sleep!

1.17   Writing Your First Speech Program in Visual Basic

If you want to create a simple Visual Basic 5 application that says "Hello World" when the program starts, you can probably expect that you would create the code for such an application the same for a speech program as you would for any other type of output application, such as a print output event, or save to file, or message box.

It is also assumed that there are already SAPI ActiveX speech controls loaded to your Visual Basic components toolbar, otherwise you would need to load the speech control you want to use before the following procedure and code would even work. So again, if you do not have the your SAPI 4.0 and Speech SDK Suite installed yet, do not worry, since we will be coming back to revisit this many times.

First, create a new project or open a project that you wish to add the automatic greeting "Hello World" to when your Windows application software is first opened.

Second, select the speech control that you want to use, which in this case is probably the general Text-To-Speech control (if you want to play the message on you PC sound system speaker, as opposed to over a telephone line or web page).

Next, drag and drop the speech control that you want to use onto the top Visual Basic form (Form1). You can reset any properties you want, or else you can just accept all defaults for our purposes right now. That's all there is to it, so simple its almost embarrassing right?

There should be nothing here that you did not already anticipate in consideration of what you have learned already today. So now lets take a look at another simple bit of code that should be almost as easy for you to anticipate and understand.

Although this is clearly very simple that you could have probably anticipated it in advance, you should also anticipate the real power in this little Visual Basic speech application is not going to be in the lines of code, but instead in how you set your properties on the TextToSpeech control, and also on how you define the speech control constants.

Each of these fine little niceties will in fact be very big efforts, and we will spend several days this week going over the details of each!

1.18   Writing Your First Simple Speech Program as a Web Script

There are several Internet programming tools that can automatically create and edit your web pages to insert ActiveX controls, or you can manually edit to insert ActiveX controls into your webpages using any file editor as sophisticated at Microsoft FrontPage or as simple as Microsoft NotePad.

Regardless of whether you use automatic ActiveX control insertion, or insert manually by edits to your HTML code, the HTML tags that you need in order to perform the same process as the previous example will involve something like the very simple HTML script that follows.

Listing 1.1. Simple HTML Tags required to initialize the SAPI DirectVoice object.

```
<object NAME="DirectVoice" TYPE="application/x-oleobject"
    classid="clsid:EEE78591-FE22-11D0-8BEF-0060081841DE">
</object>
```

In Listing 1.1, you can see the object tags that specify the speech control, as well as type. The class ID is a constant that is unique for each type of ActiveX control, and are all listed in the Appendix.

Listing 1.2. Simple Web Scripting to Say "Hello World" When Page Is Linked or Opened.

```
<script>
    DirectVoice.Speak("hello world")
</script>
```

In Listing 1.2, you can see the very simple scripting code that makes the web page say the message *"Hello World".*

Again, very simple, so simple you could probably have guessed it yourself. Also again, there are a lot more complicated properties and parameters that must be specified in order to get the web page to say the message just the way that you want it to.

We will be getting into those niceties also later this book, but by now you are probably more eager than ever to load and install SAPI.

1.19 *Summary*

Now it is time to summarize what you have learned thus far, and prepare for Chapter Two, when we will load and install the Microsoft Speech API and Speech SDK Suite. Although you may still have far to go as a professional Windows speech programmer, in this chapter you have already learned most of the basic things you need to know about in order to understand any speech software application and design your own Windows speech recognition software.

In this chapter you have learned some of the history behind the speech software programming revolution, including a look into the many underlying technical foundations. You have also learned the critical role that Microsoft and the Windows Open System Architecture have played in making speech recognition programming easy and accessible to programmers.

You have seen as well as heard of speech programs written in Visual Basic as well as Microsoft Office macros, HTML and web scripting with the capability to speak as well as listen and recognize your speech. You have also learned how the Microsoft SAPI standard and ActiveX object controls can be used to very quickly and easily build speech aware software.

If you can apply your new understanding of speech technology and your available Windows speech programming tools to your speech software applications, you should be well on your way to becoming a proficient Windows speech application software programmer by the end of this book.

Chapter Two

Introducing Microsoft Windows Speech API and Microsoft Compatible Speech SDK Suites

The three most important foundations of the Microsoft Windows speech program developer environments are the Microsoft Windows Speech API (SAPI), the Microsoft Windows Speech Software Developer Kit (SDK), and Microsoft Windows standard speech engines and standard voices.

It is very necessary for every Windows Visual Basic speech programmer to become very familiar with all of the many technical complexities of all three of these standard Microsoft speech facilities in order to be able to write Microsoft compliant Windows speech programs, regardless of whether you program Windows software using SAPI with Visual Basic, VBA, VB Script, Java, Java Script—or even just HTML!

You must also have an intimate understanding of all of the standard Microsoft speech engines and foundation sound system facilities of Windows, even if you plan to use another vendor's speech SDK or API, as well as if you may use other speech engines, since you will still have to integrate the other vendor speech engines, or your own, to the standard Microsoft Windows SAPI speech environment.

You should also be aware of the special high-level Windows speech functions and facilities that are available to you to leverage your existing Microsoft Visual Basic with Windows speech programming skills by applying SAPI ActiveX speech component controls to develop powerful and extensible fully Windows-compliant SAPI speech applications with minimal time and effort using Visual Basic.

In this chapter, we will discuss the following:

- Introduction to the High Level Microsoft Windows Speech API
- Getting to Know MS Windows Speech API and Visual Basic Speech Tool Suite Even Better
- Getting Your Own Windows Speech SDK Tool Suite and SAPI ActiveX for Visual Basic
- Installing Your Microsoft Windows Speech SDK and SAPI Visual Basic Tool Suite Software
- Exploring Your New Microsoft Speech SDK and SAPI Libraries for Windows Visual Basic

2.1   Introduction to the High Level Microsoft Windows Speech API

Although you will learn how to install and load your Microsoft Windows Speech API later in this chapter, this section will first acquaint you with the various components and facilities in SAPI 4.0.

As you may know, *API* stands for *Application Programming Interface*. The Windows API is a special set of internal high-level procedures that you can call from Visual Basic or other Visual programming languages.

The use of Windows API standard libraries serves to standardize such basic windows functions as mouse click events, window sizing, tool bar and menu *'look-and-feel'*, and also greatly speeds up the application project creation process.

For speech recognition programming the Microsoft Speech API standardizes the *'sound-and-voice'* of Windows speech recognition programming.

2.2   First Impressions of SAPI for Windows Visual Basic Speech Programmers

When you first look through all the folders and files in your new Microsoft Speech API and Speech SDK Suite library and program samples, you will probably immediately notice that almost all of the SAPI 4.0 sample programs are written in C++, with very few programs written in Visual Basic or any other language.

This is because all of the low-level Windows foundation and class library functions are only accessible using C++ and COM object calls, and this has always been the case.

However, with the February 1999 release of Microsoft Windows Speech API Version 4.0, it first became possible to use new ActiveX controls.

A set of special new COM objects which can now be called from Visual Basic, VBA, and VB Script, as well as HTML and JavaScript, in order to directly call very high-level Windows functions via changes to parameters and contents or property specifications.

This makes it possible for even new programmers in Visual Basic, Java, or even basic HTML, to write even very powerful speech applications, or add speech functions to existing Visual Basic, Visual J++, or even HTML web scripting applications!

You should be aware that when software engineers talk about *low-level* functions of the computer operating system, these are the most advanced and powerful internal functions of the elemental software platform operations, and are normally never referenced or used by most of the applications programmers who create Visual software.

On the other hand, most *high-level* software functions are built upon elemental *low-level* functions, and can be called by other software as software reuse objects, so that the application programmer never has to 're-invent the wheel'.

A SAPI speech *engine* is just such a Windows low-level operating system function program and its constituent run-time or *Dynamic Link Library*'s (*DLL's*) that does all of the actual work of recognizing speech or translating text into speech for output to a PC sound system speaker.

Most Windows SAPI compliant Speech Recognition engines convert audio input signals to that speech engine's specific phonemes, which can then be translated into text for use in other applications. A Text-To-Speech or computer speech synthesis engine does the same thing, but in the opposite direction.

All speech engines are OLE or COM objects that control recognition or generate speech according to a precise set of specifications and mode of speech recognition or speech synthesis.

This requires that you must work very closely with the available SAPI documentation for that particular object or control, and meet all specification requirements with regard to mode, engine type, or anything else that is listed in the SAPI caveats, or else your SAPI application may not always work.

Every speech engine has a different set of discrete operational technology methods and technical function processes to achieve either speech recognition or speech synthesis.

Therefore, there are many very specialized SAPI compliant Windows speech engines designed and proven effective for even very specialized speech applications, like foreign language translation and localization, disabilities access, human-machine prosthetic device programming, recreational games, and educational multi-media programming, to name but a few.

The standard Microsoft SAPI speech engines are most effective in over 95% of all speech software applications for use by the general public and should thus be regarded as your first best source for either a speech synthesis or speech recognition engine.

In this book we will assume that you will be using Microsoft standard SAPI 4.0 speech engines in your own speech programming applications, or else an MS-Windows SAPI-compatible vendor SDK, such as those available from Lernout & Hauspie, Dragon Systems for NaturallySpeaking, or IBM for ViaVoice.

You should also be aware that you can use the Microsoft Speech SDK and the SAPI 4.0 ActiveX libraries with any other SAPI-compliant speech software vendor's own SDK or API, because they have to first be certified as fully tested to work with SAPI before they can put the Microsoft logo on their website or shrink-wrap software product.

But if you do not see the Microsoft logo on the website or shrink-wrap box for any non-Microsoft speech software that runs on Windows, do not automatically assume that it is SAPI-compliant.

Always ask first for the proof of SAPI certification, or you may be sorry later when your own speech apps are not fully SAPI compliant on every PC even if they seem to work on the PC that they were first developed on.

2.3 *Windows Visual Basic SAPI ActiveX Speech Controls to the Rescue*

Before the release of Version 4.0 of Windows Speech API, all speech recognition programming could only be written either at the low-level using C++ or high-level using C++ or Visual Basic, and only some of the very high-level functions could be accessed by Visual Basic.

But after SAPI Version 4.0, Microsoft added extensive new Windows speech functionality that could be called at a very high-level even by simple Visual Basic object code, as well as a whole new set of speech functions which could be implemented using simple calls, or references to very high-level objects from within Visual Basic code.

Version 4.0 also added the ability to support Visual Basic script and several web HTML scripting languages, which are even more within the easy reach of new programmers, or even advanced computer users. These new speech functions first provided in the Version 4.0 Speech API kits were all based on the Microsoft ActiveX standard and are the primary focus of all speech programming examples in this book.

ActiveX has done more than any other development to make all of the most sophisticated technology involved in speech recognition programming readily available at a high-level to make speech recognition programming fast and easy!

ActiveX is the Microsoft technology that allows Visual Basic and other Visual programming environments to embed and share controls, and provides major productivity gains to the programmer, as well as the foundation for standardized speech interfaces to provide greater reliability and consistent look-and-feel for Windows computer users.

The ActiveX speech programming controls that are provided as part of the Microsoft Speech API and Speech SDK Suite are generally in the form of run-time control file libraries, as well as object classes and other components, that must first be loaded and added to the speech programmer IDE development platform, then can be embedded in a Visual Basic form and runtime distribution files.

This varies somewhat from the usual set-up to establish ActiveX controls into Internet applications, and both software implementation and configuration processes will be demonstrated later in this book.

2.4   How Microsoft SAPI Makes Windows Visual Basic Speech Faster and Better

In addition, the trade-offs for inherent efficiency and relative stability of the Microsoft Windows operating system, and the relative ease of getting to low-level Windows functions by Microsoft Foundation Class calls, also greatly benefits all speech programmers.

The way that Windows handles SAPI marshalling and messaging services becomes very important with regard to the need to handle concurrent instances as well as file handling on several speech software objects at the same time.

Some of these data objects can be very large and the event controls can be incredibly complex, especially in order to handle continuous natural speech and localization recognitions.

But first, you should know that the two most important external file object types that you need to know about, especially with respect to discrete versus continuous speech in all Windows environments, are known as lexicons and vocabularies.

These file types were first introduced in Chapter One with regard to their role in grammars and foreign language automated speech translation and localization, but the important thing here is the challenge of their size to external file handling which is so efficiently handled by Windows.

A *lexicon* is a database, relational table or look-up file that equates a given word to its component phonemes. The lexicon tells exactly how a particular text string for spelling a word should be linked to a particular series of IPA phonemes and speech Unicodes.

Most lexicons are regarded as *bi-directional grammars*, which means that they can be used for either speech recognition or for computer speech synthesis, or both. They are also typically fairly small and more commonly used with discrete command control speech software.

A *vocabulary* is single column table or file of word strings which can be parsed in order to determine if a given spoken word should be recognized or treated in any special way.

Most vocabularies are regarded as uni-directional grammars, and are normally used for speech recognition only. They are also typically much bigger than lexicons or localization file objects, and are more often used with continuous natural speech dictation or transcription software.

It is also important for you to know that another big reason for the demonstrated efficiency gains of Microsoft SAPI over any other current speech API, as well as the major productivity gains of speech programmers using SAPI 4.0, is related to the OLE Component Object Model (COM). This is also notably the basis as well for several other Microsoft technology innovations that have been used to improve the efficiency and usability of SAPI.

The most important of these innovations is SAPI ActiveX speech controls, which are the corner stone of Microsoft SAPI Windows Visual Basic speech recognition programming facilities.

ActiveX should already be a familiar concept to even Visual Basic 5 programmers, since it is based on.VBX and.OCX control technology that were the earliest foundations for Visual Basic form programming.

Later in this book we will explain in more detail how Microsoft and its ActiveX control technology can make Windows speech recognition programming accessible for rapid prototyping and general purpose applications.

A Component Object (CO) is either an OLE embedded or OLE cross-linked application sharing object specified in accordance with the OLE Component Object Model (COM) Windows standard.

A Component Object has a specific set of Windows interface objects that can communicate with that object, with parameter control data associated with each instance of the object as activated at runtime, and also has ability to run multiple instances of software on the same PC at one time.

It is important to mention at this point that the CO Model (or COM) objects, and their related methods and events, are the basis for about 90% (or more) of Windows speech recognition programming. Most of the programming in order to use both high-level and low-level SAPI object facilities involve C++ and Object Oriented (00) programming.

Before we jump into a lot more detail about the internals of SAPI or ActiveX speech components and other high-level speech objects and controls, you are probably now very eager to have your first look at (and listen to) some typical SAPI based speech applications similar to what you can make yourself using Visual Basic with SAPI.

So get ready to obtain and install your own SAPI speech tools. But first we will briefly review the release specifics of SAPI 4.0a, the first Microsoft Speech API to make it possible for any Windows Visual Basic programmer to create their own Windows Visual Basic speech programs and Windows add-ons based on simple ActiveX controls!

2.5   Getting to Know MS Speech API and Visual Basic Speech Suites Even Better

You should by now be aware that Windows speech recognition programming is a very complex world, but by now it should begin to be starting to be a little more clear to you how all of the many pieces fit together.

Although we will be getting into a lot more detail about the most critical internals of the major Windows speech recognition programming facilities and foundations, for now you should be starting to understand the three most important tools in the Microsoft speech recognition programming world:

- The Microsoft Speech API (SAPI)
- The Microsoft Speech SDK Suite
- The Microsoft Speech Engines

You should by now have a fairly good understanding of what the Microsoft Speech API (SAPI) is all about, at least with regard to its high-level component objects which you can use in your Visual Basic, VBA Office Suite macros, or VB Script web page applications.

You should probably also have a fair understanding of the Microsoft Speech SDK, especially if you have used a Visual Basic project design IDE or other Interactive Developer Environment to create and modify Windows object software application programs in the past.

2.6   Microsoft Speech API and Speech Engines Versus Other Speech Toolkits

Although we have not yet specifically discussed how the Microsoft SAPI Speech SDK works in Visual Basic programs, you can probably guess that it is simply an additional set of speech related object components and special speech recognition programming tools that you can add to your Visual Basic 6 component libraries and toolbars.

The concept of a speech engine may be new to you, but by now you should also have started to understand that it has to do with giving your Windows speech programs additional power and control.

You should also probably have guessed that the way that Microsoft provides for Windows compliant speech application programming is very similar to other component object models and methods that you have used in the past, and is designed to allow you to activate, control and maintain speech software by use of property specification and event handling not all that different from the same ways that you would build and operate any other Windows program.

Since you have already probably have a good understanding of each of these three speech recognition programming facilities, you can probably easily understand why Microsoft bundled them together to make a single Windows Speech SDK Suite.

2.7   *Microsoft Speech SDK Suite and the Future of Windows Speech Tools*

You should be aware that you can obtain each of the speech component facilities either separately one at a time, or else you can obtain all three of them together in the Microsoft Speech SDK Suite.

Normally it is recommended that you should obtain them all together, including all of the standard Microsoft Windows speech engines and standard voices, so that they will all be from the latest release.

If you already have speech engines from another Microsoft Windows SAPI-certified vendor, you may not want or need the Microsoft speech engines, since there may some instances where speech software can be confused with regard to which speech engine it should be using, and there may be runtime conflicts.

But for the most part, you should normally obtain all of the standard Microsoft speech engines from the same place, and load them onto your PC, since you may need them in some special speech application instances, even if they are not primary speech engines.

You should always remember that the technology foundations of Windows speech programming are changing so rapidly that it is still a good idea to stay as close to Microsoft standards as possible.

No matter how big or technically advanced another speech vendor may be in other related software technology areas, Microsoft is moving so quickly as Windows goes into the early 2000's that it may sometimes be hard for the other vendors to keep up with regard to maintaining full Windows SAPI standard compliance.

If you get too far way from pure SAPI in your speech software, you do so at your own risk. No matter what anyone may say, no one supports Windows programming better than Microsoft!

2.8   Version History of Windows SAPI Library and Visual Basic Speech Suites

From the brief history of Microsoft SAPI, you should remember that the early origins of SAPI began with the Microsoft participation in the SRAPI speech API specification developed by the Opens Systems Committee led by Novell and IBM in the early 1990's, and Microsoft developed its own Windows-specific speech API standard in early 1996.

There was no official SAPI 1.0, although there were several beta versions that were passed around throughout 1996.

In fact, the SAPI project was still officially a Microsoft R&D think-tank project until early 1997, when the first official version, SAPI 2.0 was released.

The original SAPI 2.0 was still more of an experimental API library than anything else, and to be quite frank, there were not really any high level components in SAPI 2.0. It was definitely a Windows low level library, very powerful but you had to be a fairly advanced C++ programmer to use the API.

There was still a lot of on-the-fly design changes, as well as fix patches, in the intermediate version releases of SAPI 2.0, and those releases were often unofficial patches issued only to key Microsoft partners such as Dragon Systems (now ScanSoft) and Lernout & Hauspie (also now ScanSoft), who were both very much involved in developing specialized speech engines and their own SDK's based on SAPI.

However, that is clearly to be expected given the incredibly rapid pace that had been set by Microsoft as SAPI 2.0 was developed.

The very next year in 1998, SAPI 3.0 was officially released, after a frantic build-up from COMDEX demonstrations the previous fall, when Dragon Systems ran away with numerous awards for NaturallySpeaking, the first large-vocabulary continuous natural speech dictation and transcription software to be successfully implemented using Windows.

Although it was itself based on SAPI, the Dragon products out-classed the first IBM *ViaVoice* products for Windows, as well as Microsoft's own first speech dictation products. But as Microsoft pointed out, those were giveaways with Windows 98 and not intended to compete with more sophisticated speech products such as NaturallySpeaking anyway.

The power of SAPI 3.0 was still directed mostly at C++ programmers, and programmers who were comfortable with COM and DCOM as well as Microsoft Foundation Class programming. Although there was some support for Visual Basic and there were some facilities based on ActiveX, with SAPI 3.0 you really had to be a very advanced C++ programmer to write Windows speech software.

Because of the overwhelming demand that Dragon *NaturallySpeaking* and IBM *ViaVoice* as well as a lot of other Windows speech software created throughout 1998, there was a lot of interest from Windows developers for more high level SAPI 3.0 functions.

As a result, in early 1999 the next version was released by the Microsoft Intelligent Interface Technologies (IIT) division. SAPI 4.0a greatly expanded upon the Visual Basic and ActiveX components to cover all of the same facilities that had been available before in SAPI 3.0 to low level Windows for C++ and COM programmers.

The Microsoft SAPI 4.0 libraries and associated speech engines as well as the Microsoft SDK Suite were first made available in early 1999 by Intelligent Interface Technologies (IIT) division as one of the first initiatives of the Microsoft Windows 2000 release.

The Microsoft SAPI 5.0 version of the Windows Speech API was made available in October 2001. The decision to release the software with a new version number was in fact a little bit controversial because the version 5.0 is really the same as version 4.0, with some additional tools, methods and function extensions which allow SAPI version 4.0 code to be used more efficiently with the Internet.

The new version 5.0 of SAPI also accommodates many new standards for web browsers as well as an ambitious jump from foundation on Windows 2000 to Windows XP operating system. This was even more ambitious considering that it completely leapfrogs over Windows ME operating system that was introduced between Win 2000 and Win XP.

Although this book continues to primarily focus on SAPI 4.0, the most critical and useful features of SAPI 5.0 are also demonstrated later in this book, related to integration of SAPI to MAPI and TAPI for improved high level Visual Basic ActiveX voice enabling of web and mobile wireless network software.

2.9 *Windows Visual Basic Runtime Files Needed to Use SAPI on Your PC*

Before you try to load and use SAPI in your own Windows Visual Basic programming environment, you should be aware that there are several runtime VB and Windows sound system files that you will need in order for SAPI to work on your own developer platform for Visual Basic 6.

Before you attempt to install the Windows Speech SDK Suite and use the Windows speech engines and SAPI 4.0, you should first go over the list of required files in Table 2.1 in order to be sure that you have everything that you

need in order to both run and create Windows SAPI speech application software projects.

If you do not find one or more of the listed files in your Windows or System
folders, you should immediately go to the Microsoft website and do a search
for that filename, since most of these files can be downloaded directly from the
website.

If you do not find any of the missing files on the Microsoft website, you
should contact Microsoft developer technical support, but be prepared that
sometimes due to demand it can take awhile to get the specific information or
files if you can not find them yourself.

Listing 2.1. Windows runtime files you need to use speech in Visual Basic.

```
SETUP1.EXE      Program that installs the Visual Basic
                runtime.
VB5STKIT.DLL    Part of program that installs Visual
                Basic runtime.
VB5STKIT.DLL    Visual Basic runtime dll.
STDOLE2.TLB     OLE file needed for Visual Basic on
                Windows 95.
OLEAUT32.DLL    OLE file needed for Visual Basic on
                Windows 95.
OLEPRO32.DLL    OLE file needed for Visual Basic on
                Windows 95.
ASYCFILT.DLL    OLE file needed for Visual Basic on
                Windows 95.
CTL3D32.DLL     OLE file needed for Visual Basic.
COMCAT.DLL      OLE file needed for Visual Basic.
MSMAPI32.OCX    Control needed for email sample application.
COMCT232.OCX    Common controls used in sample applications.
COMCTL32.OCX    Common control used in sample applications.
RICHTX32.OCX    Rich text control used by dictation
                applications.
RICHED32.DLL    Rich text control component.
MCI32.OCX       Multimedia control used by MAPI applications.
```

You should be pleased to learn that if your version of the Microsoft Speech
SDK Suite is SAPI 4.0 a revision or greater, these runtime Visual Basic binaries
should be included in your install files.

2.10   Get Your Own Speech Tool Suite and SAPI ActiveX Libs for Visual Basic

You will no doubt want your own Microsoft Speech SDK Suite of Windows speech software development tools and speech engines. You will have 2 options when you go to the Microsoft Speech website download center links for either a "bare-bones" or "fully loaded" version of Windows speech tools:

- SAPI4SDK.exe (7.65 MB-w/all code & samples, but no speech engines)

- SAPI4SDKSUITE.exe (39.06 MB-w/runtime code/samples, plus voices)

One of the most obvious things that will probably jump out at you when you compare these two options are the great difference in size of the version without versus with speech engines and voice files. But you will probably understand how big the individual speech engines and speech files are after you more fully understand how this technology works, since it actually required storing digitized recordings of each possible human sound as spoken by each of the individual categories of speakers as audio match signatures.

You should also be aware that you may not need the full SAPI 4.0 SDK Suite if you will be using a third-party vendor SDK (just as IBM *ViaVoice* or Dragon *NatSpeak*), since they will have their own speech engines and voice files. But even if you use other vendor high-level specialized speech SDK's that are SAPI-compliant to work on MS Windows environments, you will undoubtedly want your own Windows Speech SDK Suite. You may just want to be able to access all the Windows OSA speech foundations, facilities and tools, or have greater access to low-level operating system functions if you ever need them.

You should be aware that there are dozens of SAPI-certified Windows speech SDK vendors, and many have several specialized speech API's as well as their own very high-level Windows (or very low-level Windows) SDK's to meet either vertical or horizontal application programming needs.

Some also have specialized localization vocabularies or lexicons and grammars, but you often have to obtain their SDK in order to use their special speech localization files.

As you can probably expect, a lot of after-market Windows vendors and VARS, including both very small and very large companies, may claim to be fully Windows SAPI-compliant, but in reality they are only compliant when they want to be.

Always go to the Microsoft website or Microsoft Developer Network (MSDN) news groups to get official as well as peer professional programmer information about any other vendor speech API or SDK before you invest a lot of time and effort integrating it into your software and only find out later it is not as good as the latest and greatest from Microsoft.

2.11   Where and How to Get SAPI Software for Visual Basic Speech Programming

As everyone knows, there are not very many things in life that are free, and anything that you get for free probably has a lot of hidden strings attached.

But believe it or not, Microsoft has traditionally provided all of its versions of SAPI up to and including SAPI 4.0 and their Speech SDK Suite for web download, completely *free* of charge. This is thanks to a special commitment that Microsoft founder Bill Gates made toward the future of Windows computer speech technology, due to the special potential he has expressed in many interviews and in his auto-biography that he believes it can have on world peace and understanding between all nations.

And it is not a free trial, it is freeware, as long as you agree to carefully abide by the license agreement that precedes the download. There is one catch, however. The Microsoft Windows Speech SDK Suite is only free for download over the Internet and there is no guarantee that the offer for free download of the Windows Speech will not be withdrawn at any future date.

However, the author of this book is also committed as much as Bill Gates to the belief that SAPI, and especially SAPI 4.0, is an important resource for a better future for the world. This author will attempt to help to assure the goals of the Microsoft founder by providing a link to the MS Speech API 4.0 download site as long as it is available, and will strive to continue to make it available on a CD to anyone who purchases this book and contacts the author at his website (www.qualimatic.com) for a nominal fee to cover cost of electronic media, copying, shipping and handling.

One of the most important things that made Microsoft such a success has always been their commitment to the basic principle of making it as easy as possible for programmers to develop software products to run on Windows platforms. As a result they end up selling a lot of Windows platform software as well as related vertical applications when they give away Windows programming tools early in any new computer market penetration. So not feel sorry for Microsoft, they will make a lot more money everytime they give away a free copy of SAPI, since you have to buy Visual Basic in order to use it, right?

As you can probably expect, there has been a tremendous demand for download of this particular free SDK. So if you download the entire SDK it can take a very long time (SAPI 4.0a is 40 megabytes), which makes it very difficult to download in its entirety unless you have a high-speed dedicated line.

You can also get the complete Microsoft Speech SDK Suite, including all the speech engines, SAPI 4.0 libraries, and documentation on the Microsoft Developer Network (MSDN) CD.

So there are several ways that you can get the MSDN software, which includes just about everything in the world that any serious Windows programmer would ever want or need. But one of the easiest ways is to purchase the Microsoft Visual Studio, which includes Visual Basic, Visual C++, Visual J++, Visual FoxPro database, Visual InterDev for the web, and the MSDN libraries. And by the way, SAPI 4.0 and Speech SDK Suite are on MSDN CD number 2.

If you do decide to download the Microsoft Speech SDK Suite from the Internet, the first thing that you must do is go to the Microsoft IIT website (www.microsoft.com/iit), and you should see a link to their SAPI download center. If the link changes (as you should understand it may), you can search for it by using the words "SAPI 4.0 Download" on the MSDN search form page.

When you go to the Microsoft download center, you will have to either log in using the Microsoft Developer Network registration ID and password that you have already been assigned, or else you will have to apply for one by registering, as shown in Figure 2.2.

You can also get the latest version of SAPI 5.1+ and all of its related speech SDK software and documentation via free download from the Microsoft Download center, but first you need to register as a Microsoft Developer to provide contact information related to future updates.

2.12   *Loading Your Windows SAPI Engines and Speech SDK Suite*

As has been previously indicated, there are several download options for the Microsoft Speech SDK Suite, including the download of the entire bundle of SAPI 4.0, Microsoft speech engines, and the SDK tools to create your own speech engines, or any of these three software libraries all by itself.

Because the total size of the complete SDK Suite (40 meg) is very great versus downloading SAPI 4.0 and the speech tools only (8 meg), you may be tempted to only obtain SAPI 4.0 libraries, but if you are, you should reconsider.

Unless you have other SAPI-compliant speech engines from another vendor, and have sufficient documentation from them on how to make them work with SAPI, your Speech SDK will not work.

You always need to have some vendor's Windows speech engines. So its usually a matter of all or nothing, unless you already have another vendor's speech engines and have all of their documentation to know how to integrate them with Microsoft SAPI.

As indicated earlier there are two primary download options, which include either the SAPI libraries (approx. 8 MB) or the entire Speech SDK including both the SAPI libraries and the Microsoft speech engines (approx. 39 MB). Unless you already have other speech engines from another vendor like IBM, L&H, or Dragon you need the entire Speech SDK with SAPI speech engines. But to learn to program with the Microsoft Speech API using Visual Basic ActiveX voice controls, you only need the SAPI libraries (however, if you want to fully test and modify the examples to build your own speech apps, you need both).

You might want to put off your download of the Microsoft Speech SDK Suite till late night, or at least the end of your business day. It can take up to an hour or even more, depending on your modem speed. You should also be prepared that it can also take several attempts to do the download, since the download does not always restart easily. When and if you are able to get the complete download successfully finished, it might be a good idea to immediately back it up to any alternative media or other storage on your LAN if you have one.

You should be prepared that depending on your modem speed, download of the complete Speech SDK Suite can take several hours, or days, since the demand on Microsoft download servers can be very great. So it may be necessary to restart the download several times if there is especially heavy traffic on your ISP that results in disconnects.

2.13   Where to Get SAPI Manuals and Speech Software Support for Visual Basic

There are numerous sources of documentation and support for Microsoft Windows speech application software programmers.

The first, best source is always the online documentation that you are able to get from either MSDN or the special online SAPI speech recognition programming documentation site supported by Microsoft's Intelligent Interface Technologies (IIT) division, and by Microsoft Speech Developer partners.

Until you get your Microsoft Speech SDK Suite and SAPI libraries either from download from IIT or Microsoft Developer Network CD, you can view

SAPI documents that are on the download files or the CD by going to the IIT website at www.microsoft.com/iit (or www.qualimatic.com).

The online SAPI documentation that you can access from Microsoft IIT and MSDN websites is exactly the same as documentation manuals in Microsoft Speech SDK Suite.

The online SAPI documentation is very detailed and is in fact just exactly the same documents on web pages that you get in.RTF format as part of your Speech SDK Suite download, or on the CD from MSDN. An example of the kind of SAPI documentation that you can browse online from the Microsoft IIT and MSDN website is shown here.

But you should be aware that there are thousands of pages of the SAPI documentation online, and depending on Internet traffic, it can be very cumbersome to browse it when you are in a hurry with a problem. You should also be aware that there are over 10,000 pages of SAPI documentation in Word format that are available on both the IIT website, and in the SAPI download from Microsoft MSDN, which is another big part of the reason why it is almost 40 meg in size.

Unless you have ample time and bandwidth to wade through 10,000 pages of online documentation about SAPI, that should be a very good reason to buy this book!

There are several Microsoft Speech Technology related websites and FAQ's. You can also write Microsoft directly if you want to, but the demand is great, so responses can take awhile. But just about every SAPI speech recognition programming topic you may ever need to know about has most likely already been posted some time in the past month.

Microsoft Speech Labs has several ways that you can contact them if you need to, and they are listed on the Microsoft Speech home page. If you have problems locating the answers to your SAPI Windows speech programming technical questions (which will almost undoubtedly happen due to the size and complexity of both SAPI and the overwhelmingly detailed documentation that is provided with the Microsoft Speech SDK Suite), you can always contact Microsoft technical support via email.

Due to the incredible volume of email questions that they get, the folks at Microsoft technical support are very clear about the fact that you may have to wait a very long time for an answer to your specific problem. Therefore they always recommend that you should first scan the FAQ's as well as newsgroup topics related to SAPI.

Just to be sure that you have all your bases covered with regard to all available MSDN information about any SAPI programming problem you ever have, you should always go to MSDN search site first just so you get the most current official Microsoft information. Your first and surest way to find information about a specific SAPI programming problem is to go to the MSDN online search form.

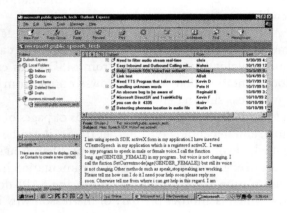

Figure 2.1.

The Microsoft Speech Technology news group is your best source of general as well as esoteric speech technology details that can have very great significance to SAPI standards and its future direction.

Due to the complexity of the SAPI specification and all of the very detailed documentation that is available on IIT and MSDN websites related to SAPI, you should always select to search ALL sections of the MSDN libraries, but you can also get help from your peers using newsgroups, as shown in Figure 2.1.

The MSDN search engine is very efficient, so it will not make much difference in search seek time, but could make a lot of difference if you miss out on the information you needed!

There are some very important SAPI speech recognition programming related news groups that you will find located on the Microsoft news server website (http://msnews.microsoft.com) that can be extremely useful to you as a Microsoft speech programmer, or for posting technical questions related to SAPI speech programming so you can get some help from other Windows speech programmers.

These news groups are:

- *Microsoft.public.speech_tech*
- *Microsoft.public.speech_tech.sdk*

Of these two news groups, the first is usually more general and related to both historical as well as future developments in the overall strategy and positioning of Microsoft as the predominant speech technology software vendor.

If you have had much previous experience with use of newsgroups as a source of quick information on new and emerging technology, you should not be surprised that a lot of the messages that are posted are not really relevant to the specific topic of the news group.

A lot of people get in a panic about a programming problem and post to both the technical and general news groups. We can all probably relate to that panic, but both newsgroups are read by Microsoft and most Windows speech programmers, so you really only need to post to just one.

Sometimes it may feel cumbersome to wade through all the messages, but it can be worth it, at least once, just to pick up on a lot of technical tidbits that you might not have known otherwise.

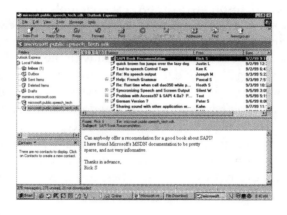

Figure 2.2.

The Microsoft Speech SDK news group is officially related to questions and comments involving particular versions of SAPI and its libraries, as they are intended to be used, as well as unique special problems that can be confounding in your own applications.

It's a good idea to browse through some of the most recent postings when you join a newsgroup, but after that it is probably best to use a search engine to find a short list of postings interesting to you.

The second newsgroup, shown in Figure 2.2, is intended more to be specifically directed at technical issues related to the SAPI libraries and using the Windows Speech SDK tools, so it is probably the most useful to answering most speech recognition programming questions.

2.14   *Running Install Programs for SAPI Speech Engines and Speech Suite for VB*

When you have either downloaded or copied your Windows Speech SDK Suite, with or without all of the Microsoft speech engines, you should first check its size against the download manifest (or the CD manifest if you get from MSDN) to be sure that you have everything that you expected.

The full Microsoft Speech SDK Suite download should be 39,063 KB, and unless it has been renamed or corrupted, it should be named as 'SAPI4SDKSUITE.EXE' and have the same file size.

Since it is a self-extracting executable, all you have to do is click on its application icon from Explorer, or run from the Start menu. After you start running the install program, the first thing you will see is 'legal-ese' for your license agreement.

Due to the fact Microsoft gives the SAPI speech tools to developers for free, but does require a few special conditions that you may not have seen before, be sure that you scroll down and read the entire agreement. If you do not read it but just click the 'Yes' button in order to get on with the install quickly, or do not care, you are still legally bound to all of the conditions Microsoft has listed.

After doing some preliminary scans to register your system to the install software, and make sure you have enough room and the basic hardware required, you will get an active window with text, to either accept or change the location where the Microsoft Speech SDK software and libraries will be installed.

Unless you have some special considerations, as for a LAN environment standards that you can not override, it is best to stay with the usual recommendations from Microsoft (which you probably already know if you are a Windows programmer).

You will be given the opportunity to change the location of the download to somewhere else if you prefer, but its normally a good idea to accept the default and download into a special folder for the Microsoft Speech SDK in the Windows Program folder.

Depending on the speed of your PC, it can take up to 30 minutes to completely load and install all of the software that Microsoft provides with the Microsoft Speech SDK Suite.

When it is finished, depending on the specific install program and version of Microsoft Speech SDK Suite that you installed, your PC may be automatically or manually restarted.

Microsoft Speech SDK Suite will download to 3 application folders. The two you may not know about yet are Microsoft Voice and Microsoft Dictation, both SAPI add-ons.

If you come back from your coffee break after running the Microsoft Speech SDK install program and find the message box to notify you that the install was successful and you are ready to reboot to register SAPI, you are all set, and ready to begin your new career as a Windows speech programmer!

2.15   Exploring Your Speech SDK and SAPI Libraries for Windows Visual Basic

The first thing that you will want to do after your new Windows Speech SDK Suite and SAPI libraries have been installed is to begin to do some exploring on your own, to check out all the folders and files to see what is what and where. That's what Explorer is for, right?

Regardless of where you specified to have your Speech SDK Suite and SAPI libraries installed, the name of the folder where it was installed should be 'Microsoft Speech SDK' (unless you change it).

You can either begin your inventory of the Microsoft Speech SDK using Explorer, or if you are most interested in taking a look at the Visual Basic sample speech programs, you can open using Visual Basic, and in either case you should see 10 subordinate MS Speech SDK folders.

2.16   A Look at SAPI Folder Sample Programs from Other Languages than VB

When you open the 'SAMPLES' folder, you will probably be overwhelmed by the incredible number of sample SAPI program code folders that you find.

When you open the 'ACTIVEX' folder in the SAPI program 'SAMPLES' folder, you will see four more folders, which correspond to the four Windows programming languages and facilities.

If you are a Visual Basic programmer, and VB programmers are the largest segment of the population in the Microsoft Windows world, you are probably most interested in the VB applications, so you might want to open the 'VB5' folder.

The main reason that so many sub-level folders are in the 'VB5' folder is because these Visual Basic capabilities related to ActiveX are new with SAPI 4.0 that they were put into just one single folder.

If you look at the high level Program Files sub-directories where the Microsoft Speech SDK was installed, you will notice two additional folders for two fully production Microsoft speech software products that are comparable to IBM ViaVoice and Dragon NaturallySpeaking, which Microsoft first demonstrated at COMDEX in 1997. Notably, this was before Microsoft decided to bundle with its own free Speech SDK instead of marketing for direct competition against versions of ViaVoice and NaturallySpeaking, since they are actually very similar but slightly less powerful products.

These two freeware products for SAPI developers are Microsoft Voice and Microsoft Dictation (which are also provided with some versions of Windows 2000, when they became part of MS-Agent).

2.17   Microsoft Voice Program 'What Can I Say' and Window Speech Help Facility

If you have used any Windows speech recognition software applications in the past, you may already be acquainted with the 'What Can I Say' Windows speech help facility (AKA, 'WCIS').

If you are not previously acquainted with 'What Can I Say' help facility, you should try it out, because it is one of the most powerful speech help facilities provided by Microsoft for SAPI compliant speech applications.

You should also know that 'What Can I Say' will probably be the main speech help facility that any SAPI savvy users of your speech software will be most likely to go to for help using your SAPI discrete speech command control dictation applications.

Don't worry about looking for a lot of instructions in how to configure the list of words and phrases that will be actively loaded for your own SAPI speech recognition software application.

The word command list to be recognized will normally be generated automatically from your grammars and special lexicon rule files using compile and external reference methods that we will begin to discuss in detail late in this book.

Although you can actually either exclude or add words or phrases using some wizards demonstrated later in this chapter, for the most part you will want your standard 'WCIS' list to be exactly the same words your SAPI speech engine grammars are defined to listen for.

The first thing you should do in order to be able to use 'What Can I Say' is to open the Microsoft Voice application.

You can try the Microsoft Voice application by running from the Windows Start menu or from Microsoft Explorer if you prefer.

But if you will be doing much SAPI speech programming and SAPI speech application testing (which we assume you will be), you should add Microsoft Voice to your '*Startup*' folder.

Depending on where you decided to download you SDK4 Suite libraries and speech program code, you should normally have Microsoft Dictate and Microsoft Voice. To begin Speech SDK configuration you should normally run executable for MSVOICE first.

Normally the first time you run Microsoft Voice, you will get a message box to explain how Microsoft Voice can be activated, and from then on the icon for Microsoft Voice will be in your Windows active task bar.

All you have to do when you want to bring up the Microsoft Voice menu is to simply right-click on the 'blue-V' Microsoft Voice icon, and one of the menu items listed will be 'What Can I Say'.

If you click on 'What Can I Say', the WCIS window will pop up with a list of words and phrases that have been defined to the currently active speech application (if indeed there is one currently active).

The instancing should start using any default grammar and vocabulary files, which should be actively recognized and executed as command events anytime that you say them, as shown in Figure 2.3.

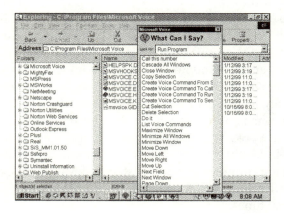

Figure 2.3.

After you run the MSVOICE.EXE application, it will add to your task bar as a "V" icon. When you right-click on the "V" icon, Microsoft Voice control menu will pop-up, and the first thing that you need to look at is the Microsoft Voice "What Can I Say" help menu.

All of the words or phrases that you see listed in 'What Can I Say', as shown in Figure 3.1, are normally easily recognized for 99% of the human population. Normally a command function list will be "localized" words, such as special technical terms that would only be relevant for a particular profession or idioms and slang for a particular geography.

You can also select individual commands to execute with your mouse just like any other scrolling list box. This will come in very handy if there are erratic problems with your microphone or the speech engine is not loaded properly (or crashes).

You can also use voice commands to scroll WCIS, as you can imagine. However, the most important tip here is that anytime you are having hardware or software problems that are causing your SAPI speech application to hang up, WCIS can and WILL be your very best way to get it working again without a 'Ctl-Alt-Delete'!

You will get a different "What Can I Say" list depending on most recent SAPI speech application, speech engine instance, and recognition grammar files currently active.

Aside from 'What Can I Say', the other almost equally as important reason to put Microsoft Voice in your 'Startup' folder and load everytime you boot up your computer, is the Microsoft Voice Help facility. When you look at the screen from the Microsoft Voice Help facility, you will probably notice that it looks very much like the general Windows Help troubleshooting facility.

In actual fact, the Microsoft Voice Help troubleshooting facility is a special extension of the general Windows Help troubleshooting menu that is loaded to your computer when the Microsoft Speech SDK Suite is first installed. It is also automatically attached to the runtime install files for your own SAPI speech software when you prepare it for distribution, as you will learn more about later in this book. Microsoft Voice is the application that contains all of the SAPI 4.0 help files and "cheat-sheets" that you may need for quick reference. Until you are comfortable with all standard Microsoft speech user conventions and technology, it is a good idea to keep Microsoft Voice active on your taskbar at all times.

2.18   Checking Out the SAPI Wordpad Speech Dictation Add-on Sample

The first SAPI 4.0 speech application program sample that we will examine at this point can be found in your 'ACTIVEX' folder in a sub-folder named 'OTHER'. This is actually a Word template, not a program. This folder will contain two files, one is a Microsoft Excel Worksheet macro program, and a Microsoft Wordpad Template macro named 'DICTATE.DOT'. The first we look at now, the latter we will be looking at later (and hopefully listening to, as well as talking to, if your sound system and microphone are installed and configured properly to be able to enter voice dictation and SAPI speech commands).

If you do not have your Microsoft Speech SDK software Suite installed yet, or if you do not even have the SAPI 4.0 software loaded on your PC yet, do not worry about that for right now. Just quickly read through the walk through of these examples shown in this first chapter. Later in this chapter we will walk you through all the detailed steps of loading and installing SAPI 4.0 including details on where you can get SAPI 4.0 and the Speech SDK Suite in a free download from Microsoft. When you finish reading this chapter, if you like you can then return to this section to actually open these samples folders and run each of the executables that we will describe. Or, if you are a really eager beaver and over-achiever, you can go immediately to begin playing with the SAPI 4.0 software installed and begin running these sample speech programs now before you go on with the chapter!

Before you decide whether or not to jump ahead and immediately install the Speech SDK Suite, you should be aware it can take up to one or two hours (or more) just to install and configure your Speech API, SDK programmer libraries, microphone and speakers. This can be much more if the software determines that your soundboard or microphone are not adequate and you have to make a trip to your local computer retail shop. Also, you should be aware that unless you already have the SAPI 4.0 software on CD-ROM, since the install program is over 40 megabytes in size, depending on the speed of your modem, it may take several hours to download over the Internet. So you might want to just look now and listen later!

You can either click on the Word template icon in Explorer, or find the executable speech program 'DICTATE.DOT' from your Start menu and Run from there, which ever you prefer. Depending on whether you have your Windows Office Macro Detection tab set 'on' or not, when you first open the.DOT, you may get a message box telling you that a macro has been detected. It may warn you that if you do not know the source of the macro it could have a macro virus, then ask you to select from buttons to either disable or enable the macro. If you got your copy of this sample speech add-on directly from Microsoft, then you should go ahead and enable the macro immediately, otherwise, you might want to scan for macro viruses first just in case. Always remember any time a.DOT macro template document is opened on any PC computer with a macro virus, it can secretly attach itself to any other open.DOT!

The first thing that you may notice is that it can take an unusually long time to load this particular macro. This is because even though it is a very high-level Windows speech object add-on, what that really means is a whole lot more additional embedded object overhead than your Word session normally carries, so it can understandably slow your overall Windows processing down a bit. The second thing you may notice when your Microsoft Word toolbar comes up, is the current active window will have a new button, with a little 'smiley face' and the message 'Not Listening'.

The other thing that you will see, if you click on the smiley little 'Not Listening' button, will be that the label on the button changes to 'Listening'. Go ahead and toggle the button on and off to see the button change in response to the click event. The next thing you should see is a message box with three little buttons, which should indicate if the active speech engine has begun recognizing.

If you move the cursor over the three buttons at the bottom of the Listening Window you will see that they do the following, respectively, when they are toggled:

- Capitalize or lower-case the last word spoken (or selected)
- Replay a recording of the word (which is saved in temp as .WAV)
- Pause or turn the active recognizer box on and off

If the speech recognizer engine is active, you will see the text '<Nothing>' while no audio input is detected from the microphone, and you will see your first Speech-To-Text recognitions scroll by before they appear in the text window of the Word application.

If everything is installed and configured properly, and if your microphone is in proper position and adjusted to the proper gain and volume level for your voice, you can toggle the active recognizer button (the one with the 'push-pin' icon), and begin talking.

Figure 2.4.

After you open SAPI Wordpad Dictation, keep saying the phrase "Hello World" until you say it the way the active Speech-To-Text speech recognition engine is expecting it to be "heard", and you see in text display the exact words that you really want it to recognize.

If you say the phrase *"Hello World"* very slowly, the result should be something like what is shown in Figure 2.4.

The phrase "Hello World" is comprised of two words, but do you know how many phonemes, or word-parts? Two? Three? Four? The answer is actually four. They sound out as: *"hel-oh wer-uld".*

That is why when you say the phrase *"Hello World"* very slowly, it may come out the first time as four misrecognized word matches: *"Hell oh were old".*

If you continue to say the phrase *"Hello World"*, a little bit faster each time, the speech engine should go from recognizing something like *"Hell oh were old"* to eventually getting the result with the meaning that you intended, *"Hello World".*

When the speech recognition engine makes a misrecognition or wrong match to either part of a word, or some garbled audio that it heard which it matched to a real word, this is known as a false positive match. When the speech recognizer engine simply fails to recognize a word that it was supposed to be listening for and the word was listed in its lexicon or vocabulary file objects, that is a false negative.

If everything in this speech recognition application is working properly, you should eventually see the text for the words that you are intending to say.

Once you get the result you want, you simply tab back to select words that you do not want and delete (either by keystrokes, or voice commands, if you already know how to do so, since this is something that you will not be taught until later in the book).

At first blush, when word recognition is not very good, most people will first think that there is either something wrong with the input microphone, or something 'funny' about the way a person may be speaking. While this would probably in fact be the case when installing new speech software on a computer user's PC, this should not be a big problem.

Later in this book we will learn more about speech diagnostic software wizards that are shipped with Microsoft Speech API that can help you solve both microphone system problems and speech training for people with unusual speaking patterns.

Again, if everything is working properly, you should end up with something like:

"HELLO WORLD!"

Congratulations, you have just 'spoken' your first speech program!

After you play with speaking words and phonemes for a little while, you will not normally have the same kind of misrecognitions that were experienced with each part of the words being heard as the wrong words. You should try playing with different speech recognizer engines, not only to create speech training files for your voice, but also to get a better understanding of how the recognizer hears your voice.

What you have just seen demonstrated here is known as prosody, which is related to the speed and tone of voice as it influences the speech recognition. Prosody is the vocal inflection, tone, timing and accent properties contained in individual patterns of speech. Prosody is the term that is most often used to refer to overall combination of properties that all contribute to a nature of a voice sounding male or female, young or old. It also reflects both individual speaker personality and the accent or dialect of each particular local area, which tend to be similar for people from each specific geographic locality.

Obviously, it is important to make sure that the prosody of a Text-To-Speech (TTS) application fully matches local accent and dialect in order to be easily understood. But it is also important to have some localization profiles that can be the default for all your speech recognition applications until the individual user's speech patterns have been trained or adapted. Both TTS input and STT/SR output speech engine parameters and properties focus on specific prosody elements, such as speed of talking and human body differences, in order to be able to control and emulate specialized speech character. These kinds of parameters are controlled by properties on the form that determine speech engine or voice, or modify the mode of the engine, or discrete prosody of the selected voice using control tags.

Control tags are a symbolic 'mark-up' language that are used in speech-to-text files to provide default or conditional long-term, as well as short-term, adjustments to properties and parameters that usually control a Text-To-Speech (TTS) computer generated speech application (similar to HTML a more commonly known mark-up language). Another thing that you have just seen is an example of the difference between discrete and continuous speech. When you speak very slowly, the parts of the word that you are wanting to say can be heard by the speech engine as gaps or pauses between words, and may try to delimit or parse the word parts as if they were entire words.

Now let's go on to another sample program, which goes to opposite direction. You have just seen a speech recognition, where the application is Speech-To-Text, now we will take a quick look at a speech synthesis, where the application is Text-To-Speech.

If you do some programming and have loaded or installed any type of development software (such as any version or level of Visual Basic, Visual J++, Visual C++, etc.) there may be some additional problems that could cause your PC to have low or erratic word recognition rates when you first install new speech software.

The problem could be that there are conflicts between the most currently loaded speech software engines or.DLL's, and some previously loaded speech software objects.

Sometimes you are not even aware that the earlier.DLL or speech software was even loaded on your computer, since it may have been loaded automatically as part of another product's install program.

For example, many non-Microsoft word processor or spreadsheet products contain either demos or even full-scale versions of speech dictation add-ons fully integrated into the base software. Later in this book, you will learn how you can check to see what other speech software objects may be loaded, and how to unload them, or if they might be causing poor performance to your Microsoft Speech API software (for yourself or anyone you give the speech programs that you develop yourself with Microsoft Speech API).

2.19   *Microsoft Dictation SAPI Speech to Text Transcription Executable Program*

The other SAPI demonstration and diagnostic speech application product that is provided with the Microsoft Speech SDK Suite is in fact and executable program, MS Dictation (AKA, 'DictaPad'). You will find DictaPad in the Microsoft Dictation folder in the default Program Files folder after installing and configuring MS SAPI Speech Suite, and when you execute it your should see something like Figure 2.5.

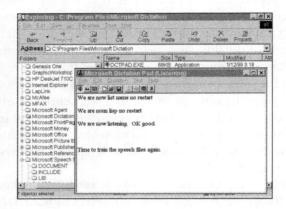

Figure 2.5.

The executable DCPAD.EXE program runs MS Dictation Pad (A.K.A., "DictaPad"), which is a standalone client that will enable Speech to Text (STT) for transcribing voice.

After you are sure that you have your microphone and sound system fully up to speed, you can put the hardware considerations behind you. You should hopefully be ready to run Microsoft Dictation.

You may remember that Microsoft Voice and Microsoft Dictation are somewhat scaled down but still very powerful SAPI Windows speech applications very comparable to IBM *ViaVoice* and Dragon *NaturallySpeaking*, which are both also based on Microsoft SAPI and the Microsoft Speech SDK. If you run Microsoft Dictation you will be able to find out if your hardware is able to handle speech recognition very quickly as you make your first attempts to transcribe voice to text.

If there is not input at all, go back to Microsoft Voice troubleshooting, otherwise your next step is to begin training your speech engine to recognize your voice. When you open and run the Microsoft Dictation application from either the Windows start menu, or from Microsoft Explorer, you will see a menu and taskbar that looks very similar to Microsoft WordPad.

If your microphone has already been tested and configured properly, when you click on the cartoon-balloon button that is first in the task bar, DictaPad will be activated and begin transcribing each word you say in continuous natural speech (or at least try). In fact, DictaPad is simply a SAPI speech-enabled version of WordPad.

Just as with Microsoft Voice, you should add Microsoft Dictation to your 'Startup' folder, since Microsoft Dictation also loads several very important speech software configuration and speech training file wizards you may need.

Use DictaPad to test voice audio quality of your microphone and room ambience around the computer where you run your SAPI speech applications. Do use DictaPad to learn and teach your users how to speak slowly and consistently to get the best natural continuous word recognition. Don't be too worried if first attempts to transcribe into DictaPad are not the best, since that is what speech training wizards are for! Expect a lot of amusing transcription "typos". And do not be discouraged, since speech technology is still very dependent on individual speaker voice transcription file training.

2.20 How to Code and Implement Your First Working SAPI Visual Basic Program

In Chapter One, you saw you very first simple SAPI speech enabled web page HTML to generate computer speech when the page was opened using a reference to ActiveX DirectSpeech control. You are now ready to take a first look (and listen) to a simple implementation of that code as shown in Figure 2.6.

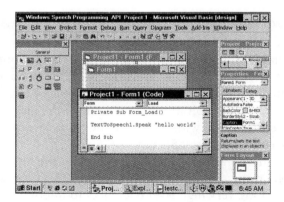

Figure 2.6

Visual Basic IDE code window for implementation of "Hello World" speech program.

In Listing 2.2, you will see your first simple SAPI speech enabled Visual Basic application form load procedure, which you can implement using your Visual Basic IDE with SAPI ActiveX controls.

Listing 2.2. Visual Basic Code to Say "Hello World" When a Program Is Opened.

```
Private Sub Form_Load()
TextToSpeech1.Speak "hello world"
End Sub
```

This simple procedure will speak the same text as computer generated speech each time that a Visual Basic form application is opened. You can try to yourself to implement this simple code as a Visual Basic project in your IDE, but good luck.

There are some obvious pieces missing, and this is in fact using DirectSpeech synthesis control, which you will learn how to implement later in Chapter Five of this book.

However, if you are an experienced Visual Basic programmer, you can probably immediately see how the ActiveX speech controls will work.

Regardless, you are going to need to install and activate your SAPI ActiveX controls to your IDE first, and there are still a few more things that you will need to understand before trying that, including your hardware requirements, and a little more about how audio I/O is processed by SAPI.

2.21   Summary

In the next chapter you will begin to learn a little more about the hardware requirements for Microsoft Windows speech software of the various types, and to configure your Microsoft Speech API and Speech SDK Suite.

You will also learn a little bit more about some of the diagnostic and troubleshooting tools that come with SAPI 4.0 and your speech engines, if you downloaded the entire Microsoft Speech SDK Suite.

In this chapter have learned a little bit more about the history of SAPI and Microsoft speech recognition programming, as well as the special role of ActiveX in establishing very high level references to internal Windows speech and sound system functions, so you can keep these things at a high logical level and not have to deal with them directly if you do not want to.

You also learned what you need to run SAPI speech software on your PC, and where you can get your own personal copy of the Microsoft Speech SDK

Suite and SAPI 4.0, as well as how to install the SAPI software and load to your own Visual Basic developer platform.

You have also learned how and where to get documentation and technical support from Microsoft and your fellow speech programmers if you ever need it for any special problems in your SAPI Visual Basic programs.

Finally, you took one last look at your Microsoft Speech SDK folders and files, to begin to get acquainted with the goodies you just got.

It may have been a little surprising, but also very significant, to see that ActiveX is only less than 10% at most of all the available options and capabilities of SAPI, since ActiveX and extended Visual Basic high-level controls were first introduced in SAPI 4.0 in 1999.

This is primarily because SAPI 4.0 was the first release to handle Visual Basic, VBA, and VB script web programming, so these are still very much cutting-edge emerging areas for Windows speech recognition programming.

But those areas will probably dominate all Windows speech programming by the next version of SAPI so it is good to stay on top of them from your earliest experience as a speech programmer if you can.

Chapter Three

Microsoft Platforms and Tools for Windows Visual Basic ActiveX Speech Programming

Before you can use your Microsoft Speech SDK Suite and your SAPI 4.0 high level ActiveX control libraries to create and modify your own speech applications you must first load and configure all of the Windows SAPI speech services type and class libraries, automation libraries, speech engines and voices. This is necessary regardless of the Windows Visual platform and language that you will be using to develop your speech software, but it is especially important with Visual Basic, VBA or VB Script web enabled software applications, which can require special runtime libraries as well.

You must also make sure that your hardware is sufficient to meet minimum requirements for each type of SAPI supported Windows speech application that you will be developing and testing using Microsoft Visual Basic, VBA or VB Script.

In this chapter, you will learn the following:

- Basic Platform Foundations for Microsoft Windows Visual Basic Speech Programs
- Basic Types of Microsoft Visual Basic Speech Applications
- Installing All the Low Level Foundations to Support Using High Level SAPI with Visual Basic
- Hardware Requirements for Each Type of SAPI Speech Engine for Visual Basic Programs

3.1 Basic Platform Foundations for MS Windows Visual Basic Speech Programs

Just as SAPI 4.0 added many new high level programming facilities for Visual Basic and VBA, there were also numerous new SAPI configuration wizards and automated diagnostic troubleshooting tools that can do most of the work, as well as make most of the decisions for you.

In order to become a true Windows Speech Programmer, it is not only necessary for you to know SAPI Visual Basic ActiveX speech controls, but it is also important that you know how to use all of the SAPI speech wizards and diagnostic tools.

You will need to know how and when to run SAPI diagnostic wizards to check your microphone, sound system, and other hardware, as well as how to create and configure individual user speech training files to help your SAPI applications match individual user voice patterns.

In this chapter, you will learn more about the Microsoft Windows Open System Architecture (WOSA) platform foundations that support SAPI and Windows speech programming using Visual Basic, as well as SAPI 4.0 tools and wizards to make your Windows speech programs defect-free.

Before you begin to prepare to fully configure and set-up your Microsoft Windows Speech SDK Suite to develop SAPI speech programs, you will first need to be sure that the computer or computers that you will be using to create as well as run your SAPI speech software will be sufficient to meet minimum specification requirements.

In order to understand requirements to configure your Windows Speech SDK, you first need to be sure you understand the basic software and hardware platform foundations for Microsoft Windows speech.

3.2 Windows Visual Basic Speech Recognition Platform Software Components

As we learned on Chapter One, the first software based speech recognition systems originated in a number of very advanced American and European academic and commercial R&D laboratories.

This included prototypes and proof-of-concept speech recognition engine software developed at M.I.T., Stanford, and Bell Labs in the U.S., and Cambridge University in Great Britain, among others, including some hybrid systems involving both specialized hardware and software for U.S. and British military commands also developed.

These software based speech recognition systems were all originally developed on Zilog 8080 CPM operating systems, with 4K and 8K memory with limitations that should be obvious compared to the more common 64K and 128K or more memory systems that we have today. Aside from that, it was not until the development of Microsoft DOS and Q-BASIC programming language (with command level hardware extensions) that software based speech recognition first became a practical reality.

These may seem like ancient history to some, but it is important to realize that the origins of speech technology at the word command recognition level were possible even with less that 1% of CPU memory that commonly available in PC desktop systems barely 10 years later.

You should not be surprised that the first speech recognition and computer generated text-to-speech software that was written as a purely software based solution that could be easily implemented by personal computer programmers was first written in Microsoft BASIC.

Although Apple had several computer generated speech software games that demonstrated speech software applications, for the most part the speech recognition programming techniques were out of reach of most desktop PC application programmers, so its clear Microsoft appreciated the great importance of making speech recognition programming easily accessible with BASIC.

Later in this chapter, we will go over some of the speech software program applications of various types that are supported by Microsoft using SAPI, but first we should review some impacts of hardware components on SAPI speech software implementation and configuration.

The SAPI Windows speech software standard is implemented as 6 ActiveX speech controls that are based upon Windows Open Systems Architecture (WOSA) technology that was first introduced in SAPI 4.0, and has not been substantially changed or enhanced in SAPI 5.0. These 6 controls are:

- *VoiceCommand*
- *TextToSpeech*
- *VoiceDictation*
- *VoiceTelephony*
- *DirectSpeechRecognition*
- *DirectSpeechSynthesis*

Figure 3.1 shows a graphical schematic of the architecture platform layers of these 6 SAPI components. Although these ActiveX controls did not change from SAPI Version 4.0, in SAPI Version 5.1 these speech components were enriched by additional platform layers that adapt them for web browsers and Internet conferencing, as well as direct integration capabilities for the Mail API and Telephony API.

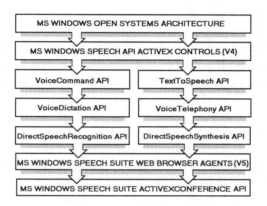

Figure 3.1.

The SAPI 5.0 Windows speech API standard and SDK provide architecture layers to support 6 SAPI 4.0 ActiveX speech control components as well as SAPI 5.1 web agents

These 6 ActiveX control components can be implemented in Visual Basic, Java or HTML speech enabling applications, and will be demonstrated throughout the rest of this book.

A summary listing of the methods, usage and properties of these 6 SAPI ActiveX speech components are provided in Appendix A of this book, and the latest technical notes are on MSDN website.

3.3   *Windows Visual Basic Speech Recognition Platform Hardware Components*

The earliest speech recognition technology was entirely based on electronic hardware systems solutions. This normally consisted of simple analog to digital audio conversion in single-board computers or microprocessor devices.

This analog to digital conversion attempted to match the entire waveform of words spoken into a microphone against *"matcher files"* of corresponding words for known audio waveform patterns.

Basically, this involves the use of *"discrete time-slicing"* of an audio input waveform or pattern of intensity or frequency of sounds into fixed length timebase durations. For example, millisecond by millisecond, which are then matched on either an individual digital item or series of digital values, between the input audio signal and known digital values for particular speech phonemes or words.

Just like *"discrete speech"*, the most critical aspect of *"discrete time-slicing"* electronics is that there is both a standard elemental unit, as well as a standard interval separator, or else can also be detected as a delimiter, between them. That already starts to sound like something you could develop a string-parsing program for, right?

The main limitation with hardware based systems for matching analog microphone or audio input against digital *"data signature"* files was that storage requirements for digital recordings, for even a small number of words, can be very cpu intensive and slow to process.

Therefore, one of the most important early developments in the history of speech recognition involved the use of the same signal modulation techniques that are commonly used in military electronics.

These are the basis for all modern data communication technology, in order to effectively limit size of *"data signature"* matcher files.

A *data signature* is simply a recognizable, and reliably recognized, pattern of digital signal numeric values that match precisely to a file of corresponding digitized speech elements. In other words, past the digitizing electronics, it is really not a lot different than any look-up table or relational database object find function you are already skilled at as a Visual Basic programmer

Electronic characteristics of the waveform, such as frequency or volume, are then measured at regular intervals.

These measures can then be used to create indexes or either numeric or mnemonic key values which can more efficiently relate a particular audio waveform pattern to a particular text word.

It should begin to be very clear just how important that computer hardware speed and file management as well as object messaging performance can be in developing effective Windows speech programs.

The next major analog to digital electronics technology involved the use of digital signal processing filtering techniques to *"exclude"* or *"spot"* insignificant words or sounds but this can pose problems. You should remember the concept of Digital Signal Processing (DSP).

In effect, such digital signal processing normally *"filters out"* noise patterns based on their electronic waveform characteristics.

Moreover, they are often used to eliminate all *"ambient"* background noises, such as machinery or music that should not be processed by the speech recognition engine software.

Accurate speech recognition directly against the data signature match files are either difficult or all too often impossible. Fortunately SAPI was effectively designed to overcome this problem in Windows, but the catch is that SAPI can be very picky with regard to the minimum hardware requirements to support these solutions.

Later in this chapter we will review in detail some of the picky minimum hardware specifications recommended by Microsoft for use of SAPI with particular types of applications.

The level of hardware speed and capabilities vary depending on exactly what kinds of Windows speech recognition programming applications and functions you are going to be developing.

But first we will review each of the major types of Windows speech software applications supported by Microsoft SAPI.

3.4   Some Basic Types of Microsoft Visual Basic Speech Applications

There are 3 basic types of Windows SAPI Speech Software Applications which are accounted for in the 6 SAPI Visual Basic ActiveX controls. These 3 basic speech application types are:

- *Text-To-Speech* and Computer-generated Speech Synthesis
- *Speech-To-Text* Discrete Command Control Speech Recognition
- *Speech-To-Text* Continuous Natural Speech Transcription

You should note that the first two speech application types are almost the same as the first two speech technologies, TTS and STT.

But you should also notice that the third type is a special variation of STT that involves much more complex vocabulary and grammar files.

Although there are other specialized speech application types such as telephony or webphone systems, these are actually integrated TTS/STT application type combinations.

If your computer hardware (or your user's computer hardware) is capable of supporting each of these types of applications, it can normally handle any complex SAPI speech application.

3.5   *Windows Visual Basic Text-to-Speech (TTS) Applications*

Text-To-Speech (TTS) systems first began to become commonplace in the early Seventies, when they were first used in some novelty electronic toys as well as in 'time-and-temperature' realtime information retrieval systems, which were often implemented using related to the same telephony technology that is available with SAPI 4 Visual Basic.

Even if you were too young to remember how excited people got about talking to computers on the telephone, you probably were just as amazed as a child by talking dolls and plush toys.

Although the same programming process used to make the speech sounds even 20 years ago in stuffed toys was very similar to most software speech today, you should probably appreciate that the process of engineering and programming early speech was many times more complicated and difficult than programming speech today with SAPI!

To put things in perspective, the same programming effort to make a 20-second message selective from only 8 responses from a common toy from 10 years ago took over 20 programmers 2 years to program, and now today with the power of Microsoft Windows SAPI you can do the same thing yourself in just 2 to 4 hours in one afternoon!

So in other words, the same level of speech recognition programming application project that required well over $2 Million in capital to accomplish in 1990 can now be done for less than $200 in the Year 2000. That is a 99.9% reduction of cost in less than a decade!

Aside from the incredible cost savings, this should make you all the more excited and determined to appreciate and understand the great tools that have been put in your hands as a Microsoft Windows SAPI Visual Basic programmer. You should always be aware of the great jump that was accomplished by Microsoft over all previous speech technology over the past decade.

So try to remember back and relate if you can to the speech and audio and telephone technology you have yourself known over the past decade as a way to get a broader perspective on just how really powerful and exciting Microsoft Windows SAPI Visual Basic speech technology is.

Because your own ability to fully use Microsoft SAPI Windows Visual Basic speech program technology is based on your personal experience.

All users of online email services (or anyone that has ever seen a TV commercial for AOL) have undoubtedly heard the synthetic Text-To-Speech phrases:

```
"[You have]    [MAIL]    [!!!]"
```

And even if you have not, all telephone answering machine and voice-mail system users have undoubtedly heard such a synthetic Text-To-Speech engine saying the speech in Listing 3.1:

Listing 3.1. MS Word macro convention coding for SAPI style speech enabling:

```
"[You have]  <number>  [new messages]."
```

This listing shows the Microsoft Word macro code that corresponds to SAPI macro style invocation, such as available in Dragon NaturallySpeaking, IBM ViaVoice and other third-party SDK's.

In both these cases, there is a software based SAPI Text-To-Speech engine involved in the concatenation of .WAV files (or other proprietary audio files) to speak the message.

A SAPI synthetic Text-To-Speech engine pastes recordings together for output to the sound board and multimedia PC speakers. This creates the illusion of 'speaking' either phrases or complete sentences.

Such SAPI-based Text-To-Speech applications can all easily be built from the 'ground up' or bolted onto your existing Windows application software using the Microsoft Speech SDK Suite.

3.6   Visual Basic Interactive Voice Response (IVR) Telephony Applications

The first Interactive Voice Response (IVR) systems involved a number of telephony related technologies that became commonplace during the early Eighties. These systems were more sophisticated than the simple 'time-and-temperature' systems of the previous decade.

In SAPI speech application environments today, IVR's are most often a very advanced form of discrete speech command applications, but they normally have much more demanding processing requirements, since they normally involve concurrent use of SAPI with TAPI objects.

However, the earliest IVR's were strictly Text-To-Speech applications, which is why they are mentioned briefly here.

They are still used extensively in automated banking and commercial account information retrieval, as well as automated airline reservations and flight availability information retrieval.

In addition, many features of IVR systems continue to be used in more advanced speech recognition telephony systems and used the most advanced speech technology.

These systems basically allow the caller to select from a voice 'menu' of selections which are spoken aloud by a pre-recorded audio tape 'loop', or by a computer generated digital voice.

These systems continue to be used extensively, both as turn-key audio tape hardware based IVR systems, as well as simple software based systems which can be run on a home PC.

Some people may remember that some of the earliest telephone menu systems often seemed to have a lot more realistic 'human-sounding' voices than a lot of the voice menu telephony systems that we have today. The reason is that a lot of those systems were actual human voice tape recording 'loops' that were simply activated by phone headset keypad menu selection. The only thing that involved software was that the recordings were sometimes joined together from recordings of individual words, which had a 'choppy' sound.

This particular problem of eliminating the 'choppy' sounds between software queuing of taped words in order to smooth out to a more human-sounding voice pattern was actually the basis of much of the modern speech technology in Microsoft SAPI that you can use today.

If you want the same things spoken continuously or most nearly the same every time in response to a particular Windows application software event, you can use a very similar technology to what was used in the early voice menu systems. Of course, today, instead of a tape loop, you can easily implement in Windows as a .WAV file object!

IVR's are activated by voice prompt that command the caller to enter a number on the touch tone telephone key pad (i.e., *"For Current Account Information, Press 1...To Change Account Information, Press 2...To Speak With an Account Representative, Press 3..."* etc.).

These touch tone voice menu systems continue to be used extensively for such applications as automated fax-back and pre-recorded up-to-the-minute news status or information retrieval on topics such as weather or sports. Not only over traditional or cell phones, but also now must as easily over web-phone or mobile wireless Internet.

The latest IVR telephony technology basically involves combining both 'loop' as well as 'string' techniques. Now, SAPI makes it possible to either loop or string digital elements for all possible phonemes into waveform data signature matcher files which could be indexed and rapidly accessed using IPA Unicode and conventional object oriented data base management techniques.

This also makes it possible to overcome many of the traditional limitations of phone line quality and individual differences in localized speaking patterns, as will be discussed later in this book.

3.7 Command-Control Speech Recognition and Dictation Speech Applications

The first command control dictation systems were developed by the military, both United States and NATO, as well as what is now Russia.

These highly specialized speech recognition command control technology systems were developed in top-secret military R&D labs in the mid Seventies. They were actually implemented into several prototype tanks and aircraft control systems by the mid Eighties.

The existence of these early speech recognition systems for command control dictation of tanks and high performance aircraft weapons fire control became well known during the Eighties due in large part to the number of popular movies and books of that era.

One very famous popular example was the mid Eighties Clint Eastwood movie *Foxfire*, which involved a purely fictional, but yet highly realistic speech recognition system in a high performance jet fighter aircraft. This fictional portrayal, however, had some limited capability to launch missiles based on voice commands. Unforunately, and fairly realistically, the pilot had to be "trained" as carefully as the speech recognition systems in the jet fighter, and the slightest "mis-speech" resulted in a major disaster.

True to the technology as it existed then as well as even now, the number of words that the *Foxfire* movie aircraft's speech recognition software could respond to was very small. Also, it had numerous other difficulties which added up to a considerable potential for disaster in the event of mistaken command recognitions.

These limitations were the main reason why the command control dictation technology was never widely applied in actual military applications. It has since become a popular technology for toys—which are all the more functional purposes of toys when "mis-speech" leads to amusing and less disastrous mistakes!

You should understand that not much has changed very much since then. If there is any time that your application could involve safety issues, be prepared that you will have to design in numerous 'fail-safe' override systems to make sure that misrecognized words do not cause a critical command error!

Some more conventional, and practical, applications of discrete command control speech applications might be to program your Windows software to respond to commands such as :

```
"Send an email to Mary",
"Retrieve all email from my office", or
"Turn off the computer and turn on the TV."
```

The number of different commands that any user may speak at any time can easily number in the hundreds. Also, grammar rules specifications needed to support such commands are not just limited to a "List" but can also contain other fields, like:

```
"Send mail to <name>" or
"Call {phonenum}" or
"Set VCR to record <movie> at <time> on <date>."
```

With all of the possibilities presented by SAPI object oriented software architectures, the user of a Windows SAPI Visual Basic application software program is potentially able to speak thousands of different commands. But here the effective limitation is not technological, but simply logical.

However, the important point to remember is that all possible commands must all be precisely accounted for by specification of grammars and rules for command control—(Control implies simplicity!).

Any Windows application can easily be designed to voice responses to message boxes and wizard screens using SAPI. Also, existing Windows applications message boxes can be easily retrofitted to change the buttons on existing controls to replace with SAPI speech recognition that can easily identify "Yes," "No," or other short responses.

Command control dictation and speech recognition easily enables the user to speak any one of a potentially huge set of commands, making it faster to say, "Change the font to Courier," "Use 12-point bold," or "Print the current page" than maneuvering through the corresponding sequence of windows and dialog boxes.

Command control dictation and speech recognition also allows a user speak a more natural word or phrase to activate a Windows Office suite macro. For example, "Spell check the current active paragraph" is easier for most users to remember than the CTRL+F5 key combination.

Such command control dictation and speech recognition can also provide users with the means to execute a command or verbally launch applications without the need for 'mousing' through cascading menus or Windows. Ultimately, effective design limits responses to bare essentials.

For many people, use of a mouse is even more frustrating than the keyboard. Command control dictation applications using SAPI can help to make computers accessible to all the people who have never been comfortable with any of the common interfaces to computers that have been possible up until now.

Understandably, this type of command speech recognition is much less demanding, both in terms of resources and hardware required, as well as the complexity of the SAPI programming to support such simple voice command functions, compared to continuous natural speech.

Basically, discrete command speech recognition is only listening, or 'spotting' for a very limited number of words, and normally no more than 10 to 20—so you should always start with only those functions which you are absolutely sure that everyone who uses your software will surely "ask" for.

This is a very different kind of programming problem than managing very large vocabulary files needed for continuous speech and natural language dictation or transcription.

3.8   *Continuous Natural Speech Visual Basic Applications*

One of the most significant of all innovations in contemporary speech recognition involved the many technological developments that were necessary in order to achieve continuous natural speech recognition involved in contemporary speech aware word processing transcription and speech aware spreadsheet data entry.

All of these capabilities are largely related to the very substantial and significant performance improvements that have been achieved in PC microprocessor CPU speeds and data storage access times of the early 1990s.

These improvements made it more feasible to perform highly efficient waveform data signature matcher file lookups and also to quickly process complex statistical algorithms to enable sophisticated machine intelligence and pattern recognition on PC platforms.

Just as the increasing economies of scale and greater performance efficiencies of PC hardware made possible a lot more sophisticated speech applications, it also increases the logical demands as well as opportunities as the physical capabilities of computers increase.

This creates an increasing need for efficient data management and file handling, which is supported in SAPI using all of the best data handling capabilities of Windows.

Continuous natural speech recognition is most useful for word processing document editing or vertical applications speech-to-text transcription.

This is commonly needed to permanently record what maybe said at legal meetings or hearings, when the user wishes to keep their hands on the keyboard to type only command keys, or when the user chooses to use the mouse to drag and select.

There is also the additional benefit that by virtue of the capability to simultaneously record continuous natural speech-to-text dialog, it is also possible for the software to be continuously listening for a limited domain set of discrete control dictation commands.

This can control the ongoing operation of the Windows software. For example, your SAPI enabled word processor might be instructed to listen for formatting commands like the following:

```
"change font to bold",
"change font to italic",
"change font to Times New Roman"
```

The limited context domain of each of these phrases will be recognized by the SAPI-compliant Windows word processor. They should never be found in the text transcription document, even though the application software actually heard the following:

```
"The limited context domain of each of these phrases
would be recognized by your <change font to bold>...<
change font to italic>...< change font to Times New
Roman>...SAPI speech word processor, and should never..."
```

If your SAPI grammar files and rules specification file objects are coded to handle contextual differences, it is possible to combine some aspects of both discrete speech commands and continuous speech transcription. Integrated speech software can be designed to be toggled between SAPI engines that listen for discrete commands versus continuous dictation speech.

If continuous voice entry transcription natural speech recognition is combined with text to speech playback of the recognized entry, then the user doesn't even need to look at the screen. The user can therefore focus on their physical paperwork or other work-at-hand in front of them.

There is no longer any need to sit in front of a keyboard, and you can speak to your computer from across the room, or even talk to a computer via a wireless headset that connects to a computer in another part of the world using wireless Internet.

In order to accomplish the full benefits of SAPI over the future wireless Internet, you need to be able to integrate Microsoft SAPI with its sister components in MAPI and TAPI.

This should help to explain why Microsoft makes all of these 3 API's available in a manner that allows that to be used easily together within a single framework under Windows Open Systems Architecture (WOSA). This was in many ways Microsoft's answer to the frustration that their senior management felt in dealings with SRAPI committees.

The most important thing to begin to understand about integrated discrete command and continuous natural speech recognition is not as restrictive as the keyboard. You can use SAPI to 'multi-task' and thereby do several things in a hands-free environment at one time.

3.9   *Installing Low Level Foundation Visual Basic Support to High Level SAPI*

Now that you have a better understanding of the hardware and software foundations that are the basis for supporting the high level SAPI functionality that you will be learning in this book, we need to make one last stop to be sure you have everything that you need on the low Windows level to be able to fully install configure your computer to support high level SAPI facilities.

In order to run the VB5 sample programs in SAPI 4.0 and Microsoft Speech API, or to be able to use either VB5 or VB6 sample code in your own Visual Basic applications, you should first review again the list of Windows runtime files in Table 2.1 first introduced in Chapter Two.

If you want to be able to run the VB5 SAPI ActiveX high level speech programming examples and sample code in your SAPI speech programs, you should look in your Windows and System folders, as well as run '*Find*' from Windows Start menu to determine if you have the runtime files on your computer.

If you have SAPI 4.0a or a later release of the Microsoft Speech SDK Suite, you may already have these files in the SAPI install library. Even if you can not find them, you should be able to locate them on the MSDN website and download them from there.

If you cannot find them in your Windows or System folders, copy them to the Windows folder, and you are all set to use the SAPI samples from VB5 folder.

Microsoft also supplies several OLE Automation libraries in the Speech SDK Suite which operate in a similar manner, but at a lower level than the new

ActiveX control objects first provided with SAPI 4.0. These should be either already loaded or else can be loaded and configured from the References library window.

Although these OLE Automation libraries operate on a lower level than the new SAPI ActiveX controls, they are still considered high level SAPI services, and they also have properties and methods that are very similar to the SAPI ActiveX services.

These types of libraries can be used in Visual Basic as well as any VBA compliant software, including all of the Microsoft Office Suite, such as Excel, Work, Access, FoxPro and others.

These two OLE libraries were first provided with SAPI 3.0, and were designed primarily to handle speech add-on support to Microsoft Office Suite macro applications. The OLE libraries are:

- `VTXTAUTO.TLB for OLE text-to-speech services`
- `VCAUTO.TLB for OLE speech recognition services`

If you may want to add speech add-on capability to any of your VBA applications, or Windows Office Suite product macros that you would like to add speech to, then you should load and configure the OLE Automation object libraries that you expect you are likely to use.

To load either or both of these OLE Automation libraries, you can simply go to the 'Tools' menu, and then to the 'References' drop-down menu, which should be in any Office Suite OLE-compliant Microsoft Windows software product, or any VBA-enabled Visual Suite programming environment. You can then configure them using the Advanced button.

This will be similar to the process you will use to configure your SAPI 4.0 ActiveX component libraries, except that SAPI 4.0 has more sophisticated wizards and tools to recommend how to specify the ActiveX speech control configuration settings.

3.10　Loading OLE Voice Text Library Services for Visual Basic

When you open the 'Tools' menu and 'Reference' sub-menu item, you should see a window box with an embedded check list of every OLE object and other objects, and you can tell if it is loaded already if it has a check next to it.

If your computer does not have an object library that you want already loaded, you can load the object simply by clicking the empty box to turn on the check.

You should know that you are looking for the Voice Text X.0 Type Library, which should have a location with a file name at the end of '*VTXTAUTO.TLB*'.

If you can not find the particular OLE Automation library object that you want on the list, you may have to go to the MSDN website to download if you do not have a CD from MSDN.

You can either accept the default configuration parameters for the OLE Automation Voice Text object, or you can click on the '*Advanced*' button to change them if you prefer.

You should now be finished with the load and configuration of the OLE Automation Voice Text object. Click '*OK*' to accept the '*References*' window changes if you are finished, or if you want the complimentary speech recognition object, continue on to the next section.

3.11   Loading OLE Voice Command Library Services for Visual Basic

If you want to load the OLE Automation Voice Command and speech recognition object library, you should know that you are looking for the Voice Command X.0 Type Library, which should have a location with a file name at the end of '*VCAUTO.TLB*'.

You can either accept the default configuration parameters for the OLE Automation Voice Command object, or you can click on the '*Advanced*' button to change them if you prefer.

You should now be finished with the load and configuration of the OLE Automation Voice Command object.

Click '*OK*' to accept the '*References*' window changes when you are finished and ready to update the VBA speech configuration registry.

We will discuss the specific properties and methods of these two OLE Automation libraries in more detail later, as well as provide some initial examples with respect to their use in the sample SAPI 4.0 speech add-ons for VBA and Microsoft Office Suite macros.

You should also be aware that if you are going to be creating or changing speech applications using Visual Basic, there will also be several VBVOICE constants and class libraries that must be loaded. But because the process for loading and configuring those objects are really more specific to the Visual Basic speech recognition programming process, they will be described in more detail later.

3.12   Comparison of Traditional Hardware Versus SAPI Software Speech Engines

Before you attempt to fully install and configure your SAPI speech engines for use with SAPI and your Microsoft Speech SDK Suite tools, you should first be sure that you have at least the bare minimum of the recommended hardware resources for the types of SAPI speech applications that you expect to be running on your computer.

The latest recommended minimum hardware should be obtained from MSDN, but the original hardware requirements for SAPI 4.0 are discussed in detail for each SAPI type in this rest of this chapter.

In order to understand the unique hardware requirements for each type of SAPI speech engine, it is first of all important to remember the critical speech component hardware technologies. These digital electronic technologies are the basis of SAPI as well as all other speech software technologies.

The first critical speech technology is known as Pulse Code Modulation (PCM). The Pulse Code Modulation (PCM) encodes an analog voice into a digital data. First the voice input signal is sampled, then the sample values are recoded into binary data according to rule logic so that the resulting signal can be switched, transmitted or stored for processing by a computer.

The second critical speech technology is known as a Digital Signal Processor (DSP). This adjusts the signal so it is not too loud, not too quiet, and most importantly so that the listening range can be predicted in order to keep extreme variations to a minimum. The purpose of a DSP is to very simply to help 'clean' or 'pre-process' the incoming speech data.

The computer speech Digital Signal Processor (DSP) is usually a micro-chip designed to electronically receive and pre-process audio inputs from a microphone or data communications line. It can usually both convert an analog or continuous signal into discrete or time-sliced digital values.

The all-hardware speech architecture is summarized graphically in Figure 3.2. As can be seen, the PCM is a separate local process that consists of a modulator and digitizer, which are the methods by which the signal is sampled and encoded. The encodings of the PCM are then sent to a remote process known as the Audio Compression Module (ACM).

This is the process by which a hardware speech engine interfaces the encoded digitized signal data to functions that perform the routine processing of signals for speech recognition. This involves high-speed search and find operations that retrieve and match data signatures for audio waveforms to speech phonemes and their corresponding computer speech.

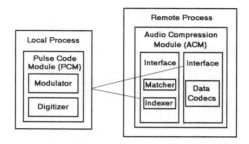

Figure 3.2.

All hardware speech processing architectures consist of a Pulse Code Modulator (PCM) which is a local client digitizing process, and an Audio Code Modulator (ACM) which is a remote process for high-speed hardwire codecs to match and translate sounds to text.

Microsoft was the first to make this a reliable technique that could be ported to a personal computer using SAPI and diphonic concatenation. Microsoft Speech API integrates speech engines as functions to encode and string together short digital audio segment as parts of words and phrases to be spoken over the sound system speakers, in an efficient manner that emulates hardware signal processing.

As can be seen in Figure 3.3, the SAPI software standard uses voice and audio objects that function like "sockets" to interface digital data patterns that are unencoded by the SAPI software speech engines. They are then matched by voice and audio objects to equivalent computer speech digital patterns and text strings which are retrieved, matched, and output using high-speed data management processes.

Understandably, this is does not sound like a very radically complex architecture, and it is not much different than any of a number of other conventional data management technologies.

However, what is most impressive about the Microsoft SAPI standard and objects implemented in the 6 ActiveX speech controls are so programmatically elegant and efficient to enable speech and audio waveform data signature retrieval and matching. And with sufficient speed and accuracy to approach human perceptual response, which is clearly an incredible technical achievement. Thus it is also easily understandable effective use of SAPI depends on minimum hardware requirements, which are assumed for even simple speech applications, and increase with increasing complexity of the speech complexity.

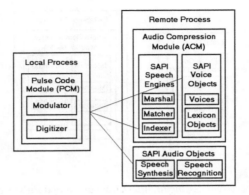

Figure 3.3.

The Microsoft SAPI architecture uses software objects that include both speech synthesis and speech recognition ActiveX controls that perform Audio Compression Module (ACM) translations by virtual connections that match audio waveforms as digital patterns that are linked to corresponding digital computer speech and text equivalents.

3.13   Minimum Hardware for MS Visual Basic SAPI Text-to-Speech Applications

Text-To-Speech engines that are fully SAPI-compliant typically require no more than a bare-bones vintage Intel Pentium 90Mhz or faster processor (if you can still find one—we are talking "P1" here).

On the average, Text-To-Speech SAPI engines use only about 16 MB of RAM. You should also have at least 1 MB of disk space for the TTS engine, and at least 2 MB for each of the basic and special 'voices' that you plan to make available and support using with your software.

Almost any sound card will work for Synthetic Text-To-Speech, including any SoundBlaster, Media Vision, and ESS Technology compatible cards that have been certified to interface with the Microsoft Windows Multimedia Sound System.

Additionally, headphones or freestanding microphones may be used, depending on the nature of the SAPI application. *And always remember— MICROPHONES are the MOST important SAPI hardware!*

Typically, this type of special SAPI recognizer engine provides a pre-generated library of human voice sounds and allows the application developer to transfer its intonation and speed to the text being spoken. Although text with prosody attached requires more storage than ASCII text (1K per minute compared to hundreds of bytes per minute), it requires considerably less storage than prerecorded speech, which uses at least 30K per minute.

Obviously, if you have a "P4" or above, you can easily generate TTS to support even your own Alvin-style "Chipmunk" voices if you want to.

3.14   Minimum Hardware for MS Visual Basic SAPI Telephony IVR Applications

Although Interactive Voice Response (IVR) telephony is not one of the basic SAPI speech application types, it is mentioned here because it is the best example of an integrated speech software application that is likely (or possible) to combine all 3 SAPI base application types.

What this means is that the minimum hardware required to process IVR speech applications for phone based voice menus will normally be the same microprocessor speeds that are required for continuous natural speech applications. These are the most demanding of all SAPI speech applications software with regard to resources, and add for all the rest, as will be described in more detail later in this section.

Storage and temp storage required to process IVR applications are also normally the same as continuous natural speech, if the IVR application must be able to do sophisticated word-spotting and be intelligent enough to handle menu back-out events if the user is getting frustrated or not responding as expected.

But you should be aware that such temp storage requirements, as well as RAM memory, are 'additive', so storage and RAM needs are DOUBLED if there will be an IVR or other integrated Windows speech software running concurrently with a continuous natural speech localization database or vocabulary file processing application. In summary, IVR is normally only practical with "P3+" microprocessor PCs.

3.15   Minimum Hardware for MS Visual Basic SAPI Command Control Dictation

The discrete speech command control dictation speech recognition engines currently on the market that are SAPI compliant typically require only an Intel Pentium 120MHz or faster processor.

On the average, speech recognition for discrete command control dictation consumes at least 16 megabytes of RAM in addition to the required RAM needed to run the speech enabling application.

The speech engine and voices for a typical discrete command control dictation software application can use between 20 to 30 MB of additional high-speed RAM memory. Total memory for command control speech should never be less than 40 MB (aside from anything else that will be running concurrently with your SAPI speech command software).

You should also be aware that the sound system as well as microphone requirements for discrete speech recognition are much more demanding than the requirements for TTS and computer speech applications.

You need to get the best SAPI approved close-talk, headset or handset microphone that you can afford, and you will need at least a 8 KHz, 16-bit sampling rate sound card to handle the input audio stream DSP. Thus, command control speech recognition is suitable for MS/CE, PDA's, or even digital cellphones.

3.16   Minimum Hardware for MS Visual Basic SAPI Continuous Natural Speech

The hardware requirements are much greater than any of the application domains that have been discussed previously. Typically, continuous voice entry transcription and natural speech recognition engines currently on the market normally require a Pentium 166 MHz or faster processor, with 2+ GHz cpus preferred (and again, you really need at least "P3+" in order to support the complexity of continuous natural speech). All continuous transcription software relies upon external software objects and add-ons to support the digital signal processing and statistical pattern matching complexity.

As you have probably surmised at this point, all of this is basically due to the fact that continuous voice entry transcription is actually a hybridized combination of both a basic speech-to-text recognizer engine and has a much more complex full-blown discrete command control dictation recognizer running in the background.

On the average, this combination of speech-to-text recognition and discrete command control dictation will use a minimum of at least between 32 to 48 MB of RAM, and more typically between 64 to 96 MB of RAM, in addition to what is required by all running applications.

As always with memory intensive applications software, the more memory the better. For the more sophisticated applications no less than 64 MB should ever be attempted (and 1 GB+ is most desirable).

You should be aware that the minimum hardware requirements that Microsoft recommends with regard to each of these types of SAPI speech applications are in fact just that, very bare minimum.

If your hardware meets these minimum specifications, then your speech application should work most of the time, but you should be aware that depending on the efficiency of the software and its degree of compatibility to SAPI Windows standard. It will probably run out of resources on an erratic basis unless you have quite a lot more hardware than the minimum recommended levels.

Here, fast hard drive storage is also most desirable, and you want the fastest 20+ GB hard drive storage you can get (for each 20,000+ word lexicon or vertical dictionary file you will need to support).

Like all good system designers, you should always 'over-engineer' your applications, and a good rule-of-thumb is to always take these minimum speed and storage requirements and *DOUBLE* them just to be sure you have enough horse power and storage resources!

You can probably anticipate that the hardware requirements to use your Microsoft Speech SDK Suite are typically exactly the same as the hardware required to run the most complex SAPI speech applications that you plan to develop using your Speech SDK.

However, you should also know that you will need an additional 85 MB of temp disk space available to run the Speech SDK Suite after it is fully installed and configured.

You should also probably anticipate that this storage is separate from any other temp storage and RAM you need to multi-task multiple IDE or Visual programming environments concurrent with your Speech SDK and any active speech engines.

3.17 Hardware Requirements for SAPI Speech Engines for Visual Basic Programs

Most people both love and hate Microsoft Windows Wizards (and usually both). Not too many people either completely love them or completely hate them, because they are almost always extremely useful, but sometimes they can create problems. It's always a matter of tweaking options.

The great thing about wizards is they can very quickly and easily set up default configurations or templates based on a series of question boxes, and get you up and running without having to do a lot of studying to know in advance how you need to set things up.

This is also the case with SAPI 4.0 speech environment configuration wizards. However, the not-so-great thing about wizards is that they may be able to get you set up to handle most common situations, but the exceptions and special situations can require a lot of going back to change specific control parameters or property tabs.

Again, this is also very much the case with SAPI 4.0 diagnostic wizards. You just have to learn how and where to adjust option tabs!

Any time that you seem to be having a problem with your SAPI speech recognizer engine, the first thing you should do is jump to the Microsoft Voice control menu and run the Microphone Wizard.

3.18   Windows SAPI Audio Microphone and Sound System Diagnostic Wizards

In Microphone Wizard you can see your first example of one of the many speech software and hardware diagnostic wizards that are provided with the Microsoft Speech SDK Suite.

This particular wizard performs diagnostics and helps to select and calibrate your microphone, which can be critical when you are trying to troubleshoot or test your software on another computer than the one where it was first developed. Each of the SAPI 4.0 speech software and hardware diagnostic wizards has a long series of message screens that vary based on the way that you answer the questions.

If you have ever used or developed a Windows software wizard, you know that it is a long linear process flow more similar to an Microsoft PowerPoint presentation than what you are commonly used to as a Visual Basic or other Visual object event programmer.

An example of a screen to remind you to check to make sure your microphone is plugged in. Like with most Microsoft Wizards, the Microsoft Speech SDK Suite wizards are usually smart enough to know what questions to ask. Usually this screen would not show up unless there was either no audio or very limited audio signal strength to indicate the microphone might not really be plugged in.

The Microsoft Voice Microphone Troubleshooting Wizard may remind you of some very obvious potential speech audio input problems, but it is smart enough that it will not do so unless it has some real indication from its many inputs this may really be the problem.

The Microsoft Speech SDK Suite diagnostic wizards will also ask you a series of questions, and give you instructions for adjustments, or tell you what to do next. For the Microsoft Speech SDK Suite microphone diagnostic wizards you will always be asked to read text from a script in your normal voice.

The Microsoft Voice Microphone Wizard as well as the Sound System Wizards will first ask you to make some variable adjustments in volume, also known as "gain" to those of you who are electronics experts. If the Microsoft Voice Microphone Wizard is still not getting the response that it expected, it will try to make some intelligent adjustments to make the most of the audio signal it has. But first it will let you know you can override and try one last time to make your own attempts at adjusting the audio input.

Microsoft Voice Microphone Wizard, as well as all the other speech tool suite wizards, will either automatically fix the problem or else just give up. It will usually be able to fix any problem but if it can not it will normally let you know. You might notice that there is also an 'Advanced Info' button on the final screen of the wizard, and this is also pretty standard for each of the SAPI diagnostic and configuration wizards. The 'Advanced Info' button will take you to a summary report window that show you the results of the wizard's diagnostics, and may also give you opportunity to either accept or modify one of the parameters used in diagnosis, or start over and run the wizard again. When you are completely done with a SAPI speech diagnostic wizard, it will give you a 'Finished' button to exit the wizard.

3.19   *Windows SAPI Speaker Training Wizards and Troubleshooting*

In your first attempts to use DictaPad, do not be too worried if there are a substantial number of misrecognitions before or during training. There are actually pretty good results from any speech recognition that uses standard default speech files and has not been individually trained for a specific user.

As soon as possible after any SAPI speech software, including the Microsoft Speech SDK Suite, is first loaded and installed, you should activate the Microsoft Speech Recognition Training Wizard shown in the active window in Figure 3.4.

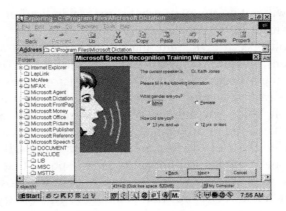

Figure 3.4.

The first thing to do each time you start SAPI Training is check sex and age of speaker.

In order to get to the Microsoft Speech Training file wizard, you should only need to right click on any active SAPI speech software application from the task bar, and then click on the menu item for Speech Training. You can create a new speech training file or modify your existing speech training file at any time by activating the Microsoft Speech Recognition Training Wizard.

The first thing that you will see after the Microsoft Speech Recognition Training Wizard is activated will be a series of screens that will collect information about the person who will be reading aloud to train the wizard. The first most important voice information involves your sex and age.

It should not surprise you that sex and age are by far the two most important factors that control speech. It should also be no surprise that the SAPI linguistic algorithms give most of the control to these two simple factors as most important to define the elemental voice properties.

However, you may be surprised to learn there are actually dozens of specific voice properties, including such things as anatomical and personality differences that must be measured and estimated by the Microsoft Speech Recognition Training Wizard in order to develop a statistical model of an individual speaker's voice. The most important factors to determine the prosody of any individual person's speech are sex and age which should not be any big surprise, but you should be aware that they are also the most important control properties you can adjust to control both speech input and output.

After the Speech Recognition Training Wizard has collected the basic information to compare your voice against the standard and special Microsoft SAPI speech engine voices, you (or the user you want the software to more easily recognize) will be asked to read a script from a series of window boxes.

As the subject reads the script out load, the text will be reverse highlighted as each word is recognized by the standard SAPI speech engine selected by the wizard, as shown in Figure 3.5.

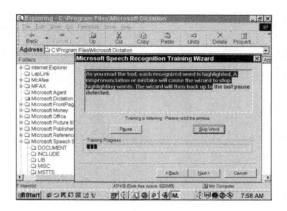

Figure 3.5.

As you train you will reverse text that is expected to be spoken when it is first recognized. As you read along, if your SAPI microphone and audio input system is working, you will see progress made by the active speech engine as it recognizes each expected word.

Just under the highlight speech recognition text script window, there is a sliding bar to show how much of the words that have been recognized by the speech engine have been compared to the standard voice selected according to sex and age.

The actual speech training process can take many sessions adding up to several hours to actually get a near-100% accurate training file just for the one individual. The speech training wizard needs to hear the subject say all of the basic phonemes, and basic words, many times in order to get a good statistical analysis that can be extremely reliable.

Because you do not have to train the speech file all in one session, you can break out at any time by clicking the 'Cancel' button, and you can start again anytime you have a few minutes to spare, and you get 'full credit' for past training time. Microsoft designed the Microsoft Dictation Training Wizard to be very flexible, you can use it or not, and stop anytime or add to it any time.

You can stop the speech recognition wizard training process at any time, and restart from the same point at any future time if you wish. SAPI is really just collecting statistics about your voice and how you speak relative to most other people that it knows about, not just simply checking off words!

You can create as many new training files as you want, even for the same person, in order to be more specific about a particular voice quality, or ambient background noise, during a particular voice training session, or sessions.

If you want to 'get credit' for the time you just spent on reading aloud to help train the SAPI speech engines in your individual voice characteristics and speaking patterns, you must first save the data collected by the Microsoft Speech Recognition Training Wizard to an.SPK file.

Before you end your SAPI Speech Recognition Wizard voice file training session, you must first specify either a new 'speaker file' or else an existing speaker training file that you want to update to. If you do not your training session will be lost.

3.20   Speech Dictation and Speech Recognition Engine Control Default Settings

There is one more set of speech configuration settings that you need to be aware of. These settings are found in the Dictation Options which are another one of the menu items you should see when you right click on Microsoft Dictation in the active taskbar.

When you activate the Dictation Options or preferences menu item, you should see a screen which should have at least the following 6 tab items:

- User Dictation Definitions
- General Dictation Definitions
- Dictation Glossary Definitions
- Intellisense Speech Parameters
- Advanced Speech Parameters
- Computer Voice Parameters

There are several dozen SAPI installation speech dictation and speech control options that can be customized from these tabs.

All of these tab properties can be used to configure or re-configure the defaults that will be used to create your standard SAPI environment, for a given computer, user, or SAPI speech software application.

Many of the Microsoft Dictation options correspond to other tab options and preferences that you are probably already acquainted with in other Microsoft applications.

Undoubtedly you are already familiar with the SAPI speech API format's equivalent to the standard Intellisence "look-forward" formats you are probably already used to setting in Excel.

If you have not used IntelliSense tab settings before, you can simply click on the IntelliSense tab of the Microsoft Dictation Options, and then you can modify, add or remove 'IntelliSense' elements, which are really auto-formats for speech, similar to format styles in Word or Excel. Some of the Dictation Options tabs may be unlike anything you have ever seen before, and specifically related to SAPI object control properties and defaults.

One example of this is IntelliSense sliders which control the sensitivity of the speech recognition engines with regard to your preferences for more or less risky match assumptions to achieve the recognition levels that you want or need for your own SAPI speech applications.

You should probably already have guessed that these Dictation Options are the default speech engine defaults, similar to control settings for your mouse, or any other Windows input or output device.

You should also probably know that each of these speech parameters or preferences can be reset dynamically from within a given SAPI speech software application by that programs local properties or parameters.

There is one more tab that you should get a final look at before you close the Dictation Options, and that is the Computer Voice options that are the default for your SAPI speech applications.

The most important item to notice in the Computer Voice options box is the drop-down combo list box that has the names 'Brutus', 'Freddy', and 'Mary'.

These names correspond to standard and special voices that are provided with SAPI 4.0 and the Microsoft Speech SDK Suite.

These voices should be regarded as 'voice templates' that correspond to the basic categories of sex and age criteria that was noted before which determine the nature of any voice's properties.

Figure 3.6.

The final Microsoft Dictation Options tab is 'Computer Voice', which may not be the most sophisticated speech programmer control, but is probably the most fun, since it controls all standard and special SAPI voices.

These basic voices can be added to by loading new voices that you get in the future from Microsoft (there are some very unusual special new voices that will be introduced later in this book), or from other vendors, or you can even create and load your own custom voices. The Dictation Options tab used for selecting all loaded voices is shown in Figure 3.6.

Basically, a 'voice template' as far as Microsoft is concerned involves the basic set of parameters and properties under the SAPI specification. These can be adjusted to either change the sound of a computer generated TTS voice, or used to generate different default speech recognition match STT training files, according to which of the standard or special SAPI voices that are specified.

We will learn more about the standard and special Microsoft SAPI voices later in this book. But now we are ready to summarize this chapter and what you have just learned.

3.21   Summary

In this chapter you have learned a little bit more about the underlying software and hardware needed to support Microsoft SAPI speech technology, including the minimum hardware requirements for each of the basic SAPI supported speech application types.

You have learned some of the diagnostic and troubleshooting tools and wizards that you can use to both quickly configure your Microsoft Speech SDK Suite environment on your computer and go back to customize at any future point in time.

You also learned how to load and configure Microsoft Voice and Microsoft Dictation speech applications and use some of the associated diagnostic wizards and tools, including Windows Speech Help and 'What Can I Say?'.

In the next chapter, you will not only learn about the Microsoft SAPI standard and special voices for use in Visual Basic speech programs, but you will also learn more about the specific techniques and events that can be implemented or controlled by use of SAPI high level ActiveX speech controls for Visual Basic speech applications. You will also learn how to apply this knowledge to get fullest benefit of Windows low-level services.

Chapter Four

Understanding Microsoft Windows SAPI Foundations for Visual Basic Speech Applications

Now that you have been introduced to the Microsoft Speech API, loaded and installed your Microsoft Speech SDK Suite development platform, and configured your computer and SAPI tools, you are ready to take a closer look 'under the hood' at the SAPI platform foundations.

There are two most important aspects of the Microsoft Windows Speech API foundations that are intrinsic to your understanding of the Visual Basic programming model that is built into the SAPI 4.0 specification.

These two primary Microsoft Speech API foundations are used to build each of the 3 primary types of SAPI Windows speech applications introduced earlier in this book, simple Text-to-Speech (TTS), simple Speech-to-Text (STT), and integrated STT/TTS speech applications, which may involve both discrete command control dictation as well as continuous natural speech transcription.

These 3 primary types of Windows speech applications each have 2 SAPI ActiveX control components first introduced and enhanced in SAPI 4.0, for a total of 6 major SAPI high level ActiveX controls, which you will learn to use in Visual Basic and VBA web speech programs later in this book.

In this chapter, you will learn the following:

- Voice Technology Foundations Used in Microsoft Windows Visual Basic SAPI Text-To-Speech
- Using Microsoft SAPI Windows Text-To-Speech in Visual Basic Voice Text Applications
- Voice Technology Foundations Used in Microsoft Visual Basic Speech-to-Text
- Using Microsoft SAPI Windows Speech-To-Text in Visual Basic Voice Command Applications
- Voice Technology Foundations Used in Microsoft Visual Basic Speech Recognition
- Using SAPI Windows Dictation Object in Visual Basic Continuous Speech Applications
- Understanding the Windows Speech SDK Suite Sample Visual Basic Programs

4.1   *Visual Basic Voice Technology Foundations Used in Text-To-Speech*

Now that you know a little more about SAPI platform architecture, standards, libraries and tools, you are ready to learn more about what SAPI high level ActiveX objects can do with them in particular types of Windows Visual Basic speech software applications.

First you will learn more about the simples of the 3 most critical SAPI voice technology foundations, which are used Visual Basic to generate computer speech from text.

4.2   *Word Separation and Windows SAPI Voice Synthesis Quality*

The first critical voice technology used by SAPI in Visual Basic computer generated speech involves the use of word separation techniques to improve voice synthesis quality.

As you may remember from Chapter One, this involves software methods that are compatible with, and virtual extensions of, the digital electronics methods used to break up analog audio signals into digital *'sound bytes'* by time-slicing. As you may also remember, Microsoft Windows SAPI uses a comparable method to combine IPA Unicode sound elements into text for processing by Visual Basic.

A Text-To-Speech SAPI synthetic voice engine that uses conventional subword concatenation methods combines a pre-determined series of short digital-audio waveform segments together and performs simple statistical wavelet smoothing to produce a continuous sound.

This is equivalent to using bigger bricks or blocks to build a wall. You may build it faster, but you might also easily have a lot more rough edges to polish off.

In the more sophisticated diphonic concatenation, on the other hand, each segment consists of two phonemes—one that begins the sound pattern, and another one that terminates the sound sequence.

In this respect, you should probably appreciate that diphonic concatenation allows you to get the benefit of a 'delimiter' that will enable SAPI to parse the word-part phonemes more efficiently.

Thus, with diphonic concatenation, the word *"hello"* consists of the phonemes:

"h-eh-l-æ"

and the corresponding concatenated subword segments using diphonic methods are:

```
<silence/"(white noise")> h-h-h-eh-eh-eh-l-l-l-œ-œ-œ
<silence("white noise sound")>.
```

The most important thing about diphonic concatenation is the white noise, as well as the regular time duration gaps between phonemes. You have probably also noticed in this example that the phonemes are repeated or *"echoed"* 3 times.

There is an important reason for this. (No, the intent here is not to create a stuttering computer generated animation for the TV old show *'Max Headroom'*—although if you are trying to achieve the same effect for a game animation, you can in fact create the stuttering *'Max Headroom-syndrome'* by creating loops of diphonic concatenation echoed more than 3 times!).

The triple repetition sustains and reinforces the diphonic concatenation. This is actually in many ways very similar to the *'bleed-over'* method that some of the most advanced color graphics printers use to provide the best possible coverage to close up and smooth the gaps between digitized elements.

It has to do with word-part phoneme sounds actually continuing to be output to the PC audio speaker for a very small discrete time period after the next one has begun.

To the human ear (and more importantly the human brain) this creates a much more human-sounding computer generated voice.

After you learn a little more about how to actually specify IPA speech phoneme unicode to your Windows Visual Basic speech programs later in this book, you may want to experiment with this concept. It will demonstrate very effectively one of the most important reasons why Microsoft SAPI was first able to make major advances over all previous state-of-the-art in human sounding speech.

If you remove this triple-repeat of the diphonic concatenation of phonemes, you will hear a much more mechanical sounding computer voice. It is much more similar to the robot-like computer generated speech that you heard before Microsoft SAPI than the much more convincing human voices that you will be introduced to in the next chapter.

Thanks to diphonic concatenation, SAPI generated computer voices are not only very human sounding, but can very powerfully convey both age and gender as well as emotions, which will all be under your direct control using SAPI ActiveX voice text properties and control tags.

As long as you do not repeat the diphones more than once, the result is still both recognizable and is a very simple but very effective way to smooth across gaps.

You may by now probably be wondering, 'If it repeats 3 times, doesn't that make it really a *"triphonic"* concatenation?'

But the answer is 'no'. Diphonic concatenation always refers to the specific join between two consecutive phonemes, not how many times you join the same repeated phoneme.

Sub-word segments used in diphonic concatenation are derived for use in SAPI after recording many hours of a human voice and painstakingly identify the beginning and ending of phonemes.

Although this can produce a more realistic voice, this is one of the reasons it takes a considerable amount of work to create a completely new SAPI voice.

This is one of the reasons why you do not really want to even attempt to make your own new SAPI voices. You are better off to start with the standard voices and manipulate their properties and control tags in order to get as close as you can to the voice you want to use in your speech application.

As you will soon see, SAPI makes that such an easy and painless process that you should always start with the standard voices that Microsoft provides and modify using SAPI. The important point to emphasize here is that SAPI does just about everything that you would really rather not do automatically for you if you will let it.

And the result is a much better Windows Visual Basic speech program than you could have ever developed yourself without SAPI, even if you had all the time in the world to try to duplicate even a small part of the many hundreds of cumbersome things that SAPI does for you.

Although many other SAPI-compatible vendor text-to-speech engines from Dragon and IBM and dozens of others can parse and interpret word separation as well SAPI itself, there are very few that can approach the ability of the standard SAPI voices and speech synthesis engines to put together words and phrases for truly human sounding speech.

4.3   *Windows SAPI Speaker Intonation and Prosody*

All typical SAPI synthetic computer Text-To-Speech software engines generate sounds similar to those created by the human vocal cords. Various statistical sampling and software based audio waveform filters have already been applied and are part of the SAPI software.

But in order for Microsoft to accomplish the incredible feats of duplicating the various types of human voices that are provide with SAPI and the Microsoft Speech SDK Suite, there had to be a lot of research to determine how to apply parameters to mimic human voices.

Microsoft and a great many linguists had to precisely measure a very large number of people and run a lot of computer simulation models to be able to adequately simulate *throat length, mouth cavity, lip shape,* and *tongue position* parameters. You will probably be very glad that you do not have to worry about having to do that yourself!

Then they had to confirm ability of those specific init parameters to achieve reasonable human sounding SAPI speech in opinions of the vast majority of all people who might ever use Windows speech software.

You may be somewhat taken aback to see that all Windows synthetic Text-To-Speech SAPI engines are so concerned with parameters that relate to your vocal cavity measurements.

But thanks to Microsoft, that is just one more wheel that does not to be reinvented by every aspiring speech programmer. Thanks to SAPI you will not have to write your own vocal chord biometric simulations and biomechanical speech recognizer engines the way that most past speech programmers had to do before the first Microsoft Speech API.

Several other speech intonation factors also influence the quality of a SAPI compliant Microsoft Windows synthetic Text-To-Speech voice.

Localization of speech engines to support voices with a wide diversity of accents and dialects is fairly easy for languages with phonetic alphabets.

But it it has always been very difficult in the past for computer software to make accurate recognitions of names or personal pronouns, especially if they may be easily mispronounced.

This has primarily been because even with the use of IPA standardized Unicode, when very small differences in the accent or intonation from other languages have to be applied to large vocabulary files or even fairly small lexicon files, the time and effort can be staggering.

Implementing localization into synthetic Text-To-Speech using SAPI, on the other hand, typically involves specification of a robust set of grammar-based pronunciation rules to translate text into phonemes.

The difference is that by using this approach invented by Microsoft, SAPI is able to achieve a faster and more efficient speech localization.

4.4   *Windows SAPI Phonemes and Vocabulary*

The processes that are involved in duplicating human speech, as well as taking human speech apart in order to know how to put it back together has been an especially overwhelming task.

Yet SAPI has been able to do this better than any previous software technology because it takes advantage of fundamental Windows component object model and its underlying foundations.

Even with all of the many components that SAPI has to juggle, such as text analysis, prosody, phonemes, signal processing, each of which can involve multiple external object files and contingent processes that must be coordinated and communicated across object boundaries

SAPI is by far the most efficient computer speech technology that has ever been easily available to the public.

At the very highest level, SAPI dynamically handles files and messaging at many numerous complex levels that you are better off to have handled automatically for you by SAPI, but you can still access any of the lower level functions for special applications if you need to.

If a Synthetic Text-To-Speech engine mispronounces a word, the only way that the user can change the pronunciation is by entering either the phonemes, which is not an easy task, or by choosing a series of *'sound-alike'* words that combine to make the correct pronunciation.

The synthetic Text-To-Speech voice provided by even the best power programmer enhanced SAPI compliant engine is always going to be noticeably different from that provided by a digital-audio recording.

Also, mixing the two in the same utterance can be disturbing to the user, and can usually make the synthetic Text-To-Speech voice sound worse by comparison. The process used by SAPI to overcome this basically involves a combination of the use of sound-alike words and phoneme groupings at the software level.

This also involves use of intelligent 'look-ahead' caching similar to the same way that we learned in Chapter One that digital signal processors do at hardware level, within the best efficiency available using Windows OSA architectures.

The process of converting speech audio input into text output is easily one of the most difficult of all data messaging and data management challenges in the world today, and no one does it better than Microsoft Windows using SAPI and the WOSA architecture.

4.5 Using SAPI Text-to-Speech in Visual Basic Voice Text Applications

Text-to-speech also offers a number of other important benefits, which are all based upon both the complex Windows OSA efficiencies involved in coordinating and communicating processes across objects. This assures the simplicity of single-threaded processes running only a single SAPI process, and doing it well, such as the simple Voice Text object process.

If speech application is single-threaded or dedicated to a single processor, SAPI is even more powerful and does one thing at a time better than it does many things at one time.

In general, synthetic Text-To-Speech based on SAPI Voice Text is normally most useful for short phrases or for situations where there is not a lot of complexity in deciding what to say and when.

If there are quite a bit more than just a few dozen phrases at most that are involved in your software applications range of responses, as opposed to the limited number of computer voice phrases that would be repeated over and over by automated voice response systems used by the airlines (or a "1-800" phone information businesses), then it is probably better to use a more powerful SAPI text dictation object.

4.6 Typical Applications of Visual Basic Text-to-Speech Voice Text Object

There are many computer speech applications for which SAPI Voice Text is a perfect choice, both with regard to efficiency and precision.

SAPI Voice Text object is a powerhouse for computer speech involving a small number of repetitive phrases or fairly small set of messages.

For example, audible synthetic Text-To-Speech based proofreading of numbers, which are actually a fairly small number of words in a small grammar that can be systematically concatenated using diphonic methods very efficiently by SAPI Voice Text, can help CPA's and accounting users catch errors missed by visually checking reports.

But this is of course assuming that somebody has to actually be carefully listening to each of the numbers being read, so from a design stand-point, a scrolling text verification window is always a very good idea for this kind of Windows speech application.

In addition, the numbers or Windows form entries can be routinely read back as they are input in order to get a verbal confirmation of data entry, as well as either for book-keeping or word processing.

Synthetic Text-To-Speech based on SAPI Voice Text is also especially useful for support of automated messages or utterance of phrases for exception reporting or status messaging in real-time monitoring when it is less expensive or safer to have an actual human listening to messages rather than get terminal text messages or printout reports.

SAPI Voice Text also works especially well for context-driven informational messages. For example, to inform the user that a print job is complete, such a context-driven SAPI Voice Text application might say:

```
"The printing of your file <xxx.doc> submitted for
print at <date> <time> with total pages of <pp> is
complete and can be picked up at printer <ptr_num> at
<location>"
```

A similar equivalent message for email announcement might say:

```
"The email from <name> with attachment file <xxx.doc>
that you need for your meeting on <subject> has been
received and automatically forwarded to <dist_list>"
```

It should be apparent that this kind of voice messaging application can be much more informative and helpful than simply displaying a message box and requiring the user to click 'OK'.

4.7   Special Handling of SAPI Voice Text in Visual Basic Speech Applications

Yet, in spite of the fact that SAPI Voice Text can be extremely useful and more friendly to the user than paper reports or message boxes, it should be used only for non-critical notifications.

If Voice Text is the only messaging, there could be a problem with a critical message not being heard, in the event that the computer's sound off is offline, or when users are out of hearing range at a critical time.

In order to overcome this, you should always design your Voice Text messaging software to give concurrent or redundant messaging, either to some kind of log file or accumulate message windows, as long as the log file is routinely reviewed (and the accumulated message windows are forced to tiled rather than cascaded!).

Software may also need to issue alternative visual warnings as well as possibly send email or pager notifications when the computer's sound system is turned off, or there is no response to a critical voice message within a user-definable range of time.

The important point here is that if a particular message notification application is either critical to receive human attention or response then it may turn out that the application will have to involve some level of messaging to other multi-tasked applications that may need to run concurrently with the SAPI Voice Text application. However, with WOSA, this is easily handled by Windows.

4.8   Voice Technology Foundations Used in Windows SAPI Speech-To-Text

There are also several critical impacts of voice technology foundation concepts that you have learned about previously in this book, which have special importance with regard to their usage in SAPI Voice Command based Speech-To-Text (STT) and speech recognition for discrete command control applications (which all involve conversion of speech to text that is spotted and then input as commands).

Speech synthesis applications have been neglected by many vendors, since it was the first speech technology, but SAPI gives more direct control, both high level and low level, to generation of computer Microsoft speech that arguably sounds more like real speech than any other Windows third-party vendor.

4.9   Microsoft Windows SAPI Word Matching Technology

Word matching, which you have learned is based upon a very close integration, or even direct linkage between the speech recognizer software—and also the digital electronics and embedded systems firmware involved in creation of data signatures and pre-bundling of data signature packets into critical event signals by DSP 'matcher' systems—are both increasingly critical to two very important discrete command and speech recognition applications categories.

The first area is biometric 'speech-print' security systems, including facility access and identity verification software.

The second area is for phone information voice menu based systems which are designed to give confidential information only to the persons who are authorized to receive that information.

Neither of these applications is quite as critical as some of the other military prototypes involving some potentially dangerous consequences in the event of misrecognition.

Yet it may still be somewhat surprising that discrete command control dictation and speech recognition would be used in security access or confidential information applications.

The answer is that the marriage of SAPI with the digital signal processor and intelligent firmware speech technologies is actually almost as reliable and precise as fingerprints are unique.

Because of the great economic value of this particular technology, it will probably be increasingly integrated into future as well as current SAPI specifications.

It important to be aware of with regard to the many potential benefits that can be achieved by the integration of SAPI high level speech recognition programming with low level SAPI Windows programming access to DSP and embedded systems processors, and be watching this technology!

These capabilities are actually normally only available to Windows speech programmers who are able to code both SAPI high level ActiveX as well as low level SAPI 4.0 with C++/COM objects, but this may change with future versions of SAPI which expand ActiveX controls.

Also, it is necessary not only to get from low level SAPI to DSP, but these applications may require bridging across Microsoft Telephony API (TAPI) or the Speech Verification API (SVAPI) as well.

4.10   Microsoft Windows SAPI Word Spotting Localization

Pronunciation rules in SAPI word spotting, or filtering of selected words to listen for, seldom fail on either speaking or recognizing common English words.

But they almost always fail on non-English words, especially on names that are unusual or of non-English origin.

This may not be a much more than an annoyance to non-English speaking people for a computer speech application.

But for a critical command speech recognition application, it can be a very serious problem.

Again, the big problem relates to the fact that even with IPA Unicode standards, some non-English phonemes may be difficult to combine into words, or broken down from non-English words into phonemes, which can be easily handled by SAPI or any speech standard.

This should especially be kept in mind when designing and developing speech recognition software for Asian or Eastern European language localization.

The biggest part of the problem involves the lack of a standard alphabet of manageable size that can be used to achieve the benefits of 'look-ahead' and diphonic concatenation which were previously described as such a benefit to SAPI speech synthesis.

The solution for such applications (which become increasingly more important with true globalization of the Internet for e-Commerce, with the growing number of non-English speaking tourists and residents in the U.S.), normally involves very simple but aggressive application of word spotting. This usually involves simply adding grammar code to 'spot' for only the 'top-3' words and 10 numbers.

Always remember, the *'top-3'* most important words to spot for in the grammar rules of localized discrete command or critical voice response speech recognition applications, in any English as well as non-English software are, quite simply:

```
"Yes", "No", and "Help" <!!!>
```

4.11   *Microsoft Windows SAPI Individual Speaker Training*

In the previous chapter, you learned how easy, yet time consuming, it can be to training your SAPI speech software using Microsoft Dictation wizards.

Although there are several new technologies that are being tried by Microsoft and other speech vendors to make SAPI and all speech technology more reliably speaker independent, for the foreseeable future, individual speaker training is the only way to improve the reliability of speech engine recognition for any one person to 100%.

The significance of this is that there are only two options that are available to speech recognition application programmers.

If you have a critical discrete command application, you are either going to have to insist, and make absolutely certain, that the proper speech training sessions are completed and speaker files are properly created. And if the application is life critical, you may be under some intense legal obligation to guarantee that your application speech training is done properly.

Your only other option is to limit the grammars to word-spot for simple *'yes-no'* recognitions. There should be none of these problems or considerations if the application does not involve any life critical or safety impacts.

Therefore, SAPI Voice Command can be used without any concerns or special precautions whatsoever in most conventional speech recognition.

This includes multi-media recreational games, non-critical news information, communications or education, and hospitality as well as travel industry automated availability, and even moderate sized transaction e-Commerce software applications.

As a general rule of thumb, SAPI Voice Command object, and its sister object SAPI Voice Telephony, are most appropriate for use in limited word response grammar speech recognition applications that can be designed as menu based software.

This has in fact been the most common and effective use of these SAPI ActiveX objects thus far.

4.12   Using SAPI Speech-to-Text in Windows Visual Basic Voice Command Apps

Any discrete command control application can use speech recognition based on SAPI Voice Command objects if the responses can be defined, and can be forced, to be said in a specific enough manner.

Discrete command control speech recognition applications based on either SAPI Voice Command or SAPI Telephony Command cannot ever effectively be used to enter names.

Yet, these two SAPI ActiveX controls are nevertheless very good for creating Windows software for entering numbers.

Even for saying keywords to select items out of a small selection list of up to no more than one hundred or, more ideally, many less items.

The Microsoft Dictation help facility 'What Can I Say' is a perfect example of a 'long list' voice selection box which is based on SAPI Voice Command.

Any user that has learned to use 'What Can I Say' will probably be very comfortable using any Windows speech application that is designed to look-and-feel like 'WCIS' and programmed using Visual Basic with SAPI Voice Command ActiveX controls.

4.13 Typical Visual Basic Applications of Speech-to-Text Voice Command

Almost all SAPI Voice Command Windows speech applications are highly integrated with one (single SDI) or more (multiple MDI) menu-based Windows forms or even multiple Windows software menus across applications.

One of the greatest benefits of Windows SAPI is that it makes the most of WOSA and Microsoft Component Object Model standards in order to support multiple multi-tasked concurrent speech applications.

This can even include the concurrent use of both SAPI Voice Command and SAPI Voice Telephony objects and ActiveX speech controls to receive voice input from either local Windows PC microphone or voice modem telephony, or both.

Discrete command control and speech recognition based on SAPI Voice Command or Voice Telephony can be an essential part of any application that requires hands-free operation.

It can also provide an alternative to the keyboard for users who are unable or prefer not to use one. Users with repetitive-stress injuries or who cannot type may use speech recognition as the sole means of controlling the computer.

While speech recognition can especially enhance the realism and fun in many computer games, it can also provide a very simple and effective alternative to keyboard-based control of games using SAPI Voice Command and Visual Basic ActiveX speech controls.

4.14 Special Handling of Voice Command in Visual Basic Speech Applications

Before any discrete command control speech application based on SAPI Voice Command or Voice Telephony starts a recognizer engine in active listening mode, it should first give the recognizer a 'short list' of specific command words or phrases to listen for.

The list might include commands like:

```
"minimize window,"

"make the font bold,"

"call <phone number>," or

"send email to <name>," or

"check flight availability tomorrow to {Seattle}".
```

If your Windows speech software user speaks the command words exactly as they are expected, which is to say, the way they are defined in the active grammar rule for the active SAPI speech engine, then your speech software will get very good accuracy.

However, if they say the command in any way differently, and the application wasn't provided the alternate wording in its default grammar to exclude by word-spotting, then the recognizer engine will either not recognize anything.

Or, even worse, it will recognize something completely different (i.e., the meaningless recognition *"Sea Tattle"* rather than the real city *"Seattle".*).

You should always design all your discrete command control speech application software to have a 'push-to-talk' button in your Windows control panel for your SAPI application, just in case no 'mute' button in provided with either the microphone or speakers on the PC.

When the user pushes the button, the computer's audio output is muted and speech recognition is turned on and toggles to turn it on or off.

Another common voice command control speech application trick that can be used very effectively with SAPI Voice Command is to give the application a name that it will recognize and respond to when spoken to, like *"Computer,"* or *"Rover",* or *"HAL"*, and then turn on all other command speech recognition.

This can also be implemented exactly like the 'push-to-talk' button, except that the speech recognition application also toggles itself on and off whenever it hears its name.

If you use this technique, just be sure you give it a unique name, not a common word spoken in 'front' of the computer (like 'computer') otherwise it will get annoying when it starts up its speech engines when you do not want it to.

It can be done, but you really have to write a very complicated SAPI grammar to be able to give your speech application the smarts to know when you are talking *to* your computer versus talking to someone *about* your computer!

When you design any discrete command speech recognition application, it is most of all important to communicate to the user that your application software is speech-aware, and immediately provide them with the most important commands that it is expecting to hear.

It is also important to provide command verifications that are consistent and complete, and which do not permit any possibility of misinterpretation.

Both of these functions can be most easily provided using a standard Visual Basic form to present a Windows message box visually at the same time that the speech software waits or expects a particular voice command.

Or, on the other hand, you may simply prefer to always notify the user of what the speech recognizer engine thought that it just heard.

Anytime that the command that was just recognized could be regarded as in any possible way to be potentially dangerous or undesirable (such as deleting files or rebooting the computer!)—you should use this same Windows message box technique with a button, or require some other word to be spoken and recognized before the action is taken.

Just as with the 'OK' button window for GUI applications, with speech it is always best to ask the user one last time before doing anything that cannot be undone, or undeleted, just to be safe.

4.15 Voice Technology Used in Windows Visual Basic SAPI Speech Recognition

All SAPI compliant speech recognition applications, including the sample programs you were provided with as part of the Microsoft Speech SDK Suite, contain some form of grammar rules. Or else they may alternatively reference default grammars that are defined using text files with handles similar to what you may already be acquainted with as.INF or.INI files.

The grammar, vocabulary or custom speech translation dictionary inputs normally are made up of a number of sections, with each section identified by a preceding line, with the section name in brackets (again, just like an.INI file).

Each section has a number of values, identified by a value name, followed by an equal sign, followed by the value.

As you would expect, speech grammar coding comments can be used in the file either by starting a line with a semicolon (;) or with double slash (//).

Listing 4.1. Example of a very simple grammar to control Windows.

```
[(WINDOW Commands)]
// This is a list of commands the grammar is listening for
1=open (WINDOW)
2=close (WINDOW)
3=set the time to "Time=" <time>
4=set the date to "Date=" <date>

[(WINDOW)]
// Different names for window
=the window
=a window
=window
```

Notably, the simple SAPI speech recognition grammar specification shown in Listing 4.1 enables recognition of any number of command variations, but it specifically listens only for those words:

"Please Open a window...Next Close the window."

"Now Set the time to uhhhh how about eight oh six A M."

"OK Set date to December thirty one two thousand and three."

"Ahh Set time back to ten P M now lets test midnight."

"I want to try Setting date to January one Year 2000."

"Please Open the window NOW...I said RIGHT NOW!!!"

Thus, if any word or phrase that was spoken in these examples is not listed in the very simple SAPI grammar in Listing 4.1 then those words or phrases may be spoken—but will never be "heard"!.

4.16   *Microsoft Windows SAPI Rule Grammars*

When any grammar is referenced anywhere in any Visual Basic program object or project, the speech applications active or default rules are automatically compiled in.

Unless the grammar specification file contains an explicit definition to use its own customized default rules, then your active SAPI speech engine's own default rules supercede any other rules definition. This is very important, so it is a good idea to try to imagine consequence of a few examples.

This may sound simple but it can in fact be particularly complex.

Sometimes a given speech application may involve multiple SAPI speech synthesis TTS as well as speech recognition SST engines, with multiple voices, and use both multiple standard Microsoft SAPI high level ActiveX object as well as multiple third-party low level speech API objects coded in C++/COM.

However, you should not be too worried about all of this complexity as long as you have a basic understanding of object oriented software concepts, including architecture layers and encapsulation inheritance.

In fact, thinking about encapsulation or nesting of object events as well as inheritance of object attributes should help you to understand that depending on what and how each rule or grammar object is instanced and referenced.

In fact, this is actually pretty much how grammars and all other speech objects work.

Thus, as you might expect all of the usual rules for object oriented programming apply in determining whether or not a particular rule or grammar is active with regard to a particular SAPI speech object or its associated resources.

All the same, sometimes it helps to simply draw a diagram exact in order to help understanding (or explaining) what object has control of which specific speech resource in a given instance.

SAPI will do just about everything most application programmers will ever want at the high level, but one of the greatest accomplishments of SAPI is that Microsoft also provides it access for even very low level Windows capabilities by VAR vendors.

A much more complicated integrated speech recognition application is particularly important to flowchart.

Even though a particular application does not involve near as many external components and object layers, an application may actually be very complex in its own right.

For example, it may necessarily select and control multiple grammars based on events and conditions, and it must also control and manage messaging between the grammars and their results objects, some of which are shared.

Complex speech recognition applications can easily be designed and developed in confidence by professional object programmers, according to the same standards and conventions used to develop any other Windows Visual application in VB, C++ or J++.

Of the previous two figures, only the latter is indicative of the kind of high level SAPI speech application that can be created based only upon ActiveX object controls and Visual Basic or VBA.

The earlier of the two figures related to a complex integrated application that could only be linked together with COM and C++.

The basic default definition for SAPI recognition grammar rules is shown below in Listing 4.2. This SAPI grammar rules specification is very simple and should be very easily understood.

Some customized special professional technical or localized foreign language grammar rules specifications, on the other hand, can sometimes be many hundreds, or even thousands, of lines long.

Listing 4.2. A simple default SAPI speech recognition rules grammar.

```
RuleDefault definition<Start>The
<Start> rule, by default, is defined as:"
<Start> = [opt] (JunkBegin) (Commands) [opt] (JunkEnd)".
```

```
<PhoneNum>Recognizes phone numbers.
<Year>Recognizes years.
<Month>Recognizes month names.
<date>Recognizes dates.
<time>Recognizes times.
<Dollars>Recognizes dollars.
<Digits>Recognizes a sequence of one or more digits.
<Digit>Recognizes one digit.
<Fraction>Recognizes fractions.
<Natural>Recognizes natural numbers.
<Integer>Recognizes integer numbers.
<Float>Recognizes floating point numbers.
<PluralNumber>Recognizes plural numbers, like "nineteen
fifties."
```

As you can see, SAPI grammar rules specifications look very similar to style and template definitions that are often times standard across all Microsoft office products.

Usually you will not normally see a grammar rules file like this, since they are often compiled into executable objects and in runtime libraries for distribution with a particular default speech engine.

In early versions of SAPI you had to manually insert and maintain SAPI grammar rules files, similar to early versions of HTML tags.

But beginning with SAPI 4.0, most of the rules object files, and many other grammar rules can be much more easily created and maintained using SAPI dictation wizards.

In fact, some types of grammar objects can only be accessed using wizards.

Every speech recognition application software grammar must have a header section that informs any compiler that may be used to build the grammar rules into an executable of exactly what language you used to define the grammar.

It is also necessary that you always specify usage mode, and exactly what type of grammar the commands, words, settings and defaults should be compiled as.

A typical SAPI grammar header compile option format is shown in Listing 4.3:

Listing 4.3. Example of a generic SAPI grammar header template.

```
[Grammar]
LangID=language ID
Dialect=dialect string (optional)
```

```
Type=cfg, limited-domain, or dictation (optional)
CompileTo=cfg, limited-domain, or dictation (optional)
TypeFeatureCFGParseRules=Grammar
TypeCompilesTo=CFGCFG, Limited-Domain, or Dictation
DictationFrameLimited=Domain or Dictation
```

4.17   Microsoft Windows SAPI Context-Free Grammars

Context-free grammars are a special type of grammar that can also contain sections that define *Parse String Rules*. In SAPI these sections are identified by the rule name surrounded with a '<' and '>'.

Each line of the section contains a sub-rule, which is an alternative of the main rule. Sub rules are not visible outside of the main rule.

Parse string rules are similar to conventional linguistic rules language specifications. An example of a SAPI parse string rule grammar specification for an airline reservation automated voice response SAPI application is shown in Listing 4.4:

Listing 4.4. Example of a Context-Free Grammar for a voice menu based SAPI telephony Airline Reservations application.

```
[<Reservation>]
<Reservation> = "Reservation" reservation [opt] PNR
<Reservation> = "Reservation:" <Seating> reservation [opt] PNR
<Reservation> = "Reservation:" <Seating> [1+]
<AndSeating> Reservation [opt] PNR
<Seating> = FirstClass "FirstClass"
<Seating> = Business "Business"
<Seating> = Coach "Coach"
<AndSeating> = [opt] and "+" <Seating>
```

The above rule named '*<Reservation>*' is defined for global inheritance, which can be seen by all other rules.

The rules for '*<Seating>*' and '*<AndSeating>*' are only available to the '*<Reservation>*' rule and cannot be seen or be affected by other rules.

If there is another rule called '*<Seating>*' then it is not used in that generation of the '*<Reservation>*' grammar parse rule.

Each rule line represents an alternative case that is valid only within the limited context of its own hierarchy.

In SAPI parse rule grammar specifications, a rule hierarchy definition always begins with parser rule name, followed by an equal sign, followed by the number of special speech parsing operators.

These operators are conditions that must be met to satisfy the rule. Otherwise, you know what happens (the engine never "hears" a word!).

4.18   Microsoft Windows SAPI Limited Domain Dictation Grammars

The SAPI grammar rules words section is used in both limited-domain and dictation grammars. It is titled '*[Words]*' and contains one or more words used in the grammar.

For SAPI limited-domain grammars, it lists the valid words that will be listened for because of their conditional or context relevance to potential actions that have been identified by usage case scenarios.

As you can probably guess, this is where you define filters or limited word recognition sets for recognizer '*spotting*'.

This is probably the section that most people would expect to be defined into a speech recognition grammar, vocabulary or dictionary.

An example of SAPI limited domain dictation grammar '*[Words]*' and '*[WordGroups]*' specifications for our sample airline reservation telephone voice response system is shown below.

If the words and word groups are not in the grammar rules specification, the speech recognition program will not listen for it.

This is where you might choose not to specify obvious words or any anticipated words you want to intentionally exclude if the necessary response may be not to do anything, as in Listing 4.5.

Listing 4.5. Example of a Limited-Domain Dictation grammar with WordGroups

```
[Words]
=flight
=connection
=availability
=upgrade

[WordGroups]
=Status
=Airports
```

```
[Status]
=wideopen
=overbooked
=ontime
=delayed
=cancelled

[Airports]
=Kennedy
=LaGuardia
=DFW
```

In other words, if you do not want to even acknowledge any requests for information on any of your competitive airlines make sure you exclude all words in their names!

Of course that would be wrong, and probably lead to a fair trade complaint to the government, right? So if your application actually retrieves competitive airline fare and schedule information, don't even think about it!

On the other hand, you can probably already think of a lot of reasons to use such exclusion methods so that the computer will ignore certain words. You will especially want to do this if your users may be using your speech software when they are very emotional, agitated or frustrated (which is also a high likelihood if your application involves airline information systems!).

4.19   Using SAPI Dictation Objects in Windows Continuous Speech Applications

For many people, keyboards have been the main reason why they never become comfortable with computers to begin with. To this day, many busy executives do not know (or want to know) how to use a keyboard to enter typed commands into a computer.

Yet there are many other people who would like to be able to type at a keyboard but simply cannot. Either they were either simply frustrated from being unable to hit the right keys, or experienced pain from even the first attempt. To a large degree, many older people have overcome this, but there are still a large number of seniors who for medical reason simply can not type on a keyboard even if they want to.

4.20   Typical Applications of Windows Visual Basic Continuous Speech Dictation

The most common continuous natural speech software applications are based on one or more of the 3 SAPI voice dictation object components, and most commonly involve very large vocabulary grammars, often with multiple rules and lexicons. They also tend to be the most resource intensive.

The voice dictation objects are most commonly used in continuous natural speech, and are thus most often used in transcription and word processing or voice email applications.

Continuous natural speech SAPI ActiveX voice dictation object components are also increasingly used in language localization and bilingual, or even multilingual, translation applications.

A continuous voice entry transcription application can be designed and implemented using SAPI in almost any language, including the ability to recognize different accents or dialects.

Still, most SAPI speech engines support only five or ten of the major languages, for example, European languages and Japanese or Korean.

Localization of a speech-recognition engine is time-consuming and expensive, requiring extensive amounts of speech data and the skills of a trained linguist, so it is not something that you want to ever attempt on your own.

Because of this, in the past there were not many affordable or reliable foreign language word processors, but it should not surprise you to notice that since SAPI was first released, there are now many that can be used in Visual Basic speech programs.

Most SAPI based continuous natural speech transcription and dictation systems provide discrete dictation against a specialized lexicon subset of the overall vocabulary, allowing users to speak up to 50 words per minute, which is as fast as some of the fastest typists.

Or the same systems, if they are based on SAPI dictation objects support continuous natural speech transcription up to 120 words per minute, which is as fast as most people can talk.

4.21 Special Handling of Dictation Objects in Windows Speech Applications

Some users will have unrealistic expectations, and expect all speech aware software to correctly transcribe every word that they speak, understand it, and then act upon it in an intelligent manner.

You should convey as clearly as possible exactly what your speech application can and cannot do and emphasize that the user should speak clearly, using words the application understands.

Sometimes a continuous voice transcription speech recognizer may 'hear' an ambient noise sound, like a slamming door, and attempt to translate it into words based on default grammar rules (which will result in absolute garbage phonemes, as we saw earlier).

There are several potential ways that you can help to prevent this from happening.

The user should be able to turn the continuous natural speech software off quickly if ambient noise gets out of control (a barking dog, crying child, or noisy neighbor).

This can be accomplished by use of the keyboard, mouse, voice, or joystick.

Again, always remember to provide a 'push-to-talk' or 'mute' button. This can be a key on the keyboard, mouse button, hot-spot for the cursor, a joystick button or form button.

Continuous natural voice transcription speech recognition engines can be very temperamental and like to hear commands with no surprises. They like to hear that if the user is having a phone conversation in the room while speech recognition is listening. The recognizer will continue to respond as if the user is still speaking directly to it, and yet it may hear unrecognized words.

Of course, any well designed Continuous Voice Entry Transcription application will use filters, word-spotting, or limited domain grammars, as you have learned about earlier in this chapter.

Your SAPI continuous speech application should be programmed to provide mechanisms to scan large lists of active commands or programmed with the ability to prompt the user for the most common voice responses through visuals or text-to-speech.

For example, your continuous natural speech application might say:

"Do you want to save the file? Please say' Yes' or' No'."

A good graphic user interface can provide continuous natural speech voice transcription application software users with tremendous feedback about what they can do by displaying menus, buttons, and other controls on the screen. If the application does not recognize a command, you can provide more extensive help. For example:

> "Please say Yes or No, or say Help if you need more
> information."

Continuous natural speech voice dictation engines often make mistaken recognitions that are correctly spelled and often grammatically correct.

These often times amount to nothing meaningful but can carry with them embarrassing indications that either the speech recognition software was limited, the speaker did not speak the native language well, or they might have actually 'meant' something else.

Unfortunately, the mistaken recognitions sometimes mean something completely different than the user intended.

These errors serve to illustrate some of the complexity involved in speech communication, particularly because people are not accustomed to attributing strange wording to speech errors.

To minimize some of the mistaken recognitions, your Visual Basic speech applications should always be designed be made to allow users to easily correct mistakes.

Provide easy access to a 'Correction Window' so the user can manually correct mistakes that the recognizer made.

Allow the user to easily toggle the continuous speech recognizer on and off easily multiple ways, including speech, keyboard and the usual Windows mouse facilities.

Typical continuous natural speech voice entry transcription and large vocabulary dictation speech recognizers commonly listen for 20,000 to 100,000 words.

Yet, typically one out of every fifty words a user speaks isn't recognized because it isn't in the vocabulary file of words supported by that engine. (This is even worse in bi-lingual and multi-lingual natural speech transcription software applications).

You can make life a lot easier on your users (and yourself), if you always include both voice and keyboard functions to allow them to quickly and easily add unrecognized words to your vocabulary files.

As you learned in Chapter Three, there are some Dictation Options that let you add words to a recognizer file.

But you and your users will have less problems if you design such a function directly into your own natural speech applications, so they will not have to bother to leave to go to Microsoft Dictation Options and come back.

Also, as you will learn in the next chapter, it is often easier and faster to develop applications which detect word recognition problems and immediately redirect the user to a new window where they can use Microsoft Dictate to enter text with more powerful default speech engines. You can also give the user wizards that will enable them to add special word spotting, or to simply activate *"What Can I Say".*

Even if it is active in the taskbar, it is easier for you to use Visual Basic database management facilities from within your own speech application, so you have complete control and can use OLE Automation to routinely update vocabulary files with new words so they automatically compile if needed.

4.22 *Understanding Windows Speech SDK Suite Sample Visual Basic Programs*

Now let's take just a little more detailed look at some of the Visual Basic code and property settings behind the use of some of the ActiveX speech controls in SAPI 4.0 sample programs which are related to many of the things that you have learned about in this chapter.

As you have probably learned already in your Visual Basic programming career, the best way to understand Visual Basic programming models is to open and "take apart" the code in working programs.

4.23 *Analyzing the SAPI Animated Mouth TTS Visual Basic Speech Program*

You may remember that you got your first look at the *"Talking Mouth"* Visual Basic SAPI ActiveX speech program ('BASICTTS.EXE') in Chapter One.

Now we will be looking at it again in much more detail in the next chapter in order to demonstrate the great variety of standard and special voices that are shipped with SAPI 4.0 Microsoft speech engines and the Microsoft Speech SDK Suite.

For the moment, we are only going to look at the Visual Basic code behind the *"Talking Mouth"* SAPI speech engine activation that controls the speaking of text box entry over the current active combo box selected voice. This method uses the current mode selection of the speech engine in order to control the synchronization of the animation to voices.

In Figure 4.1 you can see the *"Talking Mouth"* as we last saw it in Chapter One. Here it is speaking the text *"Hello World!"*, and with the default voice is set to *'Mary for Telephone'*.

If you wish, you can take another look at the *"Talking Mouth"* by running the *"BASICTTS"* executable in the VB5 ActiveX sample folder.

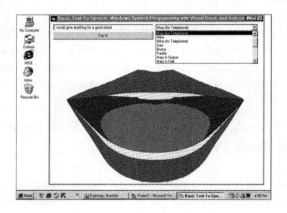

Figure 4.1.

The standard default speech engine for the "Talking Mouth" application is usually the female voice 'Mary' on a telephone, with big red lips, because many years of R&D has demonstrated that all people, including men and women, prefer to hear a female voice!

In Listing 4.7, you can see the Visual Basic code that is used in order to perform the 3 steps that you will always use to start up any speech application, in Visual Basic or any other language:

- Find and load the most appropriate speech engine
- Set the current active speech recognizer mode
- Select active voice and initialize its property settings

As you can see in this very simple Visual Basic code, the SAPI application is instructing Windows to find and load the Microsoft speech engine that is defined by the default SAPI controls to be the best at speaking female voices.

If you run the program yourself with the settings switched back and forth to speak both genders, you will hear voices as different as male and female, to any human ear!

Listing 4.6. Visual Basic code to activate the default speech engine for Female voice.

```
engine = TextToSpeech1.Find("Mfg=Microsoft;Gender=1")
'0=male 1=female
TextToSpeech1.CurrentMode = engine
```

The speech engine may or may not be changed at any time during any application session if the gender property is reset to male, or if other changes to properties such as active voice are changed and detected by event handling that changes speech recognizer mode.

You should notice in this example that the speech engine is activated by the SAPI ActiveX speech control for simple TextToSpeech SAPI ActiveX controls.

You should be aware that you can have multiple speech engines active at the same time, which does not hurt any thing, but it can greatly slow the processing and result in a lock-up or even GPF crash if there are not enough resources.

If you want to make sure you stay with the same speech engine for an entire session, you must write code to restrict active engine or mode changes, since the default is for SAPI to allow and support multiple speech engine instances.

As you can guess from Figure 4.1, when the drop-down combo box selection of voice is changed from female to male voice, not only does *"Talking Mouth"* voice change—but animation for the lips change from full female-looking lips with red lipstick, to more masculine lips that are thin and less red!

If you try changing the voice to each of the different voice settings by selecting a new standard or special voice name in the drop-down combo box you will be able to see how the lips are changed.

If you try all of the voices, including the robot and child voices, you should find out that the animation of the lips change to very full and red only for those voices that begin with the name Mary.

This sample SAPI Visual Basic application always knows when voice is female, and when it is not, and changes backgrounds based on that. All other voices that are not female have the same narrow lips.

Although the *"Talking Mouth"* lip animation is not a SAPI ActiveX or even a low level SAPI function, it is an example of how SAPI ActiveX properties and parameter settings can be used to control other types of functions or contingent events in any speech software application.

The use of animations, and especially lip animations that are well synchronized to the sounds of the voice speaking, can make all of your SAPI speech applications more interesting and fun, as well as friendly (and as you have now seen, potentially even "sexy") to the users of your speech applications.

By using the simple techniques shown here to directly link both the initial speech engine and mode settings, as well as any events that change those settings to your control of the speech synchronized animations, are almost certainly bound to make all your speech applications a very big hit!

The Visual Basic code that controls this change from full red female lips back to narrow male lips, and vice versa, is based on the dynamic change in SAPI voice gender property when the current mode of the Microsoft active speech engine is changed to handle any change in the active voice selected in the drop-down combo box, as shown in Listing 4.7. This is yet another clever little trick you can probably think of a lot of uses for especially in games or animation programs!

Listing 4.7. Visual Basic gender animation and voice based dropdown combo box event.

```
Private Sub Combo1_Click()
    TextToSpeech1.CurrentMode = Combo1.ListIndex + 1
    If (TextToSpeech1.Gender(TextToSpeech1.CurrentMode) = 1)
    Then TextToSpeech1.LipType = 0
        'female full red lips animation
    Else TextToSpeech1.LipType = 1
        'male thin pale lips animation
    End If
End Sub
```

You can easily use this same method to link any event or property you can think of to drive some kind of animation event or context control, which includes selecting or changing active grammar rules!

Although we will not make any changes to the sample Visual Basic "Talking Mouth" application at this time, you can open the 'BASICTTS' project in your Visual Basic IDE, and beginning looking over properties that are defined for the SAPI ActiveX speech control for TextToSpeech, as shown in Figure 4.2

You should begin to think about how you might use each of these properties in order to control linkages to other form objects or control events that can drive animation or add more intelligence and friendliness to your own SAPI speech application software.

When you have finished looking at each of the SAPI ActiveX control properties for TextToSpeech in SAPI Visual Basic "Talking Mouth" application, you can shut the BASICTTS project, but not your Visual Basic IDE, since we will use it again to look at the next SAPI sample Visual Basic speech application.

4.24   Analyzing the SAPI Word Recognizer STT Visual Basic Speech Program

The next SAPI sample program that we will look at in order to help reinforce some more of the things you have learned about today can also be found in the ActiveX VB5 folder, and is named 'BASICCMD'. If you open the BASICCMD folder and run the 'BASICCMD' program, you should see an active pop-up window with two form boxes and 3 buttons.

The "Basic Voice Commands" application is very basically a speech to text database management program. You say it, and it tells you what it heard, so you can confirm if you want to add it.

If you remember this SAPI Visual Basic speech application from your own explorations of the sample programs earlier in this week, you may know that this program listens for English words using a command dictation grammar list and performs some useful vocabulary file management functions.

When you speak a color or any other word, this program will first attempt to recognize it against the current active vocabulary file that is the default for command dictation grammars.

If the word is recognized, it will be displayed in the single word text entry box and a message above the box will display it as the last heard word.

You then have the option to use the 'Add' button to update the last heard word to the word list in the 'Listening For' box at the left.

You have probably already anticipated what this little sample SAPI Visual Basic speech application is doing. It is updating a wordlist in an active grammar!

You may remember that we discussed earlier that it would be nice to program a code object to create your own form to add unrecognized words to a discrete command grammar or continuous natural speech vocabulary file.

Remember the suggestion to link to a SAPI wizard from Visual Basic form exception handling from within your own speech application, so your users will not have to exit out to the Dictation Options?

This is it! You should be able to use this sample application for that purpose.

However, we will not get into too much detail about the techniques used in this sample Visual Basic program. There are still several things we want to show you briefly before we look at some other Visual Basic applications that do some of the same things in more detail tomorrow in the next chapter.

The first thing that you need to look at is the UpdateList procedure Dim statement declarations and their data types as shown in the Listing 4.8, which is typical of the explicit variables that you will need to use the SAPI Voice Command and other ActiveX speech controls.

Listing 4.8. Visual Basic data type declaration for Voice Command ActiveX control.

```
Private Sub UpdateList()
Dim i As Long
Dim command As String
Dim description As String
Dim category As String
Dim flags As Long
Dim action As String
```

As each new word is spoken and recognized, if the 'Add Item' button is clicked, the text string for that word is added to the list of words to listen for.

If you say a new word and this application does not recognize it, the previous word stays in the input text box, until you add the same word again, speak a new word it recognizes, or remove it by keyboard.

You have probably noticed that this application is not doing exactly what it has indicated it is doing, or to be more precise it is doing a bit more.

It is not only listening for the words in the listbox on the left.

It is also listening to recognize all English words that are defined to the large vocabulary file that is the default for the SAPI Voice Command for this Microsoft speech engine!

As you can imagine, this could lead to loading a very large resource intensive storage and require a lot of messaging resources as well.

So what is the real purpose of this little sample SAPI Visual Basic speech recognition application program, and what can it really be used for?

Its purpose is to create a 'short-list' of words that can be used to build a limited-domain grammar.

So you can use it not only to build objects to support fairly small lexicons or rules for word-spotting, but you can also use it to create or update a much smaller vocabulary or lexicon files for localization applications!

Or alternatively, for vertical professional applications such as for medical doctors or lawyers, you can also create a much larger vocabulary or lexicon file.

You should be aware this application does not have any functions to support either creating or updating either external file objects, record set objects or database updates. You must add that yourself.

In Listing 4.9, you can see the control loop that gets the data for each of the variables defined earlier in the UpdateList procedure, which will be used to perform the actual AddItem when 'Add Command' button is clicked.

Listing 4.9. Visual Basic control loop to handle results of Voice Command recognition.

```
List1.Clear
tcount = Vcommand1.CountCommands(gMymenu)
For i = 1 To tcount
    Vcommand1.GetCommand gMymenu, i, command,
        description, category, flags, action
    List1.AddItem command
Next i
End Sub
```

If you open the project for BASICCMD with your Visual Basic IDE, you will see the form pretty much as you saw it when it was running as an active pop-up window.

But if you look carefully there should be one notable exception that you may not have seen on any Visual Basic form before now. So what is that 'little ear' icon above the 'Stop Listening' button? And why does it not appear on the application active pop-up window?

Can you guess? And the answer is: *'That's the SAPI ActiveX Voice Command control!'*

So if you single click on it you can move it around the form and will be able to view its control property settings, and can look at its Visual Basic code. Which of course you already know how to do, but it is still very interesting to take your own look at some of the types of property settings that you can use to control SAPI speech!

If you open the Visual Basic code window for Form1, you will be able to see some of the code we already reviewed, as well as a lot more.

As you scroll down the code, you will come to the Form_Load procedure shown in Listing 4.10, which includes several SAPI ActiveX Voice Command statements.

As you can see, this is clearly a fairly typical Visual Basic form intialization procedure, with the 3 colors 'red,blue,green' as the initial list box items.

What should also probably be new to you is that the actual creation of the menu as well as its updates are performed under direct SAPI ActiveX Voice Command control.

That is because this is a speech aware menu and everything that you would normally do with a menu or form component control is being done entirely by ActiveX Voice Command.

Listing 4.10. ActiveX Voice Command control Visual Basic form initialization process.

```
Private Sub Form_Load()
Vcommand1.Initialized = 1
gMymenu = Vcommand1.MenuCreate(App.EXEName, "state1", 4)
Vcommand1.Enabled = 1
Vcommand1.AddCommand gMymenu, 1, "red",
      "when you say" + "red",
      "listen list", 0, ""
Vcommand1.AddCommand gMymenu, 1, "blue",
      "when you say" + "blue",
      "listen list", 0, ""
Vcommand1.AddCommand gMymenu, 1, "green",
      "when you say" + "green",
      "listen list", 0, ""
UpdateList
Vcommand1.Activate gMymenu
End Sub
```

If you look at Form_Load carefully, you will notice that there are at least 5 usages of the SAPI ActiveX Voice Command in this event driven procedure.

We will not go into too much detail about this particular sample SAPI Visual Basic procedure at this time, but you should look it over carefully before you close the project and Visual Basic IDE (since this might be related to a good question for your daily exercise).

4.25 *Analyzing the SAPI ActiveX Web TTS Voice Animation HTML Script*

You will undoubtedly also remember the SAPI *"Web Talking Lady"* HTML ActiveX computer speech synthesis application, which was first seen in

Chapter One, since this is usually regarded by most Visual Basic programmers as the most popular and memorable of all the sample applications first provided in SAPI 4.0.

When you use Microsoft FrontPage, Microsoft Explorer, or any MSIE4 compatible browser to go to the SAPI ActiveX program sample folder 'WEB' and its sub-folder 'LADY', you can open 'LADY.HTM'.

She may or may not be saying anything yet, unless you let her know what to say by typing something in!

If you remember the "Talking Lady" web application, it should not surprise you that she can say anything you want her to. But you should try to put that aside for now and notice the black background.

The other thing that you may notice if you look at the far right and bottom of 'LADY.HTM', is that there is a large area that is blacked out. It remains blacked out even if you try to use scroll bars to center the image the blacked out area remains where it started out.

If you close 'LADY.HTM' and go back to the file list, you should open 'LADY1.HTM' next. If you are in MSIE or FrontPage, go ahead and open the view to 'Source', or click on the HTML tab, and you will see the HTML tags for the BODY section, as shown in Listing 4.11.

The two things that you should notice here are the way that the background.JPG image file is referenced, and the object reference section with the ActiveX speech object name, type and classID as you used to write one of your first SAPI speech programs in Chapter One.

Listing 4.11. HTML for BODY of LADY1.HTM with image and ActiveX speech objects.

```
<BODY background=sqgirl12.jpg topmargin=0 leftmargin = 0>
<TABLE CELLPADDING=0 CELLSPACING=0 BORDER=0>
<TR> <TD WIDTH="298" HEIGHT="363"> </TD> </TR>
<TR> <TD WIDTH="280" HEIGHT="100"> </TD> <TD>
<object NAME="ActiveVoice" TYPE="application/x-oleobject"
    classid="clsid:EEE78591-FE22-11D0-8BEF-0060081841DE"
    HEIGHT=120 WIDTH=135> </object> </TD> </TR>
</TABLE>
```

If you continue to scroll down HTML from 'LADY1.HTM', you will see a SCRIPT at the end of the BODY section, as shown in Figure 4.2.

Figure 4.2.

Following the body of the HTML is a web script that has values assigned for parameters that correspond to VB properties for the ActiveX control 'ActiveVoice'.

SCRIPT is SAPI ActiveX speech enabled, and uses ActiveVoice to control active speech properties when either the function SayIt() or DoIt() receives a click event.

The complete SCRIPT to support this speech enabled Web application is shown in Listing 4.12.

Listing 4.12. HTML ActiveX speech control VB script for Talking Lady web page.

```
<SCRIPT>

function SayIt()
{ActiveVoice.Speak(TB.value);}
function Doit()
{ActiveVoice.Select(2)
ActiveVoice.Speak(Fred.value)}

ActiveVoice.Initialized=1
ActiveVoice.LipTension=0
ActiveVoice.TonguePosn=0
ActiveVoice.TeethLowerVisible=0
ActiveVoice.TeethUpperVisible=0
ActiveVoice.JawOpen=0
ActiveVoice.MouthUpturn=220
```

```
ActiveVoice.MouthWidth=240
ActiveVoice.MouthHeight=0

ActiveVoice.Speak("You are getting sleepy.
                   Very very sleepy.")

</SCRIPT>
```

We will not get into too much detail to analyze this speech enabled web page HTML, since it is all very basic VB and HTML

But the most important things to notice before we go on to the final sample SAPI speech application that we will open up today relates to the way that all of the various voice properties are set and voice parameters are specified in a web script.

You should also make note of the way that the actual speaker instruction is coded for using ActiveX speech controls on a web page.

4.26   *Analyzing the SAPI Web Voice Recognition VB and JavaScript Applet*

The last sample SAPI program code that we will look today in this chapter is also a VB Script web page speech enabled application, that calls a SAPI speech enabled web Java applet.

If you go to the SAPI ActiveX sample program folder for 'JAVA' and its sub-folder 'COLORS', you will see something like a dozen files and even more sub-folders, but do not worry about all of the files for right now, as they are not all related to Visual Basic ActiveX.

For now, you should simply use Microsoft FrontPage, Microsoft Explorer, or any MSIE4 compatible browser to open 'COLORS.HTM'.

The SAPI sample Java program COLORS is a PC game similar to a popular hand-held game from the past that can be run interactively over a webpage on the Internet, or upon a local PC client using any Microsoft Internet Explorer 4.0 or greater browser.

The game works similar to a popular hand-held game called "SIMON" back in the early days before the Internet had even been built yet.

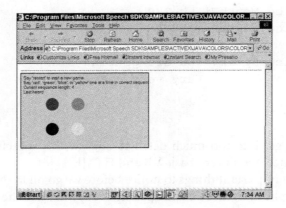

Figure 4.3.

Visual Basic ActiveX Voice Command SAPI objects can also be used with Java class objects and referenced from within HTML for web enabled speech recognition applets.

The "COLORS" program is a VB Script web based Java applet speech recognition game, which will change the brightness and hue of each color as it recognizes the word for the color, and gives you feedback messages as you try to guess a secret 4-color coding sequence, as shown in Figure 4.3.

In Listing 4.13 you can see the listing for the shorter of two Java objects needed to create and support the "COLORS" speech recognition game program, named 'colorFrame.java' (which happens to be the subordinate level object).

It is of particular significance because it handles frame looping that control speech synchronizing animation similar to something you may have noticed in Web 'LADY').

Listing 4.13. Java class object used in web based interactive speech recognition game.

```
import java.awt.*;
public class colorsFrame extends Frame
{    public colorsFrame(String str)
     {    super (str) ; }
     public boolean handleEvent(Event evt)
     {    switch (evt.id)
          {    case Event.WINDOW_DESTROY:
               dispose () ;
```

```
              System.exit(0);
              return true;
default:  return super.handleEvent(evt);} } }
```

Even if you are not a Java programmer, you will probably have noticed that there are no references to any SAPI ActiveX speech controls that you have seen thus far in this particular Java class object program. The reason is that there are not any!

The main purpose of bringing this particular Java object code to your attention is that it is doing something very much equivalent to something that was shown before in several speech synchronized animation functions in previous programs, all of which will be discussed in more detail later in this book.

If you are in MSIE or FrontPage, go ahead and open the view to 'Source', or click on the HTML tab, and depending on how your browser is set up to display Java source, you should see something similar to Figure 4.4. If not you can open 'colorsFrame.java' with Microsoft Explorer, or simply go to NotePad or WordPad (or even DictaPad!) if you prefer.

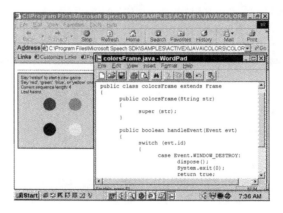

Figure 4.4.

When you open the sample source for COLORS using Microsoft Internet Explorer, or open source files for COLORS using Microsoft Explorer, you should first look at code 'colorsFrame.java', which contains nothing unusual except that it also involve frame event entries that are effectively similar to the loop animation technique in "LADY".

If you are in MSIE or FrontPage, go ahead and open the view to 'Source', or click on the HTML tab, and you will see the HTML tags for the Java APPLET section, as shown in Figure 4.5.

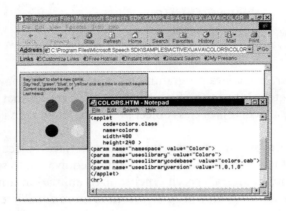

Figure 4.5.

When you open the HTML for the COLORS Java web speech recognition application, there is nothing that is unusual except that it has a reference to an applet that should be looked at in more detail later.

The complete HTML tag references for the APPLET section for the *"COLORS"* web based voice interactive game is shown in Listing 4.14.

Listing 4.14. HTML to reference a Applet for a speech recognition enabled web page.

```
<APPLET
    code=colors.class
    name=colors
    width=400
    height=240 >
<param name="namespace" value="Colors">
<param name="useslibrary" value="Colors">
<param name="useslibrarycodebase" value="colors.cab">
<param name="useslibraryversion" value="1,0,1,0"
</APPLET>
```

Again, you may have noticed that there do not seem to be any explicit references to any SAPI ActiveX speech controls that you have seen thus far.

Again, there are not any! But if you are a Java programmer, or even if you are not, the reason should be right in front of you! All references are inherited from the earlier class objects in Java or VB.

4.27 Summary

In this chapter, we have discussed all of the critical concepts that you need to understand to learn about the complex and often very confusing foundations of speech technology as well as Microsoft's own foundations to support speech programming on Windows platforms. Understanding these concepts will give you everything you need to begin writing your own Windows speech programs with Visual Basic!

In this chapter you have also learned more about the 3 most important types of SAPI speech applications. You also learned the 6 high level ActiveX speech controls first introduced with SAPI 4.0, as well how each of them can be implemented into real-world Windows speech applications software.

In the next chapter in this book, we will to look with more depth at the specifics of how SAPI voices are used by Windows Visual Basic speech programs. But you already know all the applied concepts that you need to begin using the most complex programming model conventions and high level functions for Windows speech. You can already design software applications using Visual Basic enabled speech applications that reference either ActiveX speech controls or voice enabled Java web browser applets.

Chapter Five

Using SAPI Voice Object and SAPI ActiveX Control in Windows Visual Basic Speech Programs

The availability of new ActiveX speech controls, and the enhancement of underlying Visual Basic speech services to access high-level Windows foundations that were first introduced in Microsoft SAPI 4.0, makes Windows speech programming both easy and efficient. By applying the very same basic drag-and-drop form control and traditional Visual Basic programming models, it is possible to create Windows speech software applications quickly, with a consistent 'speak and sound' interface.

The very same Visual Basic programming techniques and Integrated Development Environment (IDE) tools that Windows programmers have used in the past can be used the same way to create Windows speech programs.

By the time you finish this chapter you will understand everything you need to know to design and develop your own natural speech software applications using Visual Basic with ActiveX voice control.

In this chapter, you will learn the following:

- How to use your Visual Basic skills as a Win-Speech Programmer
- How to add SAPI ActiveX Speech controls to a Visual Basic IDE
- Ways that SAPI ActiveX relates to other Visual Basic controls
- Ways SAPI ActiveX interfaces to other Visual Basic components
- How to use SAPI ActiveX Visual Basic controls with Visual Basic scripts
- How to use SAPI ActiveX Visual Basic controls with Web scripts

- How to build and modify simple and complex Windows speech applications
- How to integrate speech input and output from Visual Basic to other applications
- How to add and control speech Visual Basic input and output to create new applications

5.1   *Introduction to Windows Voice Objects Used in SAPI Speech Engines*

Earlier in this book, you have already been introduced to the concept of the SAPI *speech engine*. To SAPI, a speech *'engine'* is the Windows speech recognition programming component model which defines all of the interactions between the various SAPI components.

Along the same lines, the specific driver level component linkages to the Windows speech program specification architecture foundations that are the *'drivers'* that support the SAPI speech engines.

One of the most critical components of the SAPI speech engines are the standard and special *'voices'*, which are the primary direct focus of all Windows events processing by all SAPI speech application software.

Voice objects in SAPI are files with data values corresponding to volume and frequency that can be used to generate or "personify" particular speaker dialects and intonations for individuals as they speak particular phonemes that make up words and phrases.

The actual content or data of the SAPI engine processing can be either the input audio speech signal that needs to be recognized as words, or strings of text that need to be spoken as words, or both. However, SAPI voices are in fact totally independent of the speech content or its processing.

In effect, SAPI voices should be thought of simply as the speech processing equivalent of Word formats or templates. They control only the form of an individual speaker's manner of speech, and the meaning or words are universal across all speakers.

SAPI voices ultimately determine the nature of how a speech signal input will be matched, or output to a sound system speaker or headphone. But the SAPI voices are actually only a series of critical parameters and property values that describe the character of the speech, with regard to the factors that most directly control the pitch and timbre, speed and duration between word elements.

These factors all combine together to determine whether the sound of the speech should seem male or female, young or old, and even human or machine.

In order to understand how SAPI speech engines work, and how you can use speech engines in your SAPI speech applications, you must first understand SAPI voice objects.

5.2 Introducing Your Basic Default Windows SAPI Speech Engine Voices

On a most basic level, SAPI voices are simply external file objects. You may have seen the names of several voice files that were loaded along with the Microsoft speech engines while the files were first being copied during your installation of the Microsoft Speech SDK Suite. Since there were quite a few of them and they were quite big, it may have taken a long time for them to all be copied (as you may have guessed the voices were the files with the extension '.VCE').

If you did not recognize the SAPI voices as they were loaded, you can see an example of one by going to Explorer and using the Tools menu to Find the files named '*.VCE'.

There are usually several dozen new voices provided with each new version of SAPI. You can usually tell which is which, because they have names that describe the voice and are normally numbered sequentially as new voices are added by type.

You probably remember the Basic Text-To-Speech "Talking Mouth" demonstration program that was introduced previously in this book.

As you probably also remember, there were several names that were listed in the combo box at the upper right of the talking form.

You can see an example of these names in the combo box in "Talking Mouth". These are the SAPI speech engine voices that are loaded and active.

Not only do you see voices for Mary versus Mike, but you also see default voices for each, as well as voices for each on the telephone. Mary even has special voices for outer space or a concert hall. So when Mary asks for a pizza, the SAPI voice engine can even mimic audio distortion over a telephone line.

5.3 Introducing Standard Optional Windows SAPI Speech Engine Voices

If you open the ActiveX program samples folder and run the "*Talking Mouth*"sample Visual Basic speech application you will be able to open the combo box and see, and hear, all of the optional voices that can be used by the SAPI speech engines to drive this speech application.

You may notice that there are normally 19 standard voices loaded to the "*Talking Mouth*" application when you first install it (if from SAPI 4.0a).

As you can probably expect, this does not mean that there are only 19 Microsoft SAPI voices, it means only that only 19 have been defined as selections to the form combo box in the Visual Basic code.

If you should count the names for the available voices, you will find that there are 6 names, and 3 of those have multiple instances of the same voice name.

You may also notice that the names are fairly descriptive of the voice characteristics.

Just in case you could not already guess, here are the basic characteristics that each of the standard voices are intended to demonstrate:

- Brutus (a rough tough kind of guy voice)
- Freddy (a young little boy kind of child voice)
- Mary (a young adult female voice)
- Mike (a young adult male voice)
- Sam (an older mature adult male voice)
- Robosoft (a mechanical robot voice)

You should try out the *"Talking Mouth"* speech program with each of these 6 basic standard voices, and you should try to listen very carefully for the very small discrete differences between the most similar standard voices.

In other words, compare Mike to Sam, Mike to Mary, Mike to Freddy, Mike to Robosoft, Freddy to Sam, Freddy to Mary, and so on, until you can begin to hear each of the voice audio properties that make it unique, as well as audio properties that you think they share.

After you have listened to the standard voices for awhile, you should begin to appreciate the many distinct and separate audio properties and parameters that define every individual SAPI voice file.

You should also probably be more than ready to use these standard voices to indicate sex, age, and personality (or lack of it), using these very basic 6 voices in your SAPI speech programs, since you probably really do not want to even try to make your own.

5.4   *Introducing Special Customizable Windows SAPI Speech Engine Voices*

If for some reason your speech application requires a computer generated speech synthesis voice other than the 6 basic standard types of voices, there are also a large number of special Microsoft speech engine voices (as well as a growing number of third-party vendor and shareware voices).

These voices are normally characterized by the ambient background noise or echo patterns that they sound like, rather than any new names.

Thus, for at least 2 of the basic standard SAPI voices (Mike and Mary), you also get at least 4 variations of their basic standard voices.

These special voices are thus able to simulate variations of their voices, with subtle changes in their SAPI voice control parameters in order to simulate the following, in addition to their basic voice:

- An Indoor Concert Hall
- An Outdoor Stadium
- Outer Space
- Talking on the Telephone

In addition, there are 6 separate Robosoft mechanical robot and space alien voice variations.

Again, you should spend some time listening to the subtle differences in the equivalent background noise environments for Mike compared to Mary, as well as comparing Mike and Mary in Space to the Robosoft voices, and you might also listen very carefully to compare the 6 different robot voices to each other.

For those of us who may be a bit tone-deaf, this exercise can get to be a little bit like being a Perrier spring water drinker asked to perform repeated taste tests to compare Pepsi with Coke.

But if you plan to do very much computer speech application programming, especially if there will be any kind of multi-media character animation involved, it is very critical that you get to where you can immediately recognize every standard and special SAPI voice, and to notice even very small discrete differences.

5.5   Customizing Basic Windows SAPI Voices for Making New Special Voices

If you are ambitious enough, and brave enough, to attempt to create your own standard SAPI speech engine voices, then you can learn how when we discuss just how you can do that later in this book, when we also discuss how to create your own SAPI compliant speech engines.

You can much more easily create your own special SAPI voices, since special voices are made simply by customizing some of the speed and pitch properties of standard voices.

This can be done using the Dictation Options Wizard that you saw demonstrated previously in this book. You can experiment with the various settings of the Voice tab slide bars to try out different ways that you might modify some simple voice properties of the standard SAPI voices in order to see how different they sound.

5.6   Understanding Visual Basic Speech Control Tags and Speaker Localization

You may have already learned earlier that 'control tags' are a special kind of 'mark-up language' (very much like HTML tags). For Visual Basic speech programming there are 'speech control tags' that can be used make very subtle changes in the active voice properties loaded at runtime by a SAPI text-to-speech application, or for localization adjustments to handle a particular accent or dialect.

You are ready now to learn a little bit more about SAPI control tags, in order to begin to understand how important they are in making very powerful adjustments in the personality and demeanor of your computer generated speech application voices at runtime.

There are three types of SAPI voice property dynamic control tags that you should be aware of, which you can use in all of your SAPI Visual Basic and VBA speech applications. They are:

*   *CHR* (Character control tag)
*   *CTX* (Context control tag)
*   *VCE* (Voice control tag)

You can probably anticipate that the Voice control tag can provide specific adjustments to all of the sex, age, and foreign language localization properties we have discussed already, but it can also change the entire language as well as accents and dialects within languages.

You should also notice that the tag for Voice Control is 'VCE', which is the same as the '.VCE' extension that you just saw on the example Voice file earlier today.

What do you think might be the significance of that fact? (*Hint*: If you think it might be a control file like an.INI, you might try to open and take a look; of course this can be dangerous, so think about it).

All of the SAPI voice character control tags begin and end with a backward slash and look something like this:

```
( '\ tagtype = 'opt1','opt2',…'optN' \').
```

Each of the 3 voice character control tags has dozens of specific options which can be used to alter discrete computer generated speech properties of SAPI standard or special active voices, and the number is constantly being expanded.

Although there are dozens of options for each type of SAPI control tag, you should probably be able to understand that they are a special kind of dynamic voice property reset or override. There is substantial opportunity for high level SAPI speech program control by setting particular control tag options in response to specific contingent events or combinations of other application form controls or their properties (an example of this will be shown later in this chapter).

Just so you can see a few examples of some of the kinds of options that you can specify for the voice character tag, take a quick look at the following selected list:

Angry	Business	Calm	Depressed
Excited	Falsetto	Happy	Loud
Perky	Quiet	Sarcastic	Scared
Shout	Sleepy	Sullen	Tense

As you can probably guess you can also create your own control tag options, which is another thing that you will learn later in this chapter.

However, you should also probably be able to guess that you can not easily add new voice character control tag types to these 3, and even if you do, you will be outside the SAPI specification, and your speech software will no longer be in 100% SAPI compliance.

So you may want to create your own new tag *options*, but not *new tags*!

Some of the character control tag options relate primarily to a particular simple option like *'Quiet'* (which you will find is quite different than the option *'Whisper'*), but many others involve very complex emotions or personality voice characteristics (like *'Tense'*).

You should immediately be able to comprehend the amazing power that these control tags give to SAPI speech recognition programming!

You will probably want to start trying to insert some of these tags in your own Visual Basic and VBA programs as soon as possible, and you will get a chance to do that later today.

You can see and example of the SAPI control tag code for a complex runtime computer voice 'personality adjustment' in Listing 5.1.

Listing 5.1. Example of direct computer speech with SAPI voice tags.

```
\chr='calm','sleepy','quiet'\
DirectVoice.Speak("I just woke up, and
      already I just want to go back to sleep.")
\chr='excited','scared','loud'\
DirectVoice.Speak("Oh no! The alarm clock
      did not off again! Now I am late for work!")
\chr='angry','shout','tense'\
DirectVoice.Speak("That does it! This old
      alarm clock is going right into the trash!)
```

You can also either create and insert new voice control tags, or else either modify or remove existing control tags using several SAPI Speech SDK Suite developer environment facilities and wizards that will be added to your IDE or developer platforms. But you should normally begin to get used to inserting your own control tags yourself, right into your speech program code.

This will give you greater control as well as awareness of exactly what tags are there. If you use SAPI wizards or menu selections to apply voice character tags, you still need to look at your code from time to time to make sure you know, and want, what is there. Finding just the right voice can be very important in setting the right 'tone' for your speech application software!

Also, as you can probably imagine from looking at this listing, voice character tags can accumulate just like format tags applied by Microsoft Word or other Office suite style template files.

So sometimes tags that you wanted did not get applied, some that you wanted to remove will not get removed when you last exit, and sometimes, as you will find, other speech applications or other speech engines may dynamically insert tags you do not want.

5.7   Managing SAPI ActiveX Speech Components With Visual Basic IDE

You will need to have at least a working model of the Visual Basic IDE to do any level of speech programming. You probably already have Visual Basic professional edition, but if you do not, there is a limited version of Visual Basic IDE (Interactive Development Environment) software application programming project management platform included in the Microsoft Speech SDK Suite.

You don't have to immediately rush out and purchase Visual Studio, which contains Visual Basic, Visual C++, Visual J++, Visual FoxPro database, Visual InterDev Web agents, and MSDN subscription if you only want to program simple Visual Basic speech enabled software with ActiveX.

If you know that you will want to be able to program Windows speech applications at both the SAPI high-level services (using languages like Visual Basic and ActiveX), as well as SAPI low-level services (using languages like Visual C++ and COM), you will need the complete MS Visual Studio IDE. Aside from the fact you will have the most appropriate high-level as well as low-level optimized Windows foundation class languages, most efficient database, most efficient Web object creation environments, and most efficient cross-platform tools, you also have the very valuable MSDN subscription.

5.8   *Making a Speech-Enabled Speak-and-Say Interface to the Visual Basic IDE*

You can also create a speech enabled interface to any Windows application software package using Visual Basic and ActiveX speech controls, regardless of what language it was written in.

This includes the Visual Basic IDE project platform and compiler menus itself! In this section, you will learn a simple technique to enable you Visual Basic IDE, so you can actual create, edit and compile any Visual Basic program using voice commands!

You can easily add speech command capability to your own Visual Basic IDE using the Microsoft Speech Suite SDK and SAPI with voice control wizards. So from now on, you can enter voice commands to control your Visual Basic IDE, and if you so desire, never have to type in code ever again!

After you load Microsoft Voice, you should be able to click right mouse button to get the pop-up menu for 'What Can I Say' speech commands, as shown in Figure 5.1.

The easiest way to speech enable your Visual Basic IDE to react to voice commands is to simply use the Microsoft Voice application to recognize voice commands as we demonstrated earlier this book, and to simply run Visual Basic while the Voice application product is active. The 5 simple steps to speech-enable your own Visual Basic IDE project platform are thus as follows:

1. Activate the Microsoft Voice application by running it.

2. Activate your Microsoft Visual Basic IDE by running it.

3. Double-click on the V-icon in your task-bar to display the Microsoft Voice main menu.

4. Click on 'What-Can-I-Say' selections to see what voice commands are defined for the IDE.

5. Activate Microsoft Dictate to enter text for VB coding, then cut and paste to IDE code window using mouse cursor or control key voice commands to navigate Visual Basic IDE.

This simple way of creating a voice-command Visual Basic IDE project platform add-in was actually developed and used by this author and a class of beginning Visual Basic programming students in a class for the disabled using Windows special accessibility functions for the visual impaired. It is also a very handy technique for teaching programming classes and training courses while walking around the classroom and helping students while wearing a hands-free wireless microphone headset.

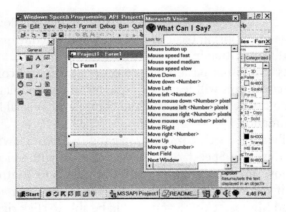

Figure 5.1.

Making a SAPI voice command interface for speech control of your Visual Basic IDE is easy using a 'What Can I Say' MS Voice, MS Dictate and SAPI control wizard tabs.

If there are any additional voice commands that you would like to add, or if you would like to customize the words to recognize, you can do this as you learned before earlier when you first installed Microsoft Speech Suite SDK by going to the Microsoft Voice Command Control tab.

You can also verbally adjust the performance of the speech recognition for your own particular voice, or perform additional speech training if your voice commands are not easily understood by your new speech-enabled Visual Basic IDE. You should also get this experience yourself to be aware of the challenges involved in making voice commands to control the mouse cursor, make menu selections, and enter text until you are fully comfortable with it, since this is what your own Visual Basic speech software users must also learn to do.

If you can not find any mouse cursor control commands when you scroll down the list box in 'What Can I Say', you may need to go to the Voice Command Control panel. But if you can not even find the Voice Command to 'Start Microsoft Visual Basic' (or any other start application commands), you also need to go to the tab for Voice Command Options, to check all of the boxes to select what you want to appear in the default voice command list.

You should be very pleased with this quick and easy way to enable existing Windows applications, and you should take as much time as you like to play with this little trick. You should also take the time to try changing or adjusting each of the Voice Command control options to get a better feel for the impact that it has on voice command of applications.

5.9   *Leveraging Your Current VB Toolkits SDK Skills for Speech Programming*

All of the same Visual Basic skills and techniques that you have learned and developed up till now in your career as a Windows application programmer can be applied directly to your Visual Basic speech programs using SAPI ActiveX speech control objects, just the same as any other objects added already to your own Visual Basic IDE tool-bars.

Any Visual Basic Version 5 or greater working model can both open and save changes to SAPI sample Visual Basic programs, and example Visual Basic high-level speech application programs in this book. However, without the full professional Visual Basic IDE you won't normally be able to distribute any SAPI Visual Basic speech programs that you created on a working model.

As you might have anticipated, one of the most important reasons that you need at least a working model of a Visual Basic IDE is that the entire Microsoft Speech SDK Suite tools are based on the assumption that you will add the SAPI 4.0 or greater ActiveX speech controls to your IDE.

Because they are designed to be easiest to use and most effective when loaded and configured to your Visual Basic IDE form control toolbar. If you have not done so already, you should install and activate your SAPI 4.0 ActiveX speech controls to your Visual Basic IDE. But first, if you do not already know how to create Windows software applications, and even if you do, it can be very beneficial to first learn how to use the Visual Basic Windows Application Wizard.

This is because a big part of the SAPI speech programming specification assumes that you will be using not only SAPI standard Windows 'speak-and-say' interfaces, but also the most basic Windows 'look-and-feel' interfaces that can be automatically built and standardized by Visual Basic wizards!

5.10   Loading Visual Basic ActiveX Controls from MS Speech Suite to Your IDE

Before you can use SAPI ActiveX high-level speech component controls in your Visual Basic applications, you have to add them to your Visual Basic IDE tool-bar and activate SAPI 4.0 ActiveX controls as components within your own Visual Basic IDE.

There are several ways to install and manage your Visual Basis SAPI components, the most powerful of which the 'Add-in Manager Add-on'. If you plan to use debug facility of Visual Basic, you should next go to the Debug Components menu and make sure that you add it first.

Next you will need to open and activate to install ActiveX speech controls to your Microsoft Visual Basic IDE. Pull down the Project menu, and select the Components sub-menu item.

The components of the Visual Basic IDE will list every control library that has been loaded but not yet activated. Highlight and select the Components selection.

After your Visual Basic IDE Components function loads, you should see the Windows check list box. Next you simply scroll through the list of installed controls, and check the box next to the speech and voice ActiveX controls.

Be prepared that when you first look at active components in your Visual Basic IDE, pre-existing and non-Microsoft ActiveX speech components which you were not aware of previously might be activated in your IDE.

This happens because when you install some speech aware products, even if you don't instruct it to do so, the install program might actually load some ActiveX components that it needs.

If you see any components checked that you were not aware of, either de-activate them by clicking to remove the check, or make note of them in case conflicts arise in the future.

The first SAPI ActiveX speech controls that you will need to activate are the two Microsoft Direct Speech components, Microsoft Direct Speech Recognition and Microsoft Direct Text-To-Speech, as shown in Figure 5.2.

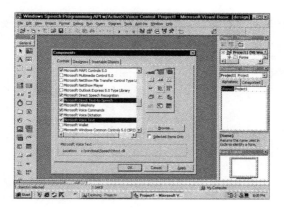

Figure 5.2.

The first controls that you want to be sure are activated and added to the form control toolbar are the two SAPI Direct Speech Controls.

The next ActiveX speech controls you should check to load and activate are the four SAPI ActiveX speech Voice controls.

The four ActiveX speech Voice controls provided with SAPI 4.0 are as follows:

- Microsoft (Voice) Telephony
- Microsoft Voice Commands
- Microsoft Voice Dictation
- Microsoft Voice Text

After you have finished checking all the Microsoft Speech API high-level ActiveX controls, click the buttons to Apply, and then click OK to exit if everything seems to be OK.

If everything did in fact load and activate OK, you should notice some new ActiveX component control icons added to the tool bar of your Visual Basic IDE. If you drag and drop them to the Form window, you can examine each of their properties, as shown in Figure 5.3.

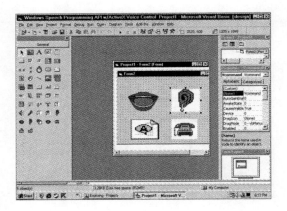

Figure 5.3.

Drag and drop each of your new SAPI ActiveX speech icons on the Toolbar menu to the default active VB project form window and you can examine its control properties.

You are now completely loaded and ready to go, so you can try out all your new ActiveX speech controls on a blank Visual Basic new project form.

All you have to do is click and drag-and-drop from the Visual Basic form component control icons for the new ActiveX speech components that you just added.

If you have not guessed already, the 4 control component icons that have been dragged to the form were all either provided with SAPI and just activated either explicitly or by indirect reference. The Visual Basic ActiveX speech control component icons that you see on the form are as follows:

- Mouth (Microsoft Voice for Speech-To-Text)

- Ear (Microsoft Text for Text-To-Speech)

- A-Bubble on Letter (Microsoft Mail API, A.K.A. 'MAPI')

- Telephone (Microsoft Telephone API, A.K.A. 'TAPI')

You should be aware that some of these icons are used for more than only just one ActiveX control component, and can also be changed to any other icon you select, but these are normal defaults.

5.11   How SAPI Speech Controls Relate to Existing Visual Basic Controls

All of the SAPI 4.0 ActiveX speech control objects for Visual Basic can be used exactly like every other component control object that you are already using in your own Visual Basic IDE.

Just like with other Visual Basic controls, once they have been installed, loaded and added to your tool-bars you can:

- Either double-click or drag-and-drop to the Visual Basic IDE Forms window (where they can be repositioned or resized at your discretion)

- Redefine or reset properties using the Visual Basic IDE Properties Window (where you can also review each of the settings and decide if you want to adjusting or tweak them)

- Write program event handlers and conditional event action processes in the Visual Basic Code Window (which uses the current settings of properties of the SAPI ActiveX speech controls or references the results of actions or events that are performed according to parameters they control)

So if you already know how to program using the controls in your Visual Basic IDE, you are already well on your way to knowing how to program speech applications using Visual Basic speech controls.

But first, it is important for you to understand a few more things about how the SAPI speech controls relate to other Visual Basic controls.

5.12   Similarities of SAPI ActiveX and Your Other Visual Basic Controls

The SAPI ActiveX speech controls are very similar to all other control components that you can use, or have already use, in Visual Basic programs.

Basically speaking, you can add, define and manipulate all SAPI ActiveX speech controls in Visual Basic exactly as you would any other control.

The only major difference is that they relate to speech enabling functions for your Visual Basic programs.

Unless you have already used some of the Multi-media controls in your Visual Basic programs, this may be new to you.

Many of the properties and events that are in all the SAPI ActiveX high-level controls relate directly to sound input and output services that interface directly to the low-level Windows sound media services.

But there are a lot more of the individual properties, methods and events in the SAPI ActiveX speech controls for Visual Basic that are related to speech pattern recognition, as was discussed earlier this week.

Although you will not normally have to worry about the similarities between SAPI ActiveX speech controls and other controls, you will certainly need to understand the special sound and speech pattern recognition characteristics of all six SAPI ActiveX speech controls.

In order to get further acquainted with how each of the SAPI ActiveX speech controls are used in typical voice enabled Visual Basic applications, you can open any of the SAPI sample library projects and examine its Form and Code windows as well as the attribute settings of each active control in its property window. Figure 5.4 shows a view of the Visual Basic IDE opened to the "Talking Mouth" project.

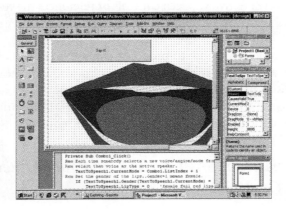

Figure 5.4.

After you have loaded the SAPI ActiveX speech controls from the Speech Suite you can open any of the sample Visual Basic programs in your IDE to examine its Form and Code windows to analyze how to implement common speech programming functions.

5.13   Relationship of SAPI ActiveX to Other Audio Resource Visual Basic Controls

The similarities between SAPI ActiveX speech controls and other Visual Basic Libraries are much more critical with respect to two other Visual Basic ActiveX libraries.

These two libraries are part of the Microsoft Windows OSA specification and can be used together with SAPI to build complex integrated speech recognition and speech synthesis applications using Visual Basic. These libraries are:

- The *Mail API (MAPI),* which can be used in combination with SAPI to build Web email applications that either speak mail messages or else enable the user to speak dictation text into email messages

- The *Telephony API (TAPI),* which can also be used in combination with SAPI to build telephone line answering systems or telephone menu entry systems that enable the caller to leave voice messages on .WAV or text files, or else speak phone menu selections and interpret voice response selections

These two libraries will be explained in more detail later in this book.

5.14   How SAPI Speech Visual Basic Controls Integrate to Other ActiveX Controls

There are several ways that SAPI ActiveX Visual Basic speech controls can be interfaced to other Windows Visual Suite platform applications, or integrate across other platforms or application suites using WOSA standard specifications. These include:

- Directly referencing or linking external objects from within your VB speech program

- Referencing or linking to your Visual Basic speech program from another VB program

- Linking to your Visual Basic speech program from any other Windows programs

These can also include external linkage of speech object files or programs using SAPI advanced low-level Windows speech services using COM and C++ as well as Visual Basic, and this topic will be covered in some more detail later also.

5.15   Integrating SAPI ActiveX Visual Basic to Microsoft Office Suite Controls

By far the simplest and easiest way to integrate SAPI ActiveX Visual Basic speech control programs to other applications involves the enabling of speech functions in existing Windows application products.

This includes such products as the Microsoft Office Suite, or even products such as the Microsoft Visual Basic IDE itself, as you will learn later today.

There are basically three ways to integrate SAPI speech controls into existing Windows based applications:

- Using the Microsoft Voice product from your SAPI Speech SDK (as will be demonstrated later in this chapter to speech enable your Visual Basic IDE to accept voice commands)

- Using Visual Basic for Applications (VBA) scripting code in macros or template code that can call SAPI ActiveX controls

- Using HTML Web scripting to reference or link speech applets coded as Visual J++ or Visual Basic class objects

Some of the simpler of these methods have already been demonstrated from the sample programs, and will be explained in more detail later in the book.

5.16   Integrating SAPI Visual Basic Speech into Microsoft Internet Applets

The final, and most advanced, technique involves integrating SAPI Visual Basic speech functions with other Windows controls that may reside on different platforms as well as in different applications, and even applications that are coded in different Windows languages.

This involves use of COM with your SAPI ActiveX control based Visual Basic speech programs, which is the technique that is used most often to build complex client-server or Web speech applications.

For the most part, this topic is beyond the scope of this book but it will be discussed and explained with respect to techniques that you can use as a Visual Basic programmer to add some object oriented speech recognition programming functionality.

5.17 Adding SAPI Voices and Speech Engines to Your Visual Basic IDE

For the most part, you have already learned most of all that you need to know about SAPI standard and special voices, and SAPI speech engines earlier in this book.

Also, you do not normally have to specifically install or reconfigure either standard SAPI voices or standard SAPI speech engines. If you selected to install the version of SAPI 4.0 with Microsoft voices and speech engines, they have already been added and configured when you first installed SAPI 4.0 and the Microsoft Speech Suite SDK.

You will in fact need to add and configure voices and speech engines if you either create your own special voices or write your own speech engines, but those are advanced topics not discussed here, but the detailed technical instructions for these tasks can be found on MSDN.

5.18 Understanding SAPI ActiveX Visual Basic Control Functions Options

You will need to understand all of the detailed SAPI ActiveX Visual Basic control functions and methods. The most current technical details for the latest version of SAPI are also found on MSDN.

The main things to understand about Visual Basic control functions and options at this point is that they must always do two simple things:

- Conform to the SAPI 4.0 specification and the Windows OSA specification
- Conform to Visual Basic specification for Windows Visual Suite programming object control properties, methods and events

5.19 Designing Complex SAPI ActiveX Visual Basic Control Interfaces

You will also need to understand all of the complex SAPI ActiveX Visual Basic control interface methods, and their latest technical details are also found in MSDN.

The main things to understand about complex Visual Basic speech control functions at this point is that they must always do two simple things:

- Conform to SAPI specification and the Windows OSA specification for integration of low-level SAPI services with high-level SAPI ActiveX controls for Visual Basic
- Conform to Visual Basic programming model for event handling using monitor loops and connecting event handlers to SAPI ActiveX controls and their properties

5.20   *Integrating Speech Input and Outputs to Other Visual Basic Applications*

Before getting too intrigued playing with your new voice enabled Visual Basic IDE, there is one more function that is important for every Windows speech programmer to get personal experience with.

As you please, you can either try the following with mouse and keyboard, or by trying out your new voice command input controls on your Visual Basic IDE (or both). Either double-click or drag and drop each of the six new SAPI ActiveX speech controls that you installed and added earlier today to a new form in your Visual Basic IDE, as shown in Figure 5.5. Examine in turn each of the properties for each SAPI ActiveX speech controls, and be making note of differences and similarities in their properties.

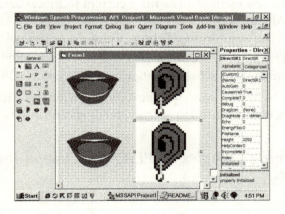

Figure 5.5.

All you have to do is drag and drop the Visual Basic Speech controls to your form and they will be shown as the mouth or ear icons as appropriate for either inputs or outputs as your particular speech application requires, using SAPI ActiveX voice control objects.

You can perform this little exercise using either the Properties Window, or Object Browser, or both. After you have done this, you have only one more voice command skill to experience for yourself. After you drag and drop the Visual Basic SAPI ActiveX controls to the form, you should see the private sub procedure code generated by Visual Basic as shown for the main 4 direct and voice components.

From here on, it should be easy for any Visual Basic programmer to learn for themselves and apply all the skills they already have to use ActiveX speech controls like any other ActiveX control object.

As shown in Figure 5.6, you can simply insert you own Visual Basic programming code into the subroutine procedures generated by the ActiveX voice controls after you drag and drop them to the form and set their properties.

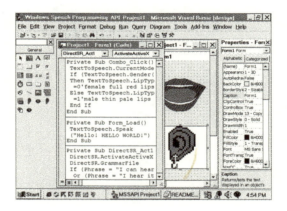

Figure 5.6.

By bringing the Code Window to the front, you can see the shell procedure code generated by each of the SAPI ActiveX speech controls.

5.21   Summary

For all accomplished, or even novice, Visual Basic programmers, learning about ActiveX speech recognition programming should have been easy and natural as an extension of what you already know about Windows programming using ActiveX.

It was probably a lot less painful than some of your earlier technology foundations, since you actually got some hands on experience writing Visual Basic speech program code, and modifying and running some real Visual Basic speech applications, thanks to the portability of ActiveX across Windows.

You have by now learned all of the things that you need to know about speech technology and speech applications as well as the Visual Basic speech recognition programming model and the basic techniques you need in order to write Windows speech programs in Visual Basic.

In the next chapter, you will learn more about detailed techniques for specifying and implementing each of the properties, methods, and events that are provided in each of the SAPI speech objects for more complex Windows applications. This will include coding of speech event and error handlers for creating new Windows speech applications using Visual Basic and ActiveX voice control components.

Chapter Six

Using ActiveX Speech Control Components to Create New Visual Basic Programs

After loading and installing SAPI ActiveX speech controls to their IDE toolbars, Visual Basic programmers can either create new Windows speech applications, or add speech controls to their existing VB applications.

Speech enabled Visual Basic applications can also be easily and reliably integrated with TAPI phone and MAPI web applications, as well as SAPI telephony interface applications.

But the most powerful use of high level SAPI functions involves use of Visual Basic ActiveX speech components to create new speech recognition programming applications.

In this chapter, you will learn the following:

- How to create Visual Basic speech application shells and templates
- How to add complex Visual Basic functions to new speech programs
- How to add SAPI ActiveX controls to existing Visual Basic projects
- How to know when and where to add SAPI ActiveX control code
- How and where to code SAPI speech event loops in Visual Basic
- How to use Visual Basic timer control loops with SAPI program model
- How to use and control Visual Basic speech error and exception handlers
- How to use multiple layers of Visual Basic handlers for speech control

- How to analyze and enhance a SAPI/TAPI phone speech Visual Basic applications
- How to make changes to rebuild SAPI/TAPI phone speech VB applications

6.1   Basic Steps to Create Windows Speech Applications in Visual Basic

If you not yet a Visual Basic programmer you may be somewhat surprised when you are first acquainted with the simplicity that is involved in creating Windows applications using Visual Basic (and that is even without using the VB Applications Wizard!).

There are only 3 basic steps to create a Visual Basic application for Windows. These 3 basic steps are:

- Create a new project
- Drag-and-drop controls to forms
- Add Visual Basic code to the generated form code

If you are already a Visual Basic programmer, but just learning to use Visual Basic for Windows speech recognition programming, you should not be too surprised to learn that these steps are exactly the same for Visual Basic speech recognition programming using SAPI ActiveX speech controls.

It may take a little while for this to sink in, both for even the most accomplished Visual Basic programmers as well as even the most novice programmers.

Because of the many new Visual Basic and ActiveX enhancements and additions that were first provided with SAPI 4.0, it is not possible to simply create projects, drag-and-drop ActiveX speech controls, and add Visual Basic code to the forms in order to quickly create powerful Windows speech aware applications. However, one thing you probably already guessed, the last step is the hardest!

The creation and enhancement of Windows speech applications software using Visual Basic is not a lot different from all other types of Visual Basic programming.

In fact, most of the Visual Basic speech recognition programming concepts that we will be discussing today are all probably very similar to Visual Basis techniques that you use already.

As we begin to get into more detail about use of Visual Basic to develop speech application software, always try to relate to similar techniques that you already used in the past to develop GUI software.

We will now begin to discuss all of the things that you need to do in order to create new Windows speech software applications, as well as to speech enable existing Windows applications, using Visual Basic.

But very briefly before we do, you need to be aware (as you probably also are used to as a Visual Basic programmer), that there are several runtime.DLL and other dynamic load library files that must be provided along with your Visual Basic executables. Also, you will need runtime external file objects for any speech program you distribute (just like you normally need to do with Visual Basic).

In the case of SAPI 4.0 and greater, Listing 6.1 shows all of the runtime files that you need to bundle and ship with all of the Windows speech programs that you create and distribute.

Listing 6.1. Windows runtime files to distribute with your Visual Basic speech programs.

```
FILE NAME       FILE DESCRIPTION
VB5STKIT.DLL    Visual Basic 5 runtime dll.
VB6STKIT.DLL    Visual Basic 6 runtime dll.
STDOLE2.TLB     OLE file needed for Visual Basic on Windows 96.
OLEAUT32.DLL    OLE file needed for Visual Basic on Windows 96.
OLEPRO32.DLL    OLE file needed for Visual Basic on Windows 96.
ASYCFILT.DLL    OLE file needed for Visual Basic on Windows 96.
CTL3D32.DLL     OLE file needed for Visual Basic.
COMCAT.DLL      OLE file needed for Visual Basic.
```

This is only a summary list, and based on the assumption that the SAPI version is 4.0, and the Visual Basic Version is either 5.0 or 6.0.

You should expect that any newer versions of either SAPI or Visual Basic may require addition runtime files.

However, for reasons of upward compatibility, you should not automatically expect that new versions in either SAPI or Visual Basic can permit excluding any files listed here (better safe than sorry, so always include all!).

6.2   Creating New Speech Projects from Your Visual Basic IDE

The procedure for creating new Windows speech applications are very simple, at least with regard to the first of 3 Visual Basic steps.

To add any Windows ActiveX speech control to a Visual Basic form, simply click on the button for the control, then drag a rectangle onto the form.

The rectangle around the selected icon for the ActiveX component can be any shape or size, and you should only be aware of the dashes around your control as you drag it to help decide where to drop it.

Release the mouse button when you feel like it is generally in the right place, and you will see the icon for the ActiveX speech control on form when you are done.

Try to put the speech component anywhere on the form that is not on top of something else. Don't worry what it looks like as far as getting perfect in positioning speech controls the way you do other controls, because speech controls are transparent, and no one can see them anyway!

If you select the object (by clicking on it) you will see its properties in the *'Properties'* window. In particular, note the *'(name)'* property.

This is the name you use to reference the control inside your basic code, which you can change anytime you want if you do not like it.

So if you want to create a simple Visual Basic 5 applications that just says "Hello World" when a Windows program first starts up, simply create a new project and follow the steps above to add a *'Microsoft Voice Text'* control to *Form1*.

All you have to do next is simply add the follow code (assuming the name of the control is *'TextToSpeech1'*, which is entirely up to you):

```
Private Sub Form_Load()
TextToSpeech1.Speak "hello world"
End Sub
```

Look familiar? Yes, this is pretty much the same code that you saw in Chapter One, your very first Visual Basic speech program!

The Microsoft Speech API uses many constants, which are defined in a separate file: *'VBSPEECH.BAS'*.

To use these constants, all that you need to do is add this file to your project. Typically, this file is located in the following folder but if you cannot find it use *'FIND'*:

```
'C:\Program Files\Microsoft Speech SDK\Samples\ActiveX\VB5'
```

If you open your 'VBSPEECH.BAS' file using WordPad or other viewer, you will see something like the following Visual Basic copy code, in Listing 6.2:

Listing 6.2. Example of lines from VBSPEECH runtime constants file.

```
Attribute VB_Name = "VBSPEECH"
Public Const SVFN_LEN = (262)
Public Const LANG_LEN = (64)
```

```
Public Const EI_TITLESIZE = (128)
Public Const EI_DESCSIZE = (512)
Public Const EI_FIXSIZE = (512)
Public Const SVPI_MFGLEN = (64)
Public Const SVPI_PRODLEN = (64)
Public Const SVPI_COMPLEN = (64)
Public Const SVPI_COPYRIGHTLEN = (128)
Public Const SVI_MFGLEN = (SVPI_MFGLEN)
```

You should be aware that this is only a small portion of even the normal default *'VBSPEECH.BAS'* file that is shipped with SAPI 4.0.

You should also understand that even though this file is initially several hundred lines long, it can be changed and expanded to add new attributes and new variables until it can be a thousand lines or more. You should appreciate that this is in fact simply a Visual Basic constants file. You should also appreciate that if you want to add public constants or global variables, this is where to do it. But if you do, be sure to remember to copy and make a back up first—but if you forget and later want to reset to defaults, you can manually reset any parameters you change to their original values as listed in the Appendix of this book.

6.3   Adding SAPI ActiveX Controls to Visual Basic Application Projects

Just like all other Visual Basic programming, before you can actually use the SAPI ActiveX speech controls that you have dropped down on your form. As usual, you must carefully review the code generated to support the Visual Basic forms for your Windows speech recognition programming software application. Then you must add all of the other Visual Basic code that you need in order to make the application do all of the other things that you want it to do besides speak.

If you are already an accomplished Visual Basic programmer, this is no surprise. But if you are not yet fully comfortable with Visual Basic, do not worry. In all cases, it is once again just like any other Visual Basic forms control enabling. Remember there are a wealth of resources on the help menu of your Visual Basic IDE if you get stuck along the way!

6.4 Understanding VB ActiveX Programming Models Used by SAPI

There are nonetheless some very specific SAPI programming model assumptions that must always be addressed in your Visual Basic speech programs. However, if you are an experienced Visual Basic programmer, you probably address most of them anyway, so this should be "old hat" for you.

All SAPI speech recognition and speech synthesis controls use an asynchronous programming model. What this means is that you can use events to handle program flow. For example, when you call the speech synthesis method 'SpeakText', Visual Basic program control returns immediately to your code, and does not wait for the text to be synthesized by the speech engine.

The SAPI computer speech synthesizer runs in the background while your code continues doing other things. When the synthesis is complete, a de-activate process event is sent. Your program can ignore the events if you want, but you must tell it!

All of this relates to something called asynchronous event processes. *Asynchronous event programming* involves processes that are paired, which means that a given activation event results in a given completion event response.

However, in '*async programming*', the activation event can occur at any time (or never), so the program has to continuously watch for it to happen. In Visual Basic this usually means activating a continuous loop process to monitor for the event.

6.5 Simple SAPI ActiveX Visual Basic Programming Model Control Loops

Many Visual Basic programmers would prefer to avoid the complications of asynchronous event handling. For example, say you want your Windows speech program to say some text and wait for a synthesizer to finish before any more processing. The obvious approach, in Visual Basic, is normally something like what we see in Listing 6.3:

Listing 6.3. VB loop with text never appearing in message box, <u>even if</u> text was spoken.

```
Private Sub Form_Load()
voice1.speak "this wont work in visual basic"
```

```
while voice1.Speaking
wend
MsgBox "this message would come up only after the text is
spoken"
End Sub
```

That doesn't work very well in Visual Basic and Office applications because other applications events (for reasons that should be obvious if you look closely at the code).

The speaking instruction never gets processed as the while loop spins (which in this case even has an active and waiting voice and speech synthesizer engine!).

A much more effective way to accomplish both text and speech processing in the right order involves coding the Visual Basic speech application code according to the following async program model, as shown in Listing 6.4:

Listing 6.4. VB async loop with text appearing in message box after text is spoken.

```
Private Sub Form_Load()
voice1.speak "this will work in visual basic"
while voice1.Speaking do
DoEvents
wend
MsgBox "this message would come up only after the text is
spoken"
End Sub
```

The frequent and repetitive iteration looping call to '*DoEvents*' lets the rest of the application handle events while you wait.

Even still, although this method will work for speech programming, it is very CPU intensive in Visual Basic, and causes sluggish response. Handling of this kind of repetitive iteration loop events is intrinsic to the Visual Basic speech-programming model and is explained in more detail in this section. To see how this works, first open the ActiveX folder and go to the ANSWER machine folder application.

You can find the most advanced and complex of the SAPI Visual Basic voice controls for speech recognition programming next to the ACTIVEX folder, which contains the ANSWER project.

A much better way to use Visual Basic to service the Windows interface for widely distributed speech applications, on the other hand, is to adapt a more basic asynchronous model.

The basic asynchronous model is actually the one used by most Visual Basic programmers to begin with. The conventional Windows programming model can also be used to add the usual error and event handling conditions with speech resources, as shown in Figure 6.1.

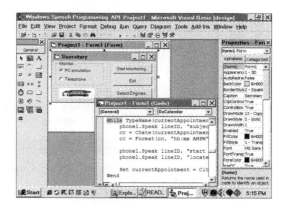

Figure 6.1.

DoWhile to Wend is one of the most effective speech event loops in VB programming.

A more conventional asynchronous way to do the same thing while supporting speech programming in Visual Basic using conventional VB programming model is as follows in Listing 6.5:

Listing 6.5. *Visual Basic async loop to support Windows speech programming.*

```
Private Sub Voice1_AudioStop(ByVal hi As Long, ByVal
lo As Long)
MsgBox "this message would come up only after the
text is spoken"
End Sub
Private Sub Form_Load()
voice1.speak "the best model"
End Sub
```

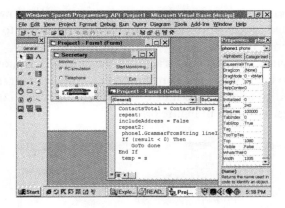

Figure 6.2.

A Visual Basic conditional loop within a selective process is a good way to combine use of error handles and exception events with speech event loop monitors.

In Figure 6.2, you can see how a conditional loop can be used to trap and handle errors or exceptions according to the particular needs and attributes of your user speech software application.

You should study the specific options and control setting properties documentation on MSDN or in the Appendix of this book for specific details about the usage of individual ActiveX voice control property settings from your IDE. This should be very familiar to you, but is shown in Figure 6.3.

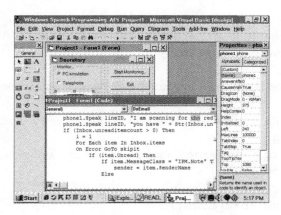

Figure 6.3.

The same techniques for telephonic speech, which includes both computer phone speech and computer phone recognition, can be used with SAPI Telephony controls, or to link SAPI controls to other Windows API components, or between SAPI and MAPI or TAPI.

You should study all property event methods, and any associated class library members that you may need to reference and customize, using object browser as your Explorer. You should also study other Windows API components related to Speech API (SAPI) voice components, Windows Mail API (MAPI) and Windows Telephony API (TAPI), as shown in Figure 6.3, if you would like to integrate web and phone messaging.

You should study all of these methods very carefully, and in fact if you also study the Microsoft SAPI 4.0 sample programs you will find that it is these methods that are used most often for Visual Basic and ActiveX voice controls for speech recognition programming applications.

When any other method is used, if you analyze the application very carefully you will find that there was a specific reason for using one of the other async looping techniques.

6.6 Using Visual Basic Event Control Loops for Speech Event and Error Handling

It should not surprise you that these 3 asynchronous looping program models all have specific purposes in Visual Basic speech recognition programming.

Every access to any ActiveX speech control, or any other Visual Basic method or property of any active control, may return error codes.

Visual Basic normally turns all errors into exceptions that must be handled with an application software exception handler. Which means that it must be coded by the Windows application programmer, and Windows speech programs are no exception when handling exceptions!

It is also useful to use such "containers" to "piggy-back" error handling checks to instancing or startup events such as loading a form, or to contain error handling in a loop controlled by an ActiveX timer control.

In Listing 6.6 you can see the recommended way to handle exceptions as an error handler for speech recognition programming with Visual Basic:

Listing 6.6. Recommended Visual Basic SAPI error exception handler.

```
Private Sub Form_Load()
On Error goto Got_An_Error
voice1.speak "exception handled"
goto finished
Got_An_Error:
MsgBox "error encountered:"
```

```
    + voice1.LastError
finished:
End Sub
```

As you can see, this method allows you to separate any errors encountered by the speech engine from the exception handling (which has benefits that should be obvious to the VB programmer).

The simplest methods are often the best, and it is clearly the easiest and most direct tried and true method, in spite of the fact that it can require coding an individual procedure for each type of error event, to simply define each anticipated error condition and handle it specifically.

6.7   Understanding SAPI ActiveX Controls for Visual Basic Speech Event Handling

Be prepared that just to be safe you may have to anticipate each possible type of critical error event for your particular speech application, and write your own Visual Basic speech event handler.

The only problem with this is it takes longer to code and execute more events.

Otherwise, it is often easier to simply insert your special error handling condition logic as a single statement or loop action within a routine start-up or application event.

Another method that is commonly used is to actually design into the error handling the intelligence to detect a problem with the user input and startup an entirely separate application in a window on top of the current open speech application.

An example is shown in Figure 6.4, which combines the use of a GoTo error handling as shown in the listing example earlier, to start the VoicePad to enter individual text with the help of wizards and potentially force retraining of the user speaker file.

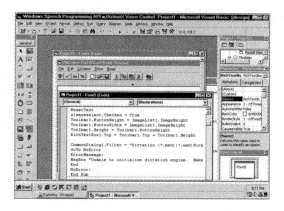

Figure 6.4.

Example of a GoTo Error handling method from the SAPI Visual Basic Dictation Pad application.

On the other hand, you can avoid exceptions entirely, but still handle errors without stopping by using 'SuppressErrors' property, as demonstrated in Listing 6.7:

Listing 6.7. *Special handler to suppress SAPI errors or exceptions.*

```
Private Sub Form_Load()
    voice1.SuppressErrors = 1
voice1.speak "exceptions suppressed"
if(voice1.LastError) then
    MsgBox "error encountered: "+ voice1.LastError
        endif
End Sub
```

Always remember that all exceptions will appear to be fatal errors or "crashes" to the end user, even exceptions which are just simply informative. So if THEY cannot handle them, either suppress then or automatically fix them without concerning the user.

This is all the more important in speech recognition programming, where the users are already pretty much overwhelmed by the technology to begin with.

However, you must always log the error first in case it is not fixed.

You should be well versed in all the methods of Visual Basic error handling and be prepared to apply this in speech recognition programming application components.

6.8   Integrating SAPI Speech Controls into Complex Visual Basic Error Handlers

You should also be aware each control in MS Speech API includes a list of error values for a control that it will only generate if it fails execution.

In addition to these values, the higher level controls can generate error values that were actually generated by a lower level component.

For example, an audio-source object can generate error values that can be passed to a speech recognition object, and then to a Voice Command control. Thus, it may come out of the Voice Control, but it may not necessarily have originated there.

When it comes time to tracking back the source of any error code or exception handler response, you should always be prepared to trace back all of the possible sources of the real source of the failure.

This becomes particularly critical with complexity of some of the possible integration of speech enabled applications and add-ons, as you have already seen in some of the complex architectural diagrams that you have seen for even relatively simple speech software apps.

This passing of error values applies to all objects in the Speech API except for those provided by the audio objects, which are the lowest level of the API.

However, the low-level errors also get complicated.

You should be prepared that the usual tools that you have grown accustomed to using when you have to trace and debug an error with your Visual Basic IDE may not always work with speech recognition programming.

This is primarily because SAPI speech services can often cross so many levels, so you are not only using high level Windows services as you may be used to, and does so many lower level services for you automatically that you may not always even be aware of!

Because speech components are local servers instead of in-process servers, it is possible for a speech object to generate an error value that does not map to any SAPI hex error values that appear in the header files.

This is because a system component has mapped the error value to an HRESULT by using the HRESULT_FROM_WIN32 macro.

If a speech object generates an error value that do not seem to be in any reasonable range, you should first strip off any bits that may have been added by the HRESULT_FROM_WIN32 macro. Then convert the error value to decimal, and finally check for a non-OLE error value that matches the error value.

As you can probably expect, this is because error codes often end up sharing the same buffer when there is a failure even if they were not designed to, and the result can be an accumulation either at the beginning or end of the buffer (or both).

So you sometimes have to dump the entire string (again, welcome to the wonderful world of speech recognition programming!).

Now that you know how to write a SAPI error handler for various levels of exception handling, and interpret the results even if there is a critical error, you are ready to take a look at some common Windows SAPI speech error codes, as shown in Listing 6.8:

Listing 6.8. Table of most common SAPI error codes and hex values.

Hex Value	Error Code
80070057	One or more arguments are invalid.
80004002	The interface is not supported by the object.
8007000E	There is no more memory.
8000FFFF	An unexpected error occurred.
00040806	The lexicon already contains data for the last word.
80040808	The buffer to receive the given word is too small.
80040805	The string contains phoneme with invalid characters.
80040802	The pronunciation or meaning of the word is invalid.
80040801	The word to pronounce contains an invalid character.
80040803	The given word is not in the lexicon.
80040804	Not contain enough space to add word to lexicon.
80040807	Buffer to receive phoneme or word is too small.

In addition to the SAPI error values described in this list, controls can pass error values generated by lower-level objects or calls to the Win32 API.

For example, the Direct Speech Recognition control might pass an error value generated by the audio-destination object.

Your error handling code should be able to trap and provide all the feedback you need to know where any error originated, and if possible stop it (or at least save a message to log where it first happened).

Obviously, before you even open any of the sample programs with the possibility of making changes you should copy and back them up first!

6.9 Analyzing and Understanding Virtual Answer Machine Visual Basic Program

We will now analyze and make some changes to an entirely new Visual Basic speech application, your own fully functional *"Virtual Answer Machine"*, located in *'VB5'* folder and *'ANSWER'* sub-folder.

Again, you should first run the program *'VBANSWER.EXE'* from either the Windows *'Start'* menu or MS Explorer as you prefer. When the application is finished loading, you will see an small active pop-up window with a telephone icon and two buttons. You should first click on the *'Simulate Call'* button, and you should then seen a second pop-up window that comes to the front, as shown in Figure 6.5.

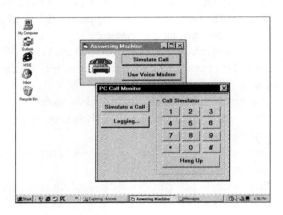

Figure 6.5.

The "Virtual Answer Machine" application is actually a SAPI update of one of the oldest voice applications since the first attempts at using .WAV files to say "Hello World". Very appropriately, this SAPI application also makes use of Windows .WAV files.

This SAPI application is actually very simple answering machine. However, when you consider all the things that an answering machine must do, you can imagine how complicated the Visual Basic program to accomplish all this can get! This voice control application must be fully able to:

- Respond to a telephone line ring to detect an incoming call
- Pick up to answer the call
- Output a pre-recorded message

- Invite a recorded message from a caller
- Record the callers message
- Save the message
- Replay the recorded message on demand

It receives a human spoken voice message, either from any real incoming telephone call if you connect it to your PC voice modem, or from a microphone (which also makes it a personal transcriber device) and then writes it to a .WAV file in a subdirectory—with a name that you give it within the application directory where it normally runs.

You should also recognize the SAPI "Virtual Answer Machine" as a multi-form Visual Basic application when you see the third pop-up window that comes to the front. This window which shows where you can specify the location and name of the subdirectory where you want to store your .WAV files, which are both your media for playing and recording messages. This function simply causes the Explorer to display the Messages directory (and creates it if needed). So each time a new message is recorded, an icon appears that can be double clicked on.

You can just double click on the icon for the Answer log message file (a .WAV file) and it will be played by your Windows .WAV file player, as is shown in Figure 6.6.

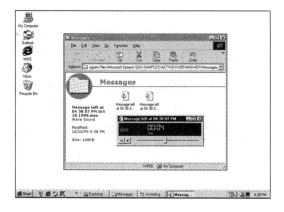

Figure 6.6.

SAPI "Virtual Answer Machine" uses MS Audio Player to record and play .WAV files.

Yet this all very simply at this point still has very little to do with speech recognition programming, and is more of a matter of basic Visual Basic external file management.

But you will be using .WAV files as both input and output media foundations for integrated SAPI speech applications, so you need to know how to code a .WAV handler, as shown in Listing 6.8.

Listing 6.9. Visual Basic procedure to record speech to an external .WAV file.

```
Private Sub ViewDirectory()
On Error Resume Next
Dim slash As String
If Right(App.Path, 1) = "\" Then
    slash = ""
Else
    slash = "\"
End If
    mdir = App.Path + slash + "Messages"
    MkDir mdir
    ChDrive mdir
    ChDir mdir
    Shell "command.com/c start.", vbMinimizedNoFocus
    Shell "cmd/c start.", vbMinimizedNoFocus
End Sub
```

The other thing that we have discussed in several instances already earlier in this book has related to integrated Windows speech and media services that are under direct SAPI high level control.

This sample SAPI application is probably the first example of that which you have seen up to this point, but as an accomplished Visual Basic, you can easily follow along.

Another non-speech related function that you need to know how to code in Visual Basic for you speech programs that is very common in integrated SAPI multi-media applications involves the use of TAPI or MAPI controls along with SAPI ActiveX controls, as shown in Listing 6.9.

Listing 6.10. Visual Basic procedure to connect SAPI to TAPI voice modem controls.

```
Private Sub Command1_Click()
    phone1.Initialized = 1 'run on emulator
    phone1.CallDialog
End
End Sub
```

```
Private Sub Command2_Click()
    phone1.Initialized = 2 'run on real phone
    phone1.CallDialog
End
End Sub
```

This function gets called each time the phone is answered, for each phone line, and as you can see it has different instances of the same SAPI Voice Telephony control and speech engine loaded and activated at the same time.

Yet as you can see from looking at the code, only one can be running to actually record a message after its own *'call pickup'* click event.

Because SAPI Voice Telephony control supports multiple phone lines, as well as TAPI, this function may be called simultaneously several times, with each version identified by line and runs on a different thread.

If you have not done so already, you should now close *the "Virtual Answer Machine"* application, and open the project *'ANSWER.VBP'* in your Visual Basic IDE.

You should see something like Figure 6.7, which shows the pop-up form and code for *'Form1'*, the highest level MDI form.

Figure 6.7.

When you begin to look at the code from this sample SAPI "Virtual Answer Machine" program you will probably notice a lot more of the types of complexity you may have seen before if you analyzed complex Visual Basic programs, since here the SAPI implementation starts to involve not only properties or events, but also object methods.

As you remember before from your previous look at .WAV file handling, a big part of such procedures in Visual Basic is to reserve enough buffer area and file handlers, and to declare your .WAV file handler variable, as shown in Listing 6.10.

Listing 6.11. Visual Basic init code to create a buffer to play or recording .WAV files.

```
Private Sub phone1_DoPhoneCall(ByVal lineID As Long)
Dim result As Long
Dim size As Long
Dim wave As Long
Dim wavefile() As Byte
Dim filename As String
```

After you have initialized your .WAV file buffer and file handler variables, you still need to reserve the buffer space. Then you can allocate it dynamically as needed in order to efficiently manage what you can probably imagine could turn into a large and cumbersome sound byte file, as shown in Listing 6.11.

Listing 6.12. Code for SAPI to speak phone message, then for TAPI to record to .WAV.

```
phone1.RecordFromString lineID, "[Prompts]" + vbNewLine + _
        "Main=Hi. We can't come to the phone right now.
        Please leave a message at the beep." + vbNewLine + _
        "[Settings]" + vbNewLine + _
        "BetweenUtt=10000" + vbNewLine + _
        "InitialBuf=30000" + vbNewLine + _
        "ReallocBuf=30000" + vbNewLine + _
        "MaxBuf=300000" + vbNewLine + _
        "NoAnswerTime=10" + vbNewLine _
            , result, wave, size
```

This code is linked to the object and its properties can be see in the object viewer window, as shown in Figure 6.8. It is dynamically linked via the Form, which contains the buttons that control the record and play action events, as well as selection of SAPI speech engines for recognition and computer speech. Obviously, this method is very powerful and has a great many speech applications!

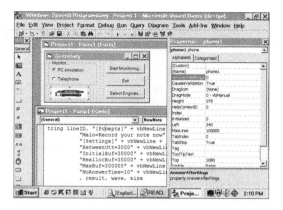

Figure 6.8.

The Visual Basic IDE Object Browser window shows properties of the TAPI to SAPI link.

Since you probably have already wondered about the difference between using a .WAV file or .WAV file loop digital recording versus a SAPI TextToSpeech engine, the answer is found in the following line of Visual Basic code as shown below:

```
phone1.WaveAddFromListString lineID, "[FromFile]"
        + vbNewLine + App.Path + "\hianswer.wav =
    Hi. We can't come to the phone right now.
    Please leave a message at the beep."
```

This line causes a recorded wave file to be used in place of the text wherever it is spoken.

Therefore, the simple answer is, if you include this statement just as it is coded, the Windows low level media player services will use its own methods to 'speak' the words that are coded in the program after '*hianswer.wav=*'.

But if you comment out this statement, or leave it out entirely, the text-to-speech engine would need to be used instead (assuming of course you would code the same message to reference SAPI control).

This method can allow you to prototype your program with both .WAV file low-level media services as well as SAPI text-to-speech.

Before you finish up your customizing of the Visual Basic speech recognition programming example Answering Machine, you should first try to change some of the Windows low-level media services .WAV messages.

Next, you should try commenting out the .WAV message statement to see for yourself what happens, and to even change the referencing to an entirely different .WAV file of your choice.

Finally, you might want to see if you can write some code to enable high level SAPI speech synthesis as well as Windows low level media services.

This gives you the flexibility to support multiple configurations if your software is going to be distributed for potential use on a lot of different PC hardware and versions of Windows. You will not only be able to configure your speech software across a wide range of platforms, but you can also use .WAV media services as a back-up in case there is some kind of problem with the SAPI speech configuration on a particular installation of your speech application software.

If you would like to write Visual Basic code to be able to handle both .WAV low level Windows media services as well as SAPI high level Windows services at the same time, it is actually a little more complicated that you may have seen in the code we have looked at. This was still a simple sample program, so you should not normally attempt this on your own until we have been able to discuss more of the detail.

Using this method, the prompts are spoken by SAPI (or played as instream .WAV file buffer strings), and then the answering machine Visual Basic program must save the caller's incoming message as a .WAV file in the Message folder.

The following Visual Basic statement 'sizes' the incoming audio, and performs the software equivalent of audio to digital time-slicing, just like a software based Digital Signal Processor (very crude DSP but very elegant Visual Basic code, and still it really is DSP), as in Listing 6.12.

Listing 6.13. VB code to size and timeslice incoming audio waveform for storage.

```
If (size <> 0) Then
    ReDim wavefile(size)
    CopyMemory wavefile(0), ByVal wave, size
    phone1.FreeWave wave
```

Next the chopped 'sound bytes' are loaded to an array in the buffer, regular copies are made, and after accumulating each sound byte block to the .WAV message file, the buffer is regularly cleared to try as well as possible to conserve resources

By defining the date and time as part of the filename, each message is sure to have a unique name so we can put into Message directory, as shown in Listing 6.13.

Listing 6.14. VB code to get date and timestamp for new name to save audio .WAV file.

```
filename = App.Path + "\Messages" +
"\Message left at " + Format(Now, "hh mm ss AMPM") +
" " + Format(Now, " mmm d yyyy") + ".wav"
```

The final step is to write the .WAV file data out to disk, so you can double click on the file to play it with Windows media recorder, and to end the procedure.

```
        Open filename For Binary Access Write As #1
      Put #1, wavefile
      Close #1
    End If
End Sub
```

End of messages, end of loop, end of procedure, end of program, end of examples, and end of chapter.

6.10 Summary

In this chapter, you have learned how to add SAPI ActiveX speech controls to your Visual Basic IDE in order to be able to add Windows Speech API controls to your Visual Basic speech application projects. You also learned a great deal about the Visual Basic programming model, and the importance of Visual Basic asynchronous loops to monitor speech events, as well as how to use control loops to write handlers for error trapping, exception handling, animation, and external event messaging coordination. You learned how to build SAPI speech synthesis programs using TextToSpeech controls, speech command recognition programs using SpeechToText controls, two-way speech and pseudo-conversation control usage, and integrating SAPI high level control services with Windows low level media services. You also learned how to dynamically compile grammars, code conditional speech rules logic, switch between .WAV files and SAPI computer speech, and how to drive external events and multi-media events via speech mode.

Next, in the final chapter, you will be looking at Visual J++ and Java applets based on SAPI ActiveX controls, and how to modify to integrate them into existing Windows programs written in an Visual Suite language. This will include support to speech applications using MS FrontPage and HTML scripting for webpage-enabled speech applets. But one last comment before we move on to the final chapter. We have gone over a lot of coding examples in this chapter, which you should yourself attempt to implement and modify yourself in many various ways until you understand a wide variety of useful variants.

Also, it should be noted that all the examples have been fully tested by the author (as well as MSDN technical support, and a great many Windows developers). They should work without any problems for most Windows PC platforms and OS versions (as specified in the accompanying documentation files in your SAPI 4.0 download). But there is never any guarantee that your PC hardware and your PC software configuration is 100% and everything will work "as-is" without some special tweaking for your PC.

If something that works OK for other programmers does not work on your PC, never assume that something is wrong with the code, assume that something is unusual about your PC configuration. This may require meticulous examination and research versus MSDN documentation as to what is assumed in order to be 100% SAPI-compatible before you begin. But your capability to do this when it is required is as much a necessary skill to be an accomplished Windows speech programmer as your ability to code Visual Basic. In fact you can expect that when you implement your Windows speech software for your end-users, you typically will have more of these kinds of configuration issues than with any other major category of Windows software support. If you still have problems, you can always go to the MSDN peer site and speech news groups as noted earlier in this book. But if you do, you will probably be able to find email chains related to similar problems by keyword searches, since most of the types of configuration problems you will encounter have already been experienced by other programmers. But if you do in fact find a problem that has not been previously identified, do not hesitate to contact MSDN tech support, or the author at the website listed in the Appendix, and added to FAQ listings for future reference.

Chapter Seven

Using Visual Basic ActiveX Speech Controls in Existing Windows Programs

By now you should have a pretty broad understanding of all of the most important things that you need to be aware of and implement as a Windows speech programmer using Visual Basic.

You should also appreciate that the best way to build upon that understanding is to get some actual hands-on experience analyzing and modifying actual Visual Basic speech application programs.

As you have probably learned already in you Visual Basic programming career, the best way to truly understand and learn the many intricacies of advanced programming techniques is to study and emulate methods used by other professional programmers sample code, and this is also true with SAPI.

You are now ready to begin getting a really in-depth understanding of when and how to apply some of these coding techniques. This is best acquired by analyzing as well as actually making changes in the sample programs provided with SAPI 4.0 and the MS Speech SDK Suite for Visual Basic programmers.

In this chapter, you will learn the following:

- How to use Speech SDK suite sample code to create your own Visual Basic speech apps
- How to customize or enhance existing Visual Basic speech template applications
- How to analyze or redesign simple SAPI computer speech Visual Basic applications

- How to make changes to rebuild SAPI computer speech Visual Basic applications
- How to analyze and redesign a SAPI 2-way TTS/SST Visual Basic projects
- How to make modifications to rebuild a SAPI 2-way TTS/SST Visual Basic projects

7.1   Analyzing and Customizing the SAPI Voice Command Visual Basic Program

The first program that you will should analyze and attempt to customize is the SAPI 4.0 sample Basic Voice Command program, which is found in the VB5 folder for 'BASICCMD.VBP' project folder. This project will contain examples of all of the Speech To Text (STT) and Text To Speech (TTS) functions that you will want to implement and modify for all of your Visual Basic speech applications. The "Basic Voice Command" project is shown opened with the Visual Basic IDE in Figure 7.1.

This SAPI Visual Basic program is really not listening for "commands", it is actually just simply listening for words that are entered into a "word spotting" list in a drop down box, then displaying the text for the last word "heard" or recognized from the word spotting list. You should define the list of words, phonemes, or phrases that you want the SAPI speech engine to "spot" and listen for to recognize, in your Visual Basic procedure code, and then it will add to the list box if you build, run or recompile.

You should be able to anticipate that this application contains an example skeleton code shell that you can modify and try out in order to understand all of the basic voice control methods for linking a Visual Basic Form selection object. This can include "speech" drop-down lists, radar buttons, or check boxes, or specific text strings SAPI default grammar objects will use to control the SAPI speech engine to recognize specific words or phrases, then output the text string last recognized to a form text box. If you go through each form object and try to change the values and properties in this sample program, you will understand all of the SAPI coding conventions and Visual Basic speech program methods for its input and output control.

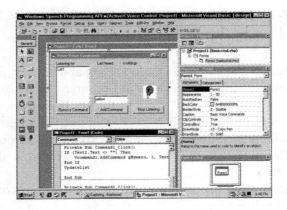

Figure 7.1.

When you look at each Code Window and Form object for the "Basic Voice Command" project you will get a good understanding of how a Visual Basic speech recognition program treats voice input strings as text to handle events based on voice string matches.

7.2   Analyzing and Customizing the Talking Mouth Sample Visual Basic Program

By now you should be well acquainted with the SAPI 4.0 sample program *"Talking Mouth"*. The "Talking Mouth" sample program not only has a lot more complex control properties than most simple Visual Basic application projects but it also has a lot that can only be controlled by code, including the ability to change animation strategy based on voice selection.

The *"Talking Mouth"* is located in the ActiveX samples folder, in the 'VB5' folder, sub-folder 'BASICTTS'. But before you locate and load it you should refresh yourself one last time regarding the difference between the code and controls for the methods and functions in the Visual Basic code for voice of Mike versus Mary. Remember that SAPI Male voice Mike has different lips than Female voice Mary. This time, rather than running the program from MS Explorer or the start menu, you want to open the 'BASICTTS.VBP' project folder.

You undoubtedly remember that this is a simple speech application that demonstrates how to pick a SAPI synthetic voice engine and speak some arbitrary keyboard entry data input from a text box.

As you may remember from your earlier look at this Visual Basic application, the heart of the program is a *Form_Load* procedure.

The most important functions are based on testing the SAPI speech engine synthesizer mode, as shown below:

```
Private Sub Form_Load()
Dim ModeName As String
```

The first step in this application (and all of your own applications) will be to choose and activate a default speech engine for an appropriate computer voice synthesizer (in this particular example, female).

This is not strictly necessary as the ActiveVoice object will normally pick a reasonable default, but it is always a good practice just to be safe (a lot like always looking in your rear-view mirror whenever you start backing your car out of the driveway).

The explicit engine selection criteria are defined to SAPI as:

```
engine = TextToSpeech1.Find("Mfg=Microsoft;Gender=1")
```

This program first sets manufacturer=*"Microsoft"* as the most important quality (rank), and gender as female(where 0=male,1=female) as the second ranked quality.

The SAPI controls will then assure that closest match will be selected.

You probably noticed that the nature of the program activation statement that was highlighted previously passes these two parameters with the assumption that SAPI will make up its own mind about which of the available speech engines is most appropriate.

And it does, based on the criteria in this case that we are requesting a Microsoft speech engine, and we want the best engine to speak a female voice, since the program defines a female voice as default at start-up. And yes, SAPI knows which Microsoft speech engine, or any other third-party engine, speaks each available voice best without distortions!

This method for choosing engines is superior to examining the actual values for each mode and picking the engine yourself because '*Find*' does a good job of ranking the quality of the other parameters even if you were not specific about those inputs (if you set '*rank=0*'). For example, although we only specify a female synthesizer made by Microsoft, '*Find*' will choose the '*Female*' driver as opposed to '*Female (for telephone)*' because the '*Female*' engine sounds better.

You might want to go back and read the last sentence again.

Did you notice how we have referred to the female voice? As a *driver*?

This is actually the best way to describe and think of SAPI voices, since the most important thing they do is serve as speaker output drivers.

Note that this sample uses the *"Microsoft Voice Text"* control, which is most effective at sharing resources with other applications.

That means changes made in this app will effect other applications, and also that it is designed not to demand dedicated resources, so it is not likely to cause other Windows apps to 'hang up' if it stops.

You can replace the control with *the "Microsoft Direct Speech Synthesis"* control which will not share resources, or have global effects, if your intent is just the opposite, to get priority to take up all the resources it needs up to the top limit of your PC.

You probably also remember how to select the engine, SAPI style.

```
TextToSpeech1.Select engine
```

You might be able to guess that this is also equivalent in Visual Basic to coding the statement:

```
TextToSpeech1.CurrentMode = engine
```

One thing that you may not have noticed yet is that the program can add the name of each SAPI compliant synthesized voice engine/mode registered on the machine to the combo box, as shown in Listing 7.1:

Listing 7.1. Visual Basic loop to get the speech end mode and give it a name.

```
For i = 1 To TextToSpeech1.CountEngines
    ModeName = TextToSpeech1.ModeName(i)
    Combo1.AddItem ModeName
Next I
```

This should not surprise you, but the way that the program 'backs' into the stack for the mode list is to create an index for access later (because it is LIFO not FIFO, in record procesing terms).

```
Combo1.ListIndex = TextToSpeech1.CurrentMode-1
```

First, the program sets the combo box to the current voice setting.

Then it subtracts one because the voice control is 1 based, but the combo list is zero based (which as you may have noted is always determined by the data types as well as properties).

You will note that setting this variable triggers a *Combo1_Click()* call, so the lip type will be switched from there also.

The next thing to notice is that each time somebody selects a new *{'voice/engine/mode'}* from the combo box, the program selects that voice as the active speaker.

Since we are now back to the index position to pull the appropriate mode, so we add back one, as shown in Listing 7.2:

Listing 7.2. Visual Basic click event function to associate current mode to sex.

```
Private Sub Combo1_Click()
    TextToSpeech1.CurrentMode = Combo1.ListIndex + 1
    If (TextToSpeech1.Gender(TextToSpeech1.CurrentMode) = 1)
    Then
        TextToSpeech1.LipType = 0
    Else
        TextToSpeech1.LipType = 1
    End If
End Sub
```

Once you have the gender from the mode, the next thing this program does is to speak the text in the text box with the appropriate sex voice.

Also note as well that animation is switched based on gender when the mouse button is clicked, which is coded as a simple function:

```
Private Sub Command1_Click()
TextToSpeech1.Speak Text1.Text
End Sub
```

That's all there is to it, and by now this simple Text-To-Speech application should be simple enough to you that you can modify it easily, which you can now try, using either properties or code.

As a very easy example, lets try to modify some name properties in our *"Talking Mouth"* Visual Basic application, as shown in Figure 7.2.

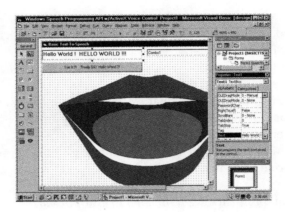

Figure 7.2.

You can change the default Text and Button object properties for the "Talking Mouth" computer speech synthesis application the same as any other Visual Basic project, except that the text string will not only be displayed, but will also be "spoken".

First, open the 'BASICTTS.VBP' project using you Visual Basic IDE.

Next, click on the text entry box.

It should highlight, and you should see its current property settings listed in the form properties window. Find the *'Text'* property.

If it has not been changed yet already, the initial setting should be:

`'Please feed me pizza'.`

Highlight the *'Text'* property text string and change its value to say instead:

`'Hello World! HELLO WORLD!!!'.`

Next, click on the button control. Its properties will be shown in the form control property window.

Find the setting for the *'Caption'* property.

If it has not been changed yet, it should still be set to say the text *'Say It!'*.

Position your cursor at the end of the *'Caption'* property text string and add to it so it now reads:

`'Say It! Really SAY Hello World!'.`

After entering the property setting changes that you just made, the result should look familiar.

If you look back to the earlier examples when this example was introduced, you should see something similar to what you now have displayed on the form in your Visual Basic IDE!

Finally, go to the IDE 'View' drop-down menu and change from 'Form' to 'Code' view in order to bring the program code to the top active window of the IDE.

Locate the Visual Basic statement that we discussed earlier which controls the initialization and finds the most appropriate Microsoft speech engine to speak a female voice, and then selects and starts it as the default speech engine for the application.

Change the value that controls the gender criteria for selecting the speech engine, and change it to optimize for a male voice instead of starting with the best engine for female voice.

Now 'Run' your changes to see if they work.

Do you notice any difference in the way that the *"Talking Mouth"* handles the male versus female voices?

Are there any differences that you can tell?

If you like the way *"Talking Mouth"* looks and sounds now better than before, save your changes to the project. If you want to save your changes, you should consider saving as a new project with a new name. Otherwise, your changes will overwrite the original.

You can always re-run the SAPI install executable to extract a new copy of the sample programs. But it is best to get in the habit of saving versions of your own speech programs and your changes, if you do not already. If you liked it better before, you can always close the project without saving it, and it will recover to the original version.

Or you can come back later if you would like to play with this some more.

But now lets go on to a new sample speech program that has not been discussed previously in this book, but it only slightly different from what you have learned thus far.

7.3 Analyzing and Customizingthe SAPI Virtual Burger Visual Basic Program

The next sample SAPI speech application is known as the Windows *"Virtual Burger"* two-way Speech-to-Text and Text-To-Speech customer order entry application. You can find the *"Virtual Burger"* application in the 'VB5' folder and the *'BURGER'* sub-folder. (Just as a side note for the really advanced eager beavers who have already downloaded and examined the SAPI 5.0 suite, this application corresponds to the *"Virtual Coffee Shop"* sample applications in the next version of SAPI).

The SAPI 4.0 sample *"Virtual Burger"* speech order entry application is far more complex than anything you have seen thus far because it not only handles multiple objects but also multiple ActiveX controls. If you have not tried out this fun little *"Virtual Burger"* speech application already, try it out by speaking the words for your fast food order from the menu items listed on the screen.

You will find soon that this is a very complex and intelligent speech application, which you can probably expect has a lot more complicated Visual Basic form controls as well as ActiveX speech—and also has a lot more complicated Visual Basic code to support all of the many things that *"Virtual Burger"* can do, which in fact it does.

In addition to the fact that this sample application involves MDI and multiple form objects, it also involves multiple speech engines in order to be able to both listen to what you say and then talk back to you. Which means that it must selectively handle repeated alternating activation and de-activation of both a TextToSpeech and SpeechToText SAPI speech engines, or TTS as well as STT.

This also means that the *"Virtual Burger"* speech application must be able to handle both speech recognition as well as speech synthesis at the same time—which as you can expect makes its speech engine startup and mode event handling especially critical.

You are probably very curious by now to know exactly how this is accomplished, so now lets open the application and look under the hood to find out. If you have not done so already, close the *"Virtual Burger"* program executable, hen open the *'BURGER.VBP'* project with your Visual Basic IDE. Try not to look at the form view for now (as interesting as it may seem), and select the *'View'* to *'Code'*.

You can scroll through the code quickly to acquaint yourself briefly with this fairly complex little application, then you need to go back to the top of the General section, and follow along as we review some of its most interesting and important features.

First of all, you should understand that there are 3 critical public declarations which are critical to control of this STT/TTS speech application.

```
Public gMode As Integer
Public gOrderedFries As Boolean
Public gRestoreGrammar As Boolean
```

As you may be able to guess, these 3 critical elements are:

- *gMode* (which keeps track of which STT/TTS mode we are in)
- *gOrderedFries* (set to True if customer says 'fries' else False)
- *gRestoreGrammar* (set to True to reload grammar after an order)

After the public control elements are set, the first step is to initialize the SAPI speech recognizer engine for use by the Virtual Burger speech enabled Visual Basic software application.

Since we want command and control to be started first, we want to find and select the best STT speech engine first, or the closest match to a simple STT speech engine that speaks a female voice, since the voice that is selected is based on Mary.

By now you should probably just about have the statements that you need in order to start your speech engine, so the following should be very familiar by now (and you should be able to locate it easily):

```
DirectSR1.Initialized = 1
engine= DirectSR1.Find("MfgName=Microsoft;Grammars=1")
DirectSR1.Select engine
```

In Listing 7.3, you can see the procedures that do form load and unload for the *"Virtual Burger"* interactive voice order menu.

Listing 7.3. Visual Basic SAPI speech enabled form load and unload procedures.

```
Private Sub Form_Load()
gMode = 0
gRestoreGrammar = False
Form1.Picture = LoadPicture(App.Path + "\Bursign3.bmp")
End Sub

Private Sub Form_Terminate()
DirectSR1.Deactivate
End Sub
```

You should make a mental note that most of the initialization is done on the first timer callback, since this speech program includes examples of multiple asynchronous event loops. You should understand there are some functions that need to be initialized later after the first timer call, or initialized at the start and then re-initialized later depending on the sequence of the events that are activated.

After the speech engine is first selected and activated, it is next de-activated to make it stop listening. Always turn off a speech recognizer engine as soon as it loaded in two-way STT/TTS apps, as there are still some things that have to be initialized on the low level graphic side of the application after the high level speech engine functions are started. Also, you do not want the speech engine to lock up resources, or to attempt to make speech recognitions before the conditional logic that selects the context for dynamic grammars are inserted and compiled at runtime.

The next step is to we get the Windows media drivers up and running, and paint the graphics image backgrounds, before we begin the CPU intensive task of running the looping code for the speech engines. An example of the kind of complexity that we can have in a speech application such as *"Virtual Burger"* that has multiple graphic images used as.BMP background for a form is shown in Figure 7.3.

Figure 7.3.

Menu area is blank in the SAPI "Virtual Burger" application.BMP background image.

The background image.BMP file for the "Visual Burger" voice order entry application should not be anything new to you, except that it confirms that the static graphics are separated from the speech API, and you should also not how it is referenced.

Finally, after all of this is done, we can now load the speech synthesizer engine, so we instruct SAPI to find and select the best engine from Microsoft that can speak a female voice for Mary.

```
voice = DirectSS1.Find("MfgName=Microsoft;Gender=1")
DirectSS1.Select voice
```

Once you have selected and activated your female voice speech engine, you can then start the SAPI computer speech voice interface.

```
DirectSS1.Speak
"Welcome to Virtual Burger. May I hear your order?"
```

You should now be prepared that there are multiple speech engines (both STT and TTS) selected and loaded, as well as multiple drivers for voice, .WAV sound, graphics and other low level Windows media services. These will all be competing for priority of resources under the SAPI control, as well as other tasks that may be in the background.

You should expect that this can be like a juggling act, and depending on the sequence and combination of events that are activated, and the resulting competition for services and resources, sometimes some kinds of unexpected things can happen, which can lead to errors.

For example, sometimes the desktop environment may come to the front while we are loading application graphics, and the battle over the image resources may lock out one of the speech engines.

This particular problem would obviously be appropriate to consider containing within the 'full stop' event lockout procedure. An example of a general failure error handler coded according to the considerations discussed earlier and are highlighted again in Listing 7.4.

Listing 7.4. Visual Basic general speech failure error handler.

```
Form1.Show
GoTo done

GeneralFail:
MsgBox
"Unable to start using text to speech or recognition."

done:
End Sub
```

As you may remember, error handling needs to be both isolated from the async loop logic in Visual Basic, which may also require that any looping logic or timer calls may need to be reset in order to clear any general failure exceptions, as shown in Listing 7.5.

Listing 7.5. Visual Basic SAPI speech engine monitor error loop timer handler.

```
Private Sub Timer1_Timer()
On Error GoTo GeneralFail
Timer1.Enabled = False
End Sub
```

After a non-fatal general failure exception error (such as would be normally caused by a lock-up due to competing services for resources) it is then necessary to have your own Visual Basic application code to recover from the exception error in an appropriate manner.

The application can be designed to either re-initialize and start over. Or else you can just continue where you left off, and resume doing more asynchronous event monitoring, and responding with appropriate event action. An example of such a conditional exception handler from our *"Virtual Burger"* program is shown in Listing 7.6.

Listing 7.6. Visual Basic conversational speech loop exception error handler.

```
If (parsed = "") Then
DirectSR1.Deactivate
If (Rnd > 0.5)
    Then
'randomly pick a message to keep from being too boring
        DirectSS1.Speak
            "I'm sorry. Can you please repeat that?"
    Else
        DirectSS1.Speak "I didn't understand you."
    End If
Else
    If (parsed = "thank you") Then
            DirectSR1.Deactivate
```

To return to the normal asynchronous Visual Basic looping logic for the speech recognizer engine, there are several more things that need to be handled in order to support command control dictation.

The speech recognizer engine must first declare variables to hold and pass phrases to the grammar for SAPI voice command word spotting, as follows:

```
Private Sub DirectSR1_PhraseFinish
(ByVal flags As Long,
 ByVal beginhi As Long,
 ByVal beginlo As Long,
 ByVal endhi As Long,
 ByVal endlo As Long,
 ByVal Phrase As String,
 ByVal parsed As String,
 ByVal results As Long)
```

This is also important with regard to managing the buffer area and file handlers not only for grammars and command word spotting rules needed for speech recognition, but also even more important when the application is conversational. This will involve intelligent computer speech synthesis of voice responses as well as word recognition.

Most sound cards cannot multi-plex recording and playing, so it is imperative to disable the listening state of the recognizer before attempting to generate sound, otherwise you will get an error when your conversation STT/TTS application tries to speak.

In order to create the impression of truly conversational speech, and that there is another real person somewhere with a microphone at *"Virtual Burger"* talking back to you each time you speak—not only does the two-way STT/TTS speech application have to recognize specific command words and phrases—but it has to use them in order to respond with an appropriate phrase or question as well.

It is a good idea to always flowchart all of the possible responses as well as responses that you want to 'force', as well as to 'script' the exact words that you want your two-way speech application to both listen for and say in response to specific words or phrases.

As you can imagine, the Visual Basic code to handle even very simple 'pseudo-conversational' speech can be very complicated. It can normally contain a lot of embedded conditional logic rules based on a lot of nested 'If' statements and case select statements that condition to what you want your speech synthesizer engine to say.

An example of such a conversational speech conditional control logic as coded in the *"Virtual Burger"* Visual Basic voice order entry program is shown in Listing 7.7.

Listing 7.7. Mainline conversational speech loop scripting logic.

```
If (gOrderedFries = 0) Then
                gMode = 2
                DirectSS1.Speak
                    "Would you like a large
                       french fry with that?"
            Else
                gMode = 3
                DirectSS1.Speak "Will that be all?"
            End If
        ElseIf (parsed = "mistake") Then
            Item = List1.ListCount—1
            If (Item >= 0) Then
                List1.RemoveItem (List1.ListCount—1)
                DirectSR1.Deactivate
                DirectSS1.Speak "Oops"
            End If
        ElseIf (parsed = "no") Then
    If (gMode = 2) Then
                gMode = 3
                gOrderedFries = True
                DirectSR1.Deactivate
                DirectSS1.Speak "Will that be all?"
            ElseIf (gMode = 3) Then
                gMode = 0
                gRestoreGrammar = True
                DirectSR1.Deactivate
                DirectSS1.Speak "Please continue your order"
            Else
                gMode = 0
                gRestoreGrammar = True
            End If
    ElseIf (parsed = "yes") Then
            If (gMode = 2) Then
                List1.AddItem "1.05 large fries"
                gMode = 3
                DirectSR1.Deactivate
                DirectSS1.Speak "Will that be all?"
            ElseIf (gMode = 3) Then
```

```
            total = 0
            For i = 0 To List1.ListCount-1
                total = total + Val(List1.List(i))
            Next i
            List1.AddItem
            "--total is: $" + Format(total, "###0.00")
            gMode = 1
            gRestoreGrammar = True
            DirectSR1.Deactivate
            DirectSS1.Speak
            "Your total will be $" + Format(total,
            "###0.00") + " at the next window please."
        End If
    Else
        DirectSR1.Deactivate
        List1.AddItem parsed
        If (Phrase = "large fries")
            Or (Phrase = "small fries")
            Or (Phrase = "medium fries") Then
            gOrderedFries = True
        End If
        DirectSS1.Speak Phrase
    End If
End If
 List1.ListIndex = List1.ListCount-1
End Sub
```

You should look very closely to understand how speech recognition of specific phrases are used to drive specific spoken responses from the speech synthesizer, and that Visual Basic conditional logic is coded to restrict the responses to be as specific as possible.

When you execute the "Virtual Burger" application, you will see the background that was displayed in the.BMP with an order entry window that appears as a list box that is dynamically filled with the text string and message strings as selected by the conditional logic of the program, as in Figure 7.4. Just as you would expect in any Windows standard application, your customer will expect the items that are displayed to be grayed when they are inactive and highlighted when they are active. This will show that the menu is no longer active and the speech engine no longer listening when the order is completed, or to highlight "Mistake" and gray out the menu when "Virtual Burger" is overloaded or "out of order".

Figure 7.4.

Menu grays out as inactive after order is totaled based on recognized voice order entry.

All you care about here is the specific phrases that correspond to complete menu items, which is the verbatim phrase heard and parsed, and is then translated to a string for the context free grammar.

For example, might want the *"Virtual Burger"* application to recognize the single word *"fries"*, since many people simply use the single word "fries" rather than the compound word "French Fries" to mean the same thing.

Also, when the single word "fries" is recognized, you might want to branch conditionally to logic that qualifies the type of "fries" that the speaker wants to order as "large fries" or "medium fries".

You should probably easily understand that this is a special case, because here the qualifier of "large" or "medium" is spoken before the word "fries". So how does SAPI know is it not a "large" drink?

This example should point out the usefulness of selective grammar spotting. We want the menu selection to be added to the order only if the complete specific phrase is spoken, such as *"large fries"* or *"medium fries"*, rather than *'large drink'* or *'medium drink'*, so what do you do? You must simply list each of the four possibilities that correspond to your virtual menu items as specific grammar entries in your code.

So we also do not want the speech recognizer to respond with a completed conditional branch to the single word *"medium"*, because we need the recognizer to hold off until it hears if the order is for a *"medium fries"* or *"medium drink"*.

However, you may in fact want to branch to a special response if only the word 'large' is recognized (for example, to speak or display the query *"We heard the word LARGE. Do you want to order a large DRINK or large FRIES?"*

and loop back to the phrase-spotted grammar)—of if only the word 'fries' is recognized (then your code might speak or display the *query* "*You ordered FRIES. Do you want to order a LARGE fries or a MEDIUM fries?*"). The branching here is done exactly the same way that you would code a request for a speaker to repeat what was said (as in examples previously explored which speak or display the prompt "*It was not clear exactly what you said. Could you please repeat that again?*)".

Part of this kind of conditional processing uses exception handlers controlled by grammars, which are in fact external file objects and isolated from the speech application program itself, as you will probably remember. However, it may not have been too clear up to this point exactly how the grammars are linked to the speech program, although you probably were able to guess it had something to do with condition logic.

When you open the "*Virtual Burger*" speech application in your Visual Basic IDE as a project, the first thing you should notice are increasing complexity of this speech application. But also notice the systematic way it begins to handle each control (not only in terms of properties but also in terms of events).

When you open both the "*Virtual Burger*" form and code side-by-side, as shown in Figure 7.5, it is much easier to see how this kind of conditional logic relates to both the fast food menu items and their corresponding phrases. Also notice the appropriate order item responses when the phrase for a particular menu selection is spoken and recognized.

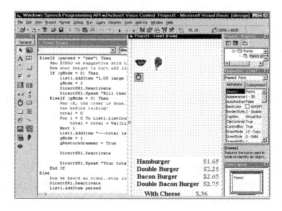

Figure 7.5.

It does not matter where the SAPI speech control icons are moved to the form because they are not visible similar to timer control, and dynamic image areas are transparent, but display labels are fixed as text box overlay that is opaque over the form background.

Conditional logic and 'If-Then-Else' constructs are in fact a big part of the answer with regard to both selecting appropriate grammars and rules in complex conversational speech applications. But they are also needed in order to actually define the physical location or names of external objects and data entity names, as shown in Listing 7.8.

Listing 7.8. SAPI speech grammar word-spotting command control procedure.

```
Private Sub DirectSS1_AudioStop
(ByVal hi As Long, ByVal lo As Long)
If (gMode = 1) Then
    List1.Clear
    gOrderedFries = 0
    gMode = 0
    DirectSS1.Speak "Hi! May I take your order?"
Else
    If (gMode = 2) Or (gMode = 3) Then
      HighLightOrder (False)
      DirectSR1.GrammarFromFile App.Path + "\yesno.txt"
ElseIf (gRestoreGrammar) Then
        HighLightOrder (True)
        DirectSR1.GrammarFromFile App.Path + "\burger.txt"
        gRestoreGrammar = False
    End If
    DirectSR1.Activate
End If
End Sub
```

You can probably guess that '*BURGER.TXT*' is an uncompiled grammar. Although all of the grammars that you have seen thus far have been uncompiled text file entries.

However, as we have discussed earlier, any external file object, including either very big as well as fairly small grammar objects, will tend to slow down the application and make it run sluggishly unless the grammar is compiled.

In Visual Basic speech applications, you can compile grammars at runtime according to dynamic conditional logic rules, as shown in Listing 7.9, from the '*Virtual Burger*' sample code.

Listing 7.9. Visual Basic code to load and dynamic compile a grammar.

```
HighLightOrder (True)
DirectSR1.GrammarFromFile App.Path + "\burger.txt"
```

You would probably like to see the exact grammar that has been built based on default menu selections as well as some dynamic conditional runtime criteria.

Rather than open up the file *'BURGER.TXT'* right now (which can be a dangerous thing to do while you have its application running or its project open in your Visual Basic IDE), you can see an example of the *'BURGER.TXT'* grammar file object specification in Listing 7.10.

Listing 7.10. Visual Basic code to specify an uncompiled command dictation grammar.

```
[Grammar]
langid=1033
type=cfg

[<start>]
<start>=large fries "1.05 large fries"
<start>=small fries ".75 small fries"
<start>=medium fries ".95 medium fries"
<start>=large drink ".99 large drink"
<start>=medium drink ".65 medium drink"
<start>=small drink ".50 small drink"
<start>=thank you "thank you"
```

Now that you have considered each one of these important features of a two-way conversational STT/TTS speech application, you are ready to attempt changes to the "Visual Burger" voice order entry application (using the same care as earlier to apply your Visual Basic skills that you have already learned).

First, try changing some of the scripted conditional logic responses. Next, try changing some command phrase recognizer values. Then, try changing some of the prices for the menu items. These are the types of things that you can expect to have to do to modify the SAPI "Virtual Burger" to customize to create your own similar voice order entry for any voice order entry application. See how easy it is?

After you have understood these 3 simple SAPI sample applications, "Basic Voice Command", "Talking Mouth", and "Virtual Burger" well enough to modify and customize them effectively, you will have gained experience with all of the most common Visual Basic speech recognition programming methods and functions that you need in order to design and implement even very complex applications, and you will understand all of the 6 ActiveX speech controls that are provided with SAPI Version 4.0.

Although you will still have to understand MAPI and TAPI as well as SAPI in order to integrate these controls with .WAV files and the WOSA Audio Services in the low level Windows architecture, these 3 sample applications can teach you to effectively use each common SAPI input and output method that you will ever need to develop your own standalone Visual Basic speech recognition applications.

Up until this point in this book, we have looked exclusively at SAPI Version 4.0 examples and controls. However, in order to apply your SAPI ActiveX controls for use across the Internet, you will need to also gain experience in understanding and using the SAPI Version 5.0+ web browser and agent controls.

7.4   Using SAPI WebBrowser Control Component for Internet Enabled Web Apps

It is actually no more difficult to design and develop an application to either open and transcribe, then send an email document, or to automatically generate an email message based on a voice command or speech recognition event, than it is to design and develop a SAPI-based Windows Virtual Phone Answering Machine, as explored in the previous chapter of this book.

In fact, almost every function and block of code that is in the previous chapter examples for the Virtual Answer Machine can be used to design and develop your own SAPI-based Windows Virtual Email Answering Robot. Because each of the functions are so similar, you are invited to develop your own virtual email responding software agents based on the SAPI 4.0 Virtual Phone Answering Machine. And if you send your Visual Basic code, documentation or compiled SAPI applications to the author at his website www.qualimatic.com and agree to the posted legal conditions, your software will be annotated and a link provided back to your website or email so that you can either distribute as "freeware" in the public domain with acknowledgement and example of your work for prospective future clients or employers—or if you prefer it may be offered as "shareware" for a fee (and potentially published in a future book if you wish).

The biggest difference between the SAPI Virtual Phone Answering Machine and any of the class of related applications, and any SAPI Virtual Email Answering machine, is that the former can make extensive use of the Microsoft Telephony API (TAPI), and the latter can make extensive use of the Microsoft Mail API (MAPI). Although TAPI and MAPI are beyond the scope of this book, the author has another book on these topics that can be obtained through the author's website that explains them in detail.

Also, as you can imagine, there are a multitude of other speech applications that would be useful to bolt to web enabled applets and web client as well as web server applications that can be implemented using cooperative implementations of SAPI and MAPI, that go far beyond email for speech enabled web domains.

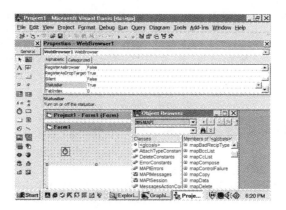

Figure 7.6.

A speech enabled WebBrowser control applet displays VB Forms in a webpage frame.

Without getting into a lot of details about the underlying component controls and properties that are available to you with Microsoft Mail API as used cooperatively with Microsoft Speech API, an example of the MAPI WebBrowser control is shown in Figure 7.6 just to give you a high level functional description of the kinds of things that you can expect to be able to design into SAPI/MAPI web enabled speech apps.

The MAPI WebBrowser control exposes a powerful and comprehensive set of methods, properties and events which allow any host application to exercise control over both cross-web integrated applications and files. This also holds for local file systems, which can be navigated, printed, drilled down, linked, refreshed, updated, searched, or any other typical browser function using speech aware recognition, or to "read aloud" or using computer speech to emphasize customized prompts based on speech control tags.

As you can also imagine, the availability of speech enabling, both in terms of computer speech synthesis as well as speech input for command control and dictation of form box entries, or extensive text entries, can be a very powerful add-on to your web pages and web-enabled applications.

But as you can probably also understand, the added-value of SAPI to web browser applications and email applications goes far beyond the use of speech itself. It can provide a very handy and accessible layer to your application architecture, in order to support conditional logic branching, error handling, and word or phrase spotting responses for designing and developing very powerful but tight applications. This is especially true for multi-media web applications that integrate multiple input as well as output modalities.

7.5   Using the SAPI ActiveXConference Control for Speech Aware NetMeetings

As you can probably also imagine, the next logical step in the progression from hybrid SAPI speech and MAPI web browser or email API applications, as well as SAPI/TAPI intelligent phone response applications, is speech aware internet conferencing applications, based on the control shown in Figure 7.7.

Just as with the SAPI/TAPI to SAPI/MAPI logical extensions, you should be able to easily adapt the sample code from the Windows SAPI/TAPI Virtual Phone Answering Machine applications in order to create your own Windows Virtual Conference Room Manager. This application could use Microsoft NetMeeting's ActiveXConference control along with the SAPI ActiveX voice controls in the same manner.

Although this is also beyond the scope of this book, as before, the functions and methods are so similar that effectively using the Windows NetMeeting ActiveXConference control with SAPI controls to build an integrated application should be a logical next step. So you are also invited to develop your own virtual web conference room management software agents. And as before, if you send your Visual Basic code, documentation or compiled SAPI applications to the author at his website www.qualimatic.com and agree to the posted legal conditions, your software will be annotated and a link provided back to your website or email so that you can distribute as "freeware" in the public domain with acknowledgement and example of your work for prospective future clients or employers. Or, again, if you prefer it may be offered as "shareware" for a fee (or potentially published in a future book if you so allow).

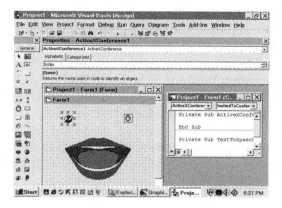

Figure 7.7.

The SAPI 5.0 ActiveXConference control component enables management of Microsoft NetMeeting for web videoconferencing and phone conferencing with automated text transcription of speech as well as computer speech pop-up messages and reminders.

The biggest difference between developing hybrid SAPI/NetMeeting applications, and any of the class of related applications that you may have developed thus far based on examples in this book, is that in this case you will probably want to begin integrating more and more multiple menus or MDI designs that can alternatively configure and instance multiple possible configurations of inputs and outputs.

For example, some virtual conference rooms may need to support both telephone audio as well as closed circuit digital video. Others may only need to support telephone audio (and in fact anonymity may be desired or required by the application usage domain), yet it may also be necessary to support multiple speakers, who must each be individually recognized using speaker verification ID speech biometrics.

Others may require only video with no continuous speech, as in a remote security camera application that only records a continuous 3-minute video loop but is continuously "listening" for one single grammar spotted word (i.e., "bomb"). Each of these have been actually designed and built by the author using SAPI.

Although each of these specialized application domains are beyond the scope of this book, the author has another book on these topics that can be obtained through the author's website that explains them in detail.

If in fact you want to use the NetMeeting ActiveXConference, or other NetMeeting controls, in your hybrid SAPI/NetMeeting speech aware web applications, you must obtain the controls from the MSDN Web Applications web site as a separate download from SAPI. You can find the relevant controls by searching for keywords "NetMeeting Downloads" on the MSDN search form page, or you can find the latest links on www.qualimatic.com, the author's website.

You should be aware that the NetMeeting ActiveXConference control is the sole COM object in MS speech scripting model for access to all popular NetMeeting features. It is easily bolted to SAPI apps to enable automated transcription of NetMeeting discussions in input web speech applications, or to speak aloud transcribed chat entries in output web speech applications, and just as easily configured both ways.

This object is designed programmatic access to NetMeeting ActiveX controls from a scripting environment using either JavaScript, or VBScript (or both).

You can also use the NetMeeting ActiveXConference control in multiple level web enabled speech applications with both SAPI and TAPI (or even SAPI, TAPI and MAPI!) at the same time, in order to build such complex and useful applications as virtual conference room applications that can:

- Place a call, which if answered and accepted, can create a new conference room "sub-room" cell

- End a sub-room side consultation call, without closing the "main" conference room transcripted call

- Make a copy of a logical sub-document created by the speech transcription, and either archive or email

And this is only the beginning of the kinds of applications you can build, the only limit is your imagination. So as indicated previously, stay tuned and visit www.qualimatic.com often, for more books and sample applications using SAPI with related API tools and announcements of new books and software in the future.

7.6   Using the SAPI ActiveX Speech Controls with Intelligent Software Agents

It should not be a surprise to you that you can also use your SAPI ActiveX speech controls to build speech aware intelligent software agents which can reside locally on clients. These can be distributed as speech aware applets across the Internet, or even reside server-side in your speech aware web pages.

You probably know "intelligent software agents" by their more popular descriptive terms, "e-Bots" or "software robots". And you probably know that they can be designed to do just about any routine task you would want to do with any file or data item collected or distributed across the web, including handling of email, mass distribution of email messages, or selective conditional email or web localization responses.

What you may not know is that this technology is a major focus of Artificial Intelligence technology, and that Microsoft has enabled SAPI to be a major platform foundation for AI over the web with MS Speech Agent. An example of MS Speech Agent dropped to a SAPI form is shown in Figure 7.8

You should understand that Microsoft Speech Agent is actually available separate from SAPI or the Speech Server SDK, but that it is actually an entirely different functionality that contains SAPI as an intrinsic part of its implementation—yet *it is entirely implemented as speech control tags within HTML!*

What this effectively means is that you do not have to know all the underlying SAPI automation control with VB or COM in order to implement in your webpage or client standalone application. However, although the purpose of MS Speech Agent was to make SAPI more easily accessible to web page content developers, as you can imagine, you can do a lot more with it if you combine with your SAPI ActiveX voice control object linkages.

Again, this is beyond the scope of this book. But in this case, since there is no software to be developed, you are not invited to submit your freeware or shareware using this facility, since there is no "software" to distribute related to use of these services. However, if you have a clever use of these tags for implementation in your client applications or web enabled objects, you are invited to share them by submitting at www.qualimatic.com). However, the Microsoft Speech Agent has a lot of expected applications in Windows Help Files and design of your own Windows Application Wizards. So there is probably an application software that is appropriate for freeware or shareware in it somewhere, so if you are able to design and develop one, and want to distribute over the author's website, feel free to submit it.

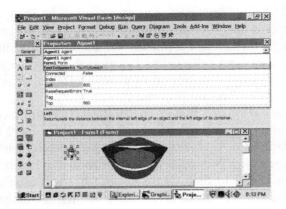

Figure 7.8.

SAPI 5.0 has expanded capabilities for using Microsoft Agent with speech enabling in order to design "web robots" to perform routine background speech recognition and computer speech synthesis as intelligent condition handlers and timer based events.

The Microsoft Agent speech services support modifying speech synthesis output for multi-media Windows web browser speech enabled or Windows standalone client speech enabled applications using special tags that are inserted in speech text specification strings, which can modify expression or emphasis.

These strings are spoken based on conditional logic in your Visual Basic, C, C++ or Java programs, and they provide all of the same control as conventional SAPI custom control tags. This also supports speech integration with MS Agent standard interface controls you are undoubtedly used to. This can include simultaneous auditory computer speech by playing .WAV files at the same time as display of a sub window frame event, usually involving one of the MS Agent animations or bubbles and balloon text.

Speech output tags for Microsoft Agent Speech follow very similar rules of syntax to SAPI, but:

- All tags begin and end with a backslash character (\);
- The single backslash character is not enabled within a tag—to do so, use double back slash (\\);
- Tags are case-insensitive—so "\pit\" is same as "\PIT\";
- Tags ARE space-sensitive—so "\ pit \" is NOT same as "\pit\";
- Unless otherwise specified or modified by another tag a speech tag remains in effect until changed.

A VB example of an MS Agent speech tag to play spoken text and display a balloon at same time look like:

```
Agent1.Characters("Genie").Speak  "This  is  \map="+
chr(34) + "Spoken text" + chr(34) + "=" + chr(34) +
"Balloon text" + chr (34) + "\."
```

You should be aware that all of the SAPI tags in the Appendix of this book are supported for control of speech synthesis voice characterization for emphasis or even emotional stress. However, some new tags including MRK and MAP can be used to input and output .WAV or other sound file-based audio "spoken" recordings as output.

7.7   *Summary*

Its been a long journey yet hopefully not very difficult. But by now you should already be not only an accomplished Visual Basic programmer, but now also a SAPI Visual Basic ActiveX voice control speech recognition programmer. So you are now hopefully at least comfortable, and ideally well prepared, to add SAPI ActiveX voice controls to your Windows programming toolbox, and all your Windows apps.

You may now want to go back to refresh yourself on all of the examples that you have explored throughout the course of reading this book, and then to acquaint yourself with the reference materials in the Appendix of this book, which include the following:

- Complete technical specification of all SAPI ActiveX Voice Control Properties, Methods & Events
- SAPI Visual Basic Speech Class ID Registrations
- SAPI Visual Basic Speech Runtime Constants
- SAPI International Phonetic Alphabet Unicodes
- SAPI ActiveX Voice Control Text To Speech Characterization Codes
- SAPI Common Error Codes
- SAPI Windows Speech Vendor Resource Listing

Appendix A

SAPI ActiveX Control Properties, Methods and Events

This appendix section presents a detailed listing of each of the properties, methods and events that are provided with Microsoft SAPI 4.0 and Speech SDK and supported as ActiveX speech controls for Visual Basic 6. These 6 Windows SAPI ActiveX speech controls for Visual Basic high level Windows speech recognition programming include:

- Voice Command Control
- Voice Text Control
- Voice Dictation Control
- Voice Telephony Control
- Direct Speech Recognition Control
- Direct Speech Synthesis Control

Although this listing of the properties, methods and events associated with each of the 6 Windows SAPI ActiveX speech controls is very comprehensive and detailed, each are described in this appendix only with a short summary description and most critical usage information.

The intent of this appendix is to provide a quick reference to enable the Windows Visual Basic speech programmer to quickly identify those properties, methods and events that have the greatest potential to most effectively satisfy all of the most critical requirements of their own Visual Basic speech recognition programming software designs.

For more extensive details about parameters, keywords, and specific usage requirement information, as well as more specific usage sample code for particular application problems, you should refer to the online SAPI documentation at the MSDN website or CD.

Also, for the sake of brevity, because many of the properties, methods and events in Windows SAPI ActiveX for Visual Basic occur across more than one control, their first instance in this appendix is usually listed in more detail than following instances in other similar controls.

A.1   Voice Command Control

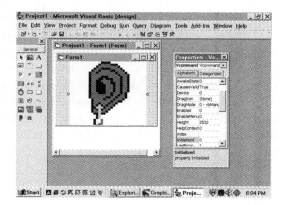

A.1.1   Properties

The Windows SAPI ActiveX Visual Basic **Voice Command** control has the following properties:

- AutoGainEnable
- AwakeState
- CountCommands
- Device
- Enabled
- EnableMenu
- hWnd
- Initialized
- LastError
- MenuCreate
- Microphone
- Speaker
- SRMode
- SuppressExceptions
- Threshold

AutoGainEnable

AutoGainEnable As Long

This property activates default automatic gain value for Voice Command control speech engines. Many speech recognition engines can automatically adjust the *gain* of the incoming audio signal for a Voice Command application, but only if the audio device supports it. *Gain* refers to the increase in signaling power, measured in decibels (dB), that occurs as a signal is boosted by an electronic device. A value of 0 indicates that automatic gain is disabled. A value of 100 indicates that the gain is set perfectly if the next utterance is spoken at the same level. A value between 0 and 100 moderates the automatic adjustments on a linear scale. For example, an **AutoGainEnable** value of 50 adjusts the gain to 50% of the level for the previous utterance.

AwakeState

AwakeState As Long

This property sets mode to wake state for a Voice Command engine. This property is TRUE if the engine is awake or FALSE if it is asleep. When the engine is awake, it listens for commands from any active voice menu for the active application. When the engine is asleep, it listens for commands only from sleep menus—those that were activated with the **Activate** method. Commands from such menus become active only when the engine is asleep, and they become inactive when the engine is awake. A sleep menu typically contains a "Wake up!" command that resumes speech recognition, and it may contain other commands.

CountCommands

CountCommands(menu As Long) As Long

This property returns the number of speech commands active on a voice menu.

Device

Device As Long

This property sets device identifier of the wave-in audio device currently used by the Voice Command engine. An application can obtain a list of devices by calling the **waveInGetNumDevs** and **waveInGetDevCaps** multimedia wave file management functions. Most standalone Visual Basic speech applications do not normally need to retrieve or set the audio device.

Enabled

Enabled As Long

This property is TRUE if speech recognition is enabled for the engine or FALSE if it is disabled. It must be set to TRUE to enable listening for the object. When speech recognition is disabled, the engine does not recognize any command from any menu, whether speech recognition is awake or asleep or any menus are active. An application would use the Enabled property to allow the user to turn speech recognition completely off, as opposed to suspending speech recognition temporarily by putting the engine to sleep. Note, however, that if speech recognition is allowed to be disabled, it is probably because the user does not want to use it. It may not be appropriate to enable speech recognition under those circumstances where users turn it off.

EnableMenu

EnableMenu As Long

This property enables the menu created with **MenuCreate**.

hWnd

hWnd As Long

This property enables the voice Window handler.

Initialized

Initialized As Long

This property equals 1 if the control has been initialized, 0 if not. The user can force the control to initialize by setting this to 1. Use of most other Windows SAPI ActiveX speech control methods and properties will automatically cause the speech control to initialize, if not initialized already.

LastError

LastError As Long

This property contains the result code from the last method or property invocation, which may be an error or exception or good return.

MenuCreate

MenuCreate(Application As String, State As String, flags As Long) As Long

This property creates a Voice Menu object to represent a new or existing voice menu for an application with the following flags:

Microphone

Microphone As String

This property assigns the name of the microphone used by a Voice Command engine. Some speech recognition engines can improve recognition accuracy by optimizing themselves for use with particular types of microphones. The microphone for a user is saved between uses even if the user shuts down the computer between sessions.

Speaker

Speaker As String

This property sets name of the current user for a Voice Command PC. Changing speaker name unloads all training for the previous speaker and loads the training for the new speaker. If no training exists for the new speaker, the application starts with default training. The speaker name is saved between sessions.

SRMode

SRMode As String

This property sets the GUID of the speech recognition mode used for the user. A speech recognition engine typically provides an assortment of modes that it can use to recognize speech in different languages or dialects. A Voice Command control uses a single speech recognition mode.

SuppressExceptions

SuppressExceptions As Short

When this property is set to 1, exceptions will never occur. You must then check the **LastError** property to get the error code of the last method or property returned results.

Threshold

Threshold As Long

This property sets threshold level of the speech recognition engine used by a Voice Command control. The threshold level is a value from 0 to 100 that indicates a point below which an engine rejects an utterance as unrecognized. A value of 0 indicates that the engine should match any utterance to the closest phrase match. A value of 100 indicates that the engine should be absolutely certain that an utterance is the recognized phrase.

A.1.2   Methods

The Windows SAPI ActiveX Visual Basic **Voice Command** control supports the following methods:

- Activate
- AddCommand
- CmdMimic
- Deactivate
- EnableItem
- GeneralDlg
- GetCommand
- LexiconDlg
- ListGet
- ListSet
- MenuDelete
- ReleaseMenu
- Remove
- SetCommand
- TrainGeneralDlg
- TrainMenuDlg
- TrainMicDlg

Activate

Activate(Menu As Long)

This method activates a voice menu so that its commands can be recognized. Once a voice menu is created and has commands, it must be activated before its commands can be recognized. When a menu is active, the engine checks the menu for a matching command whenever the engine processes an utterance via a Voice Command. The engine does not check the menu when it is inactive.

AddCommand

AddCommand(Menu As Long, id As Long, command As String, description As String, category As String, flags As Long, action As String)

This method adds a command to a menu created with **MenuCreate**. The added command is appended to any existing commands in the menu. Commands are numbered sequentially from 1 to n. New commands are added to the end of the menu, so the first command added is numbered n+1. Unlike Voice Dictation, Voice Commands support lists. If a command string includes a list name, you can use **ListSet** to set the phrases that the user can substitute for the list name when speaking the command.

CmdMimic

CmdMimic(application As String, state As String, command As String)

This method provides a voice-aware Visual Basic application with the equivalent of a spoken voice command. This causes the command engine to act as if the speech recognizer engine had actually heard the command but was in fact passed a text string.

Deactivate

Deactivate(Menu As Long)

This method in effect tells recognizer to stop listening and release the microphone/sound card resource.

EnableItem

EnableItem(Menu As Long, enable As Long, cmdnum As Long, flag As Long)

This method permanently enables or disables a menu item for the rest of a session. When a voice command is disabled by using **EnableItem**, it is not compiled into the menu. The engine cannot recognize a permanently disabled command, and no events are sent to the application when the user speaks the command.

GeneralDlg

GeneralDlg(hWnd As Long, title As String)

This method displays a default General voice dialog box, which gives the user general control of the speech recognition engine and provides the user with full access to engine-specific controls as well as general SAPI controls.

GetCommand

GetCommand(Menu As Long, index As Long, command As String, description As String, category As String, flags As long, action As String)

This method retrieves information about active status of the most current speech command.

LexiconDlg

LexiconDlg(hWnd As Long, title As String)

This method displays a Lexicon dialog box, which allows the user to display and edit his or her pronunciation lexicon. For example, the speaker can edit the phonetics of mispronounced words and load or unload personal exception dictionaries.

ListGet

ListGet(Menu As Long, List As String, Listdata As String)

This method gets the current active word list and retrieves the phrases stored in the current list for the selected voice menu. A list is associated with a menu rather than an individual command. The list must appear in at least one command string, but can be used by more than one command on the menu.

ListSet

ListSet(Menu As Long, List As String, ListNum As Long, Listdata As String)

This method sets the phrases in a list for a voice command. The user can speak any phrase in the list in place of the list name in the command string. A command that uses a list must have the list name in brackets. Example: "Send mail to <name>"

MenuDelete

MenuDelete(application As String, state As String)

This method deletes a menu from the Voice Menu database. A menu cannot be deleted if it is currently open and the application is actively listening for its commands. This method only deletes the storage in the database for the menu if it exists and will release the Voice Menu object that was created by **MenuCreate.**

ReleaseMenu

ReleaseMenu(Menu As Long)

This method releases a voice menu completely from memory. You must call **ReleaseMenu** for every voice menu that you create.

Remove

Remove(menu As Long, index As Long)

This method removes or deactivates a specified list of commands from the currently active voice menu. For best results, you should deactivate the voice menu before calling Remove. Otherwise, the menu must be deactivated, recompiled, and reactivated before **Remove** returns. If the menu is already deactivated when **Remove** is called, the menu is not recompiled until the application activates it again.

SetCommand

SetCommand(Menu As Long, index As Long, id As Long, command As String, description As String, category As String, flags As Long, action As String)

This method sets initial activation information for a command in either the global or application-specific command set.

TrainGeneralDlg

TrainGeneralDlg(hWnd As Long, title As String)

This method displays a General Training dialog box, which then enables to train a speech recognition engine by having the user speak a pre-selected set of words. After the user speaks these words and phrases, recognition accuracy should be better for that particular user.

TrainMenuDlg

TrainMenuDlg(Menu As Long, hWnd As Long, title As String)

This method displays a modal dialog box used to train the engine for the selected menu. Because the Train Menu dialog box is provided by the speech recognition engine, the controls in the Train Menu dialog box and the training it requests depend upon the speech recognition engine being used. Some vendor speech engines may not always offer this dialog box.

TrainMicDlg

TrainMicDlg(hWnd As Long, title As String)

This method displays a Microphone Training dialog box, which trains the speech recognition engine with training for a microphone. This dialog box should be displayed at the request of the engine or whenever the speaker wants to display it. Training information will be associated with both the speaker and the microphone. Ideally, **TrainMicDlg** will train the engine only for the microphone and any surrounding sounds, but it is also likely to train for the speaker's voice.

A.1.3   Events

The Windows SAPI ActiveX Visual Basic **Voice Command** control is continually notified of the following standard reference handler events:

*   AttribChanged
*   ClickIn
*   CommandOther
*   CommandRecognize
*   CommandStart
*   Interference
*   MenuActivate
*   UtteranceBegin
*   UtteranceEnd
*   VUMeter

AttribChanged

AttribChanged(attrib As Long)

This event only occurs whenever an active speech engine attribute has changed. This *attrib* parameter includes the IVCNSAC_ORIGINAPP value only if the application sets the Voice Command control's **Enabled, AwakeState, Device,** or **SRMode** properties.

ClickIn

ClickIn(x As Long, y As Long)

This event occurs anytime when the user clicks in the object's icon by voice or mouse or keyboard *x,y* coordinate inputs.

CommandOther

CommandOther(CmdName As String, Command As String)

This event occurs when a spoken phrase was either recognized as being from another application's command set or was not recognized. An application can use the **CommandOther** event to monitor utterances and inform the user what was heard. An application should not rely on this event for information about the recognition of its own commands. Most applications ignore this event. The *command* string contains the words actually spoken by the user. If the command contains a list name, the command string may not match the words of the command. For example, the Command might be "Send mail to Fred" whereas the *command* string is "Send mail to name."

CommandRecognize

CommandRecognize(ID As Long, CmdName As String, Flags As Long, Action As String, NumLists As Long, ListValues As String, command As String)

This event occurs when a spoken phrase was recognized as being from the application's command set. Along with the event, the application receives the text of the phrase and the action data that was supplied by the application when it originally defined the command. If two or more global voice menus (or two or more window-specific voice menus) contain the same phrase and the engine recognizes that phrase, the engine calls **CommandRecognize** for one menu and **CommandOther** for the other.

CommandStart

CommandStart()

This event occurs when recognition processing has begun for a command. An application can use **CommandStart** to indicate that it is still processing what the user just said.

Interference

Interference()

This event occurs when the engine cannot recognize speech properly for any known or unknown reason.

MenuActivate

MenuActivate(cmdName As String, bActive As Boolean)

This event is sent when a menu's activation state is changed. It occurs when a voice menu has been activated or deactivated, either explicitly by the application or as a result of the user switching to or from the window associated with the menu.

UtteranceBegin

UtteranceBegin( )

This event occurs when the speech recognition engine has detected the beginning of an utterance or sound. Any **UtteranceBegin** implicitly signals the end of silence, so an application can use this event to detect long periods of silence and react accordingly just as if it was a text input delimiter.

UtteranceEnd

UtteranceEnd( )

This event occurs when an utterance is finished. A speech recognition engine normally sends this event 0.25 to 0.5 of a second after the last speech utterance stops. This still does not necessarily have any bearing on the recognition of commands. An **UtteranceEnd** event merely implicitly signals the beginning of silence as opposed to speech start, so an application can use this event to detect long silence and react accordingly.

VUMeter

VUMeter(Level As Long)

This method notifies the application of the current VU level, which indicates the loudness of the digital-audio stream. If the speech recognition engine for the user install supports a VU meter, the engine sends this event about 8 times per second. This information can be used to provide feedback to the user that the Voice Command object is listening.

A.2   *Voice Dictation Control*

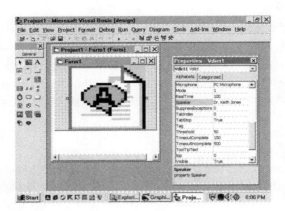

A.2.1   Properties

The Windows SAPI ActiveX Visual Basic **Voice Dictation** speech control has the following properties:

- Attributes
- AttributeMemory
- AttributeString
- AutoGainEnable
- BookmarkQuery
- CountBookmarks
- CountCommands
- CountGlossary
- CountSpeakers
- CreateDocFile
- CreateStream
- Echo
- EnergyFloor
- Flags
- hWnd

- Initialized
- IsAnyoneDictating
- LastError
- Microphone
- Mode
- Option
- OptionsEnum
- RealTime
- Speaker
- SpeakerGet
- SuppressExceptions
- Threshold
- TimeoutComplete
- TimeoutIncomplete
- wLeft
- wTop

Attributes

Attributes(Attrib As Long) As Long

This property assigns engine attributes.

AttributeMemory

AttributeMemory(Attrib As Long, Size As Long) As Long

This property sets memory size for the attribute area.

AttributeString

AttributeString(Attrib As Long) As String

This property assigns a string size to pass attributes.

AutoGainEnable

AutoGainEnable As Long

This property sets the state of the automatic gain for the incoming audio stream. A value of 0 indicates that automatic gain is disabled. A value of 100 indicates that the speech recognition engine always adjusts the gain, so that if the next utterance is spoken at the same level, the gain is set perfectly. A value between 0 and 100 moderates the automatic adjustments on a linear scale. For example, a value of 50 adjusts the gain to half the extent that the engine otherwise would. When automatic gain is enabled, the speech recognition engine may adjust the level at the end of an utterance and increase or decrease the gain. Note that if the audio source does not support **IAudio::LevelSet**, the application cannot set the automatic gain with this property.

BookmarkQuery

BookmarkQuery(Id As Long) As Long

This property sets a bookmark default for a bookmark.

CountBookmarks

CountBookmarks(start As Long, length As Long) As Long

This property counts the number of words or phrases selected by a voice bookmark command in a range of text.

CountCommands

CountCommands(fGlobal As Long) As Long

This property sets total number of commands in the global or application-specific command set. This property is only supported for legacy discrete dictation systems. New methods and properties usually replace **CountCommands** for continuous engines, or discrete engines that support continuous commands.

CountGlossary

CountGlossary(fGlobal As Long) As Long

This property counts the total number of glossary entries in the global or application-specific glossary entry set.

CountSpeakers

CountSpeakers As Long

This property enumerates the number of speakers known to the speech recognition engine.

CreateDocFile

CreateDocFile(name As String, flags As Long) As Long

This property sets the file handle reference for a new Microsoft Dictation (.msd) file. For an example of how to use **CreateDocFile**, see the Visual Basic version of the Dictation Pad sample application on SAPI 4.0 CD or MSDN Speech SDK download.

CreateStream

CreateStream(stor As Long, name As String, flags As Longs) As Long

This property sets the file handle reference for a new stream object. For an example of how to use **CreateStream**, see the Visual Basic version of the Dictation Pad sample application.

Echo

Echo As Long

This property controls the state of echo canceling on the incoming audio stream. TRUE turns on echo canceling, FALSE turns it off. When **Echo** is TRUE, the engine typically ignores low-level audio signals. The state of echo canceling indicates whether the signal should be treated as though it has residual signal on it. In general, echo canceling causes the speech recognition engine to ignore low-level audio signals so that it doesn't attempt to recognize the residual signal of the echo cancellation.

EnergyFloor

EnergyFloor As Long

This property sets the value of the noise floor, in negative decibels. For example, a value of 30 indicates an energy floor of-30 dB. An application can specify SRATTR_MINENERGYFLOOR or SRATTR_MAXENERGYFLOOR for minimum or maximum allowable values. The noise floor is the noise value in the signal-to-noise ratio (SNR) for a particular environment. In general, the higher the noise value in the ratio, the more sensitive the speech recognition engine is to background noise. For example, a quiet office would have a high SNR (low floor), whereas a noisy factory would have a low SNR (high floor). An application might send this value to a speech recognition engine if the application has information about SNR to expect from the audio stream. The engine can use the value internally to adjust its calculated noise floor in expectation of the audio stream's SNR.

Flags

Flags As Long

This property sets flags indicating the states and settings of the correction window.

hWnd

hWnd As Long

This property defines the speech Window handler reference.

Initialized

Initialized As Long

This property equals 1 if the control has been initialized, 0 if it has not. The user can force the control to initialize by setting this to 1 (the speech engines can be slow to load, so some users may want fine control over when the control initializes). Use of most any other concurrent methods and properties will automatically cause the control to initialize, if it hasn't been initialized already.

IsAnyoneDictating

IsAnyoneDictating(hWnd As Long) As String

This property determines if the application has activated dictation for the window handle, and when and if default application activated dictation methods will apply.

LastError

LastError As Long

This property receives result code from the last method or property event.

Microphone

Microphone As String

This property is the name of the current microphone assigned for this audio source. An application can use the microphone name to save or retrieve information about a particular microphone, such as the name of the microphone used to train the engine or the conditions in which the microphone is recording. For example, an application could use this information to preserve the original training when the user changes microphones.

Mode

Mode As Long

This property sets the current mode of operation on the current engine. This can be one of the values shown in the table below. The mode normally affects both Voice Dictation and Voice Command controls, if both are active in concurrent sharing applications.

Option

Option(option As String) As Boolean

The state of the option property defines whether a speech application switch is on or off. TRUE if the option switch is on, FALSE if it's off. For example, there might be a switch for "Two spaces between sentences" that will put two spaces between sentences if it's on, or only one if it's off.

OptionsEnum

OptionsEnum As String

This property sets names and descriptions of all the inverse text normalization options available in this property.

RealTime

RealTime As Long

This property holds the real-time setting for the engine. The real-time setting is the percentage of processor time that the engine expects to use during constant speech. This value can be more than 100 for non-real-time applications (for example, transcribing prerecorded speech). For most engines, the amount of processor time required diminishes markedly during periods of silence. For example, if *RealTime* is 100, the engine takes one full minute of processor time to process one minute of speech. If *RealTime* is 50, the engine takes 30 seconds of processor time to process the same minute of speech. This value is difficult to compute precisely, so it should be regarded as an estimate.

Speaker

Speaker As String

This property sets the name of the current speaker for an audio source. If *Speaker* is a new name, the engine creates a new speaker profile for a new user or a new user context.

SpeakerGet

SpeakerGet(index As Long) As String

This property contains the name of the voice, or NULL if the name of a specific user training file is not important.

SuppressExceptions

SuppressExceptions As Short

When this property is set to 1, exceptions will never occur (or will never be recognized!). You must then check **LastError** to get the error code of the last method or property invocation.

Threshold

Threshold As Long

This property sets the threshold level of the speech recognition engine. The threshold level indicates how confident the speech recognition engine must be about the validity of a given recognition in order to accept it. If the engine is not confident enough, it notifies the application that the phrase was not recognized. The threshold level is a value from 0 to 100 that indicates the threshold below which an utterance is rejected as unrecognized. A value of 0 indicates that the engine matches any utterance to the closest phrase match. A value of 100 indicates that the engine must be absolutely certain that an utterance is the recognized phrase. The optimum threshold for the average user should be 50.

TimeoutComplete

TimeoutComplete As Long

This property sets the number of milliseconds that the speech recognition engine waits before regarding a phrase as complete after the user has stopped speaking. For example, if **TimeoutComplete** is 500, a user speaking "Send mail to Fred" would see results 0.5 seconds after finishing the phrase.

TimeoutIncomplete

TimeoutIncomplete As Long

This property sets the number of milliseconds that the speech recognition engine waits before discarding an incomplete phrase because the user has stopped speaking. For example, if **IncompleteTimeOut** is 2000, a user speaking "Send mail to…" could pause for 2 seconds before the engine would assume that the user has stopped speaking the phrase. **TimeoutIncomplete** should always be longer than **TimeoutComplete**.

wLeft

wLeft As Long

This property sets the X-coordinate of the far left side of the control, relative to the left side of the screen.

wTop

> *wTop As Long*

This property sets the Y-coordinate of the top of the control relative to the top of the screen.

A.2.2 Methods

The Windows SAPI ActiveX Visual Basic **Voice Dictation** control provides support for the following methods:

- AboutDlg
- Activate
- ActivateAndAssignWindow
- AddCommand
- AddGlossary
- BookmarkAdd
- BookmarkRemove
- CFGSet
- CopyToBin
- CopyToMemory
- Deactivate
- FX
- GeneralDlg
- GetBookMark
- GetChanges
- GetCommand
- GetGlossary
- GlobalKeyHook
- GlobalMouseHook
- Hint
- ITNApply
- ITNExpand
- LexiconDlg
- Lock

- MemoryGet
- MemorySet
- PasteFromBin
- PasteFromMemory
- ReadStreamFont
- ReleaseStore
- ReleaseStream
- RemoveCommand
- RemoveGlossary
- ResultsGet
- ResultsGet2
- ResultsSet
- SessionDeserialize
- SessionSerialize
- SetCommand
- SetGlossary
- SetSelRect
- SetSize
- SpeakerDelete
- SpeakerNew
- SpeakerQuery
- SpeakerRevert
- SpeakerSelect
- StreamRead
- StreamWrite
- TextGet
- TextRemove
- TextSelGet
- TextSelSet
- TextSet
- TrainGeneralDlg

- TrainMicDlg
- Unlock
- Words
- WriteStreamFont

AboutDlg

AboutDlg(hWnd As Long, title As String)

This method displays an About dialog box that identifies the speech recognition engine and contains the copyright notice.

Activate

Activate()

This method activates a dictation session for all windows, unless preempted by another dictation session specific to a window. Speech recognition will not necessarily start listening right away after an **Activate** call. The **Mode** property must be set to a mode that enables dictation. The session will be listening if and only if **Activate** has been called AND the engine's mode supports dictation. Calling **Deactivate** will stop dictation for the session.

ActivateAndAssignWindow

ActivateAndAssignWindow(hWnd As Long)

This method activates a dictation session for a single window.

AddCommand

AddCommand(global As Long, id As Long, command As String, description As String, category As String, flags As Long, action As String)

This method ads one or more commands for dictation to support during the current dictation session. The added commands are appended to any existing commands. Commands are numbered sequentially from 1 to n. New commands are added to the end of the menu, so the first command added is numbered n+1. Unlike Voice Commands, Voice Dictation commands do not support lists.

AddGlossary

AddGlossary(global As Long, id As Long, Glossary As String, description As String, category As String, flags As Long, action As String)

This method adds one or more glossary entries for dictation to support during the current dictation session. The added glossary entries are appended to any existing glossary entries. Glossary entries are numbered sequentially from 1 to n. New glossary entries are added to the end of the menu, so the first glossary entry added is numbered n+1. Unlike Voice Commands, Voice Dictation glossary entries do not support lists.

BookmarkAdd

BookmarkAdd(ID As Long, Posn As Long)

This method adds an application-specific bookmark into the text. The meaning of the bookmark is left solely up to the application. Bookmarks move with the text so applications can place them to ensure that insertions and deletions do not put font formatting out of sync.

BookmarkRemove

BookmarkRemove(Id As Long)

This method removes the bookmark.

CFGSet

CFGSet(lang As Long, topic As String, CFG As String)

This method passes the text for a Voice Dictation Context Free Grammar to the Voice Dictation module. The grammar is then compiled and used for the topic. The CFG is persistent, so it will continue to be used by the topic until it's changed.

CopyToBin

CopyToBin(start As Long, numchars As Long, bin As Long)

This method copies data into a binary object. Each Voice Dictation control maintains "bins" where data can be moved to/from. Each bin can store a set of text and the results objects. The **CopyToBin** and **PasteFromBin** methods allow an application to cache the text (and results object) in the Voice Dictation object away to separate bins. Applications can use this to implement cut, copy, paste, and undo functionality.

CopyToMemory

CopyToMemory(start As Long, numchars As Long, mem As Long, sizemem As Long, unk As Long, sizeunk As Long)

This method copies the data from the Voice Dictation control, but rather than placing it in a bin, two associated chunks of memory are returned to the application. The first chunk is data storing information about the text, bookmarks, and results objects obtained from the copy. The second chunk contains an array of indexes to results objects.

Deactivate

Deactivate

This method tells the speech recognizer to stop listening and release the microphone and sound card resources. If you call this and the recognizer has not yet been activated, an error should normally be generated.

FX

FX(fx As Long)

This method performs an action defined by *fx* parameter as a function acting on the selected text.

GeneralDlg

GeneralDlg(hWnd As Long, title As String)

This method displays a General dialog box, which gives the user general control of the speech recognition engine and provides the user with full access to engine-specific controls.

GetBookMark

GetBookMark(start As Long, length As Long, index As Long, Id As Long, Posn As Long)

This method returns a bookmark in a range of text.

GetChanges

GetChanges(newStart As Long, newEnd As Long, oldStart As Long, oldEnd As Long)

This method nforms the applications of the changes that have occurred since the last time the application called **Unlock**. It returns where the changes started and ended in the old text, and where they now start and end in the new text. If several changes occurred since the last call to **UnLock** then they are all wrapped up into one larger change.

GetCommand

GetCommand(fGlobal As Long, index As Long, command As String, description As String, category As String, flags As Long, action As String)

This property retrieves information about a command. This method is only supported for legacy discrete dictation systems.

GetGlossary

GetGlossary(fGlobal As Long, index As Long, Glossary As String, description As String, category As String, flags As Long, action As String)

This method retrieves information about a glossary entry.

GlobalKeyHook

GlobalKeyHook(flags As Long)

This method activates a "hook" process handler that monitors all keystroke messages. When the key hook procedure receives a keystroke message, it sends a **GlobalKey** event. A hook is a point in the Microsoft® Windows® message-handling mechanism where an application can install a subroutine to monitor the message traffic in the system and process certain types of messages before they reach the target window. For an example of how to use **GlobalKeyHook**, see the Microsoft Word Embedded Dictation sample SAPI application.

GlobalMouseHook

GlobalMouseHook(flags As Long)

This method installs a "hook procedure" that monitors all mouse messages. When the mouse hook procedure receives a mouse message, it sends a **GlobalMouse** event.

Hint

Hint(hint As String)

This method gives the speech recognition engine information about the subcontext in which a document is being used. This calls right into the Direct Speech Recognition control's Hint method, and has the same functionality.

ITNApply

ITNApply(start As Long, numchars As Long)

This method finds any text within the region that could be inverse text normalized, and collapses the text to the inverse text normalization form.

ITNExpand

ITNExpand(start As Long, numchars As Long)

This method finds any text within the region, and expands any inverse text normalization sections.

LexiconDlg

LexiconDlg(hWnd As Long, title As String)

This method displays a Lexicon dialog box, which allows the user to display and edit his or her pronunciation lexicon. For example, the speaker can edit the phonetics of mispronounced words and load or unload personal exception dictionaries.

Lock

Lock()

This method effectively locks the text object so that nothing except the application can modify it. An application shouldn't keep the text object locked for long. None of the other text functions will work until **UnLock** is called. Calling **Lock** will prevent the speech engine from trying any further processing.

MemoryGet

MemoryGet(maxRAM As Long, maxTime As Long, maxWords As Long, KeepAudio As Long, KeepCorrection As Long, KeepEval As Long)

This method fills up to maximum all available memory that can be used for the current dictation session.

MemorySet

MemorySet(maxRAM As Long, maxTime As Long, maxWords As Long, KeepAudio As Long, KeepCorrection As Long, KeepEval As Long)

This method tells Voice Dictation how much memory to use for the results objects (used for correction) for the current session. If the memory constraints are tightened, MemorySet does not free up any allocated resources. Changing this will affect the settings for this session only. The changes are not permanent across invocations.

PasteFromMemory

PasteFromMemory(start As Long, numchars As Long, mem As Long, sizemem As Long, unk As Long, sizeunk As Long)

This method pastes data derived from **CopyToMemory**, back into the currently active dictation document work space.

ReadStreamFont

ReadStreamFont(stream As Long, FontName As String, FontSize As Long, FontItalic As Long, FontBold As Long, FontUnderline As Long, FontStrikeThru As Long)

This method extracts font attributes from a speech stream.

ReleaseStore

ReleaseStore(object As Long)

This method frees a storage object from memory.

ReleaseStream

ReleaseStream(object As Long)

This method frees a stream object from memory.

RemoveCommand

RemoveCommand(fGlobal As Long, index As Long)

This method removes the specified command from either the global or application-specific commands. This method is only supported for legacy discrete dictation systems.

ResultsGet

ResultsGet(start As Long, length As Long, phrasestart As Long, phraselength As Long, results As Long)

This method gets the results object for a specific selection so that an application can get more information from it, such as the digital audio.

ResultsGet2

ResultsGet2(start As Long, length As Long, phrasestart As Long, phraselength As Long, results As Long, nodeleft As Long, noderight As Long)

This method is pretty much just like **ResultsGet**, except that this method also returns the left and right node numbers that indicate where the word appears in the phrase. This way the application can determine exactly which word the results came from when using continuous dictation.

ResultsSet

ResultsSet(start As Long, length As Long, results As Long, nodeleft As Long, noderight As Long)

This method sets the results object applied to a range of text, and removes any other results objects associated with the text. Applications can use this to apply their own results to the text if the results were obtained from a recognition outside of the dictation session.

SessionDeserialize

SessionDeserialize(stor As Long)

This method loads a "serialized" session. It replaces all of the text, results object, bookmarks, and selection position information with the state of the information that existed when SessionSerialize was called.

SessionSerialize

SessionSerialize(stor As Long)

This method saves the current state of dictation to the *stor* provided. The information includes all of the text in the buffer, results objects associated with the text, and bookmarks. An application can re-load a session by calling **SessionDeSerialize**.

SetCommand

SetCommand(fGlobal As Long, index As Long, Id As Long, command As String, description As String, category As String, flags As Long, action As String)

This method is only supported for legacy discrete dictation systems. New methods and properties replace **SetCommand** for continuous engines, or discrete engines that support continuous commands. This method currently works with discrete engines only.

SetGlossary

SetGlossary(fGlobal As Long, index As Long, Id As Long, Glossary As String, description As String, category As String, flags As Long, action As String)

This method sets information for a glossary entry in either the global or application-specific glossary entry set.

SetSelRect

SetSelRect(left As Long, top As Long, right As Long, bottom As Long)

This method defines a rectangle in screen coordinates for where the selection or insertion point currently is. An application should call this whenever the window is moved or the insertion/selection coordinates change. If the user has not locked the correction window in place, then the correction window will position itself near the selection rectangle. Applications will often call this in response to a selection change notification.

SetSize

SetSize(stream As Long, size As Long)

This method changes the size of the input speech stream data object to reset number of available input buffer bytes.

SpeakerDelete

SpeakerDelete(name As String)

This method deletes all information that a speech recognition engine has accumulated in a particular user speaker file. If the speaker is currently being used, the **SpeakerDelete** method normally does nothing and returns an error.

SpeakerNew

SpeakerNew(name As Long)

This method creates and initializes a new speaker file, using the default settings provided by the engine for training. If the speaker already exists, the **SpeakerNew** method returns an error.

SpeakerQuery

SpeakerQuery(name As String, data As String)

This method retrieves the name of the currently selected speaker. If no speak is active, it returns an error.

SpeakerRevert

SpeakerRevert(name As String)

This method restores training to its original state at the beginning of the session, which is the last time the speaker information was loaded. A session begins when a speaker is selected with a call to the **SpeakerSelect** method. An application can use **SpeakerRevert** to cancel undesirable changes, such as those caused by extraneous noise or unrelated conversations during a training session.

SpeakerSelect

SpeakerSelect(name As String, lock boolean)

This method selects a speaker file to be used in a session.

StreamRead

StreamRead(stream As Long, data As String, size As Long)

This method extracts bytes from a speech input stream object.

StreamWrite

StreamWrite(stream As Long, data As String)

This method inserts data into a stream.

TextGet

TextGet(Start As Long, NumChars As Long, Data As String)

This method gets text from an internal dictation buffer.

TextRemove

TextRemove(start As Long, len As Long, reason As Long)

This method removes text from the buffer. Results objects and bookmarks are removed. The selection is moved or resized. If the selection is entirely after the move location, then it is moved forward/backwards by the number of inserted characters.

TextSelGet

TextSelGet(SelStart As Long, SelLen As Long)

This method returns the position of the text selection within the virtual text field. Applications should keep this in sync with the text they display to the user. If the selection's screen coordinates change the application should call **SetSelRect** method.

TextSelSet

TextSelSet(selstart As Long, sellen As Long)

This method sets the position of the selection. Applications should keep this in sync with the text they display to the user. If the selection's screen coordinates change the application should call the **SetSelRect** method.

TextSet

TextSet(newText As String, start As Long, numchars As Long, reason As Long)

This method replaces a text selection defined by the beginning and number of characters. The text is replaced with new text.

TrainGeneralDlg

TrainGeneralDlg(hWnd As Long, title As String)

This method displays a General Training dialog box, which trains a speech recognition engine by having the user speak a preselected set of words. After the user speaks these words and phrases, recognition accuracy should be better for that particular user.

TrainMicDlg

TrainMicDlg(hWnd As Long, title As String)

This method displays a Microphone Training dialog box, which trains the speech recognition engine with training for a microphone. This dialog box should be displayed at the request of the engine or whenever the speaker wants to display it.

Unlock

Unlock()

This method unlocks the text object so that dictation and inverse text normalization can happen.

Words

Words(words As String)

This method informs the speech recognition engine that a particular set of words is likely to be spoken. The engine can ignore the set of words. This calls right into the Direct Speech Recognition control's **Words** method and has the same functionality.

WriteStreamFont

WriteStreamFont(stream As Long, FontName As Long, FontSize As Long, FontItalic As Long, FontBold As long, FontUnderline As Long, FontStrikeThru As Long)

This method inserts font attributes into a text input stream.

A.2.3   Events

The Windows SAPI ActiveX Visual Basic **Voice Dictation** control can receive and support the following standard speech processing handler events:

- **AttribChanged**
- **ClickIn**
- **CommandBuiltIn**
- **CommandOther**
- **CommandRecognize**
- **Dictating**
- **GlobalKey**
- **GlobalMouse**
- **Interference**

- PhraseFinish
- PhraseHypothesis
- PhraseStart
- TextBookmarkChanged
- TextChanged
- TextSelChanged
- Training
- UtteranceBegin
- UtteranceEnd
- VUMeter

AttribChanged

AttribChanged(lAttrib As Long)

This event occurs when a speech attribute has changed.

ClickIn

ClickIn(x As Long, y As Long)

This event occurs when the user clicks on a speech object's icon.

CommandBuiltIn

CommandBuiltIn(command As String)

This event occurs when a spoken command was recognized and handled. The command was for the current dictation session and automatically handled by the Voice Dictation module. An application can use the **CommandBuiltIn** event to monitor commands and inform the user what was heard. Most applications ignore this event. If automatic locking is on, then the buffer is locked as soon as this event occurs. The application will have to call **UnLock**.

CommandOther

CommandOther(command As String)

This event occurs when a spoken command was recognized and handled. The command was for another dictation session. An application can use the **CommandOther** event to monitor commands and inform the user what was heard. An application should not rely on this event for information about the recognition of its own commands. Most applications ignore this event.

CommandRecognize

CommandRecognize(Id As Long, flags As Long, action As String, command As String)

This event occurs when a spoken phrase was recognized as being from the application's command set. Along with the event, the application receives the text of the phrase and the action data that was supplied by the application when it originally defined the command. You should not use the contents of the *command* parameter to identify the recognized command. Instead, use the data in the *action* parameter or the identifier in the *Id* parameter to determine which command was recognized.

Dictating

Dictating(appstring As String, flags As Long)

This event occurs when an application starts or stops dictation.

GlobalKey

GlobalKey(wParam As Long, lParam As Long)

This event ocurs when the global key hook procedure receives a keystroke message.

GlobalMouse

GlobalMouse(wParam As Long, lParam As Long, x As Long, y As Long)

This event occurs when the global mouse hook procedure receives a mouse message.

Interference

Interference(attrib As Long)

This event notifies the application that the engine cannot recognize speech properly for any known reason.

PhraseFinish

PhraseFinish(flags As Long, phrase As String)

This event informs the application that the speaker has finished a phrase and the speech recognition engine is certain about the words that were spoken. An application can use the **PhraseFinish** event to monitor what speech recognition is controlling the Voice Dictation object. An application should not rely on this event for information about the recognition of its own commands. Most applications ignore this event.

PhraseHypothesis

PhraseHypothesis(flags As Long, phrase As String)

This event informs the application that the recognition engine has a hypothesis about a phrase. For an application to accept a recognition as valid, both ISRNOTEFIN_RECOGNIZED and ISRNOTEFIN_THISGRAMMAR should be set. An application can use the **PhraseFinish** event to monitor what speech recognition is controlling the Voice Dictation object.

PhraseStart

PhraseStart()

This event notifies the application that the engine has started processing audio data for a recognition result. After sending **PhraseStart**, the engine may send one or more **PhraseHypothesis** events, but it must always conclude with a **PhraseFinish** event.

TextBookmarkChanged

TextBookmarkChanged(val As Long)

This event notifies the application that a bookmark has been changed.

TextChanged

TextChanged(reason As Long)

This event notifies the application that text has been added or removed, or that changes have been made to the data.

TextSelChanged

TextSelChanged()

This event occurs whenever an active text selection has changed. The application should lock the text, find the new position and then update using the **SelSetRect** method. Some built-in commands might cause the selection to change.

Training

Training(train As Long)

This event indicates to the application that the engine requires training for the current speaker, the current grammar, or the current microphone. The application itself must call the appropriate training dialog box for the engine.

UtteranceBegin

UtteranceBegin()

This event notifies the application that the engine has detected the beginning of an utterance or sound. Detecting the beginning of an utterance doesn't necessarily have any bearing on the recognition of words or the completion of a phrase. Because a call to **UtteranceBegin** implicitly signals the end of the silence, an application can use this event to detect long periods of silence and react accordingly.

UtteranceEnd

UtteranceEnd()

This event notifies the application that an utterance has ended. The current active speech engine sends this event 0.25 to 0.5 seconds after speech stops. This doesn't necessarily have any bearing on the recognition of words or completion of a phrase. Because a call to **UtteranceEnd** implicitly signals the beginning of silence, an application can use this event to detect long periods of silence and react accordingly.

VUMeter

VUMeter(vu As Long)

This event notifies the application of the current VU level, which indicates the loudness of the digital-audio stream. VU level returned by this function is only a rough estimate used to display a visual indicator on the screen. The engine sends this event about eight times per second.

A.3   Voice Text Control

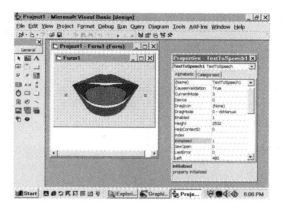

A.3.1   Properties

The Windows SAPI ActiveX Visual Basic **Voice Text** control has the following properties:

- Age
- CountEngines
- CurrentMode
- Device
- Dialect
- Enabled
- EngineFeatures
- Features
- Find
- FindEngine
- Gender
- hWnd
- Initialized
- Interfaces

- IsSpeaking
- JawOpen
- LanguageID
- LastError
- LipTension
- LipType
- MfgName
- ModeID
- ModeName
- MouthHeight
- MouthUpturn
- MouthWidth
- ProductName
- Speaker
- Speed
- Style
- SuppressExceptions
- TeethLowerVisible
- TeethUpperVisible
- TonguePosn
- TTSMode

Age

Age(index As Long) As Long

This property sets age of the active voice.

CountEngines

CountEngines As Long

This property sets number of speech synthesis voices installed on this computer. This is the highest number that can be used as an index to indexed properties and methods.

CurrentMode

CurrentMode As Long

This property sets index for the currently selected voice, as passed into the various engine information calls and properties.

Device

Device As Long

This property sets the device identifier of the audio-output device that is used for a Voice Text command. An application can obtain a list of devices by calling the **waveOutGetNumDevs** and **waveOutGetDevCaps** multimedia functions. The device identifier for a engine is saved between sessions, even if the user shuts down the computer in the meantime.

Dialect

Dialect(index As Long) As String

This property sets the dialect specific to the language—for example, "Texas" or "New York City." This property defaults to be "Standard" for the standard dialect used by the television and radio news media for American English.

Enabled

Enabled As Long

This property is TRUE if voice text is enabled for the speech engine FALSE if it is disabled. If voice text is disabled, no text-to-speech is played over the engine. Typically, starting a new application disables voice text because the user does not want the computer to speak. You should involve the user when enabling or disabling voice text.

EngineFeatures

EngineFeatures(index As Long) As Long

This property defines features specific to a particular engine. These values are definable by the engine author.

Features

Features(index As Long) As Long

This property defines Text-to-speech features that are actively available as the default for a particular custom vendor engine.

Find

Find(RankList As String) As Long

This property returns the index of an engine which most closely matches the input parameter list, ranked in order.

The syntax for RankList is:

```
<field>=<value>;<field>=<value>…
```

Where field can be:

EngineId

MfgName

ProductName

ModeID

ModeName

LanguageID

Dialect

Speaker

Style

Gender

Age

Features

Interfaces

EngineFeatures

For example, Find("MfgName=Microsoft;Gender=1") finds a female Microsoft voice.

FindEngine

FindEngine(EngineId As String, MfgName As String, ProductName As String, ModeID As String, ModeName As String, LanguageID As Long, dialect As String, Speaker As String, Style As String, Gender As Long, Age As Long, Features As Long, Interfaces As Long, EngineFeatures As Long, RankEngineID As Long, RankMfgName As Long, RankProductName As Long, RankModeID As Long, RankModeName As Long, RankLanguage As Long, RankDialect As Long, RankSpeaker As Long, RankStyle As Long, RankGender As Long, RankAge As Long, RankFeatures As Long, RankInterfaces As Long, RankEngineFeatures As Long) As Long

This property returns the index of an engine which most closely matches the input parameters and rankings. To ignore a field, set it to zero. Rank numbers are integers, 1 means lowest priority, 2 means next and so on. The higher the number the more important that criteria will be in finding a best search engine.

Gender

Gender(index As Long) As Long

This property sets gender of the voice. The **Gender** property can be one of the values. Value 1 always means female; 2 means male.

hWnd

hWnd As Long

This property sets the active speech Window handle.

Initialized

Initialized As Long

This property equals 1 if the control has been initialized, 0 if not. The user can force the control to initialize by setting this to 1. Some speech engines can be slow to load, so some users may want fine control over when the control initializes.

Interfaces

Interfaces(index As Long) As Long

This property defines interfaces supported by the active engine.

IsSpeaking

IsSpeaking As Long

This property indicates whether text is currently being spoken by a Voice Text engine. It is set to one if text is being spoken, zero if not. IsSpeaking corresponds to the Direct Speech Synthesis **AudioStart** and **AudioStop** events.

JawOpen

JawOpen As Short

This property sets angle to which the jaw is open. This is a linear range from 0xFF for completely open to 0x00 for completely closed.

LanguageID

LanguageID(index As Long) As Long

This property sets language identifier as specified for the Win32 API. Bits 0 through 9 identify the primary language, such as English, French, Spanish, and so on. Bits 10 through 15 indicate the sublanguage, which is essentially a locale setting. For example, Portuguese has two sublanguages, Brazilian and Standard. For a list of primary and sublanguage identifiers, see the documentation for the MAKELANGID macro in the Win32 SDK. Language ID codes are limited to the Windows 32 definition of LANGID. Dialect strings are specific to an individual engine.

LastError

LastError As Long

This property sets result code from the last method or property invocation.

LipTension

LipTension As Short

This property sets lip tension. This is a linear range from 0xFF if the lips are very tense to 0x00 if they are completely relaxed.

LipType

LipType As Short

This property sets gender type of lips, and can be used to also drive animation handlers. As in the sample Visual Mouth program, when set to 0, the red female lips are drawn, and when set to 1, the male pink lips are drawn.

MfgName

MfgName(index As Long) As String

This property sets name of the SAPI independent speech engine vendor—for example, "Qualimatic Software Corp."

ModeID

ModeID(index As Long) As String

This property sets GUID that uniquely identifies the mode. These GUID numbers are guaranteed by Windows foundation services to be unique, so it is not necessary to monitor and record them. In addition, the GUID is not stored or used directly by OLE, so it is not normally necessary to load it into the property registry.

ModeName

ModeName(index As Long) As String

This property sets name of the text-to-speech mode, example, "Multilingual Multispeaker Classroom" or "Betty Boop Voice."

MouthHeight

MouthHeight As Short

This property sets height of the mouth or lips. This is a linear range from 0xFF for the maximum possible height for the mouth to 0x00 for the minimum height when the mouth and lips are closed.

MouthUpturn

MouthUpturn As Short

This property sets extent to which the mouth turns up at the corners to make a smile. This is a linear range from 0xFF for the maximum upturn lips smiling to 0x00 if the corners of the mouth turn down. If this member is 0x80, the mouth is neutral.

MouthWidth

MouthWidth As Short

This property sets width of the mouth or lips. This is a linear range from 0xFF for the maximum possible width for the face to 0x00 for the minimum width to where mouth or lips are puckered. Notably, this is also known as the "kissing" speech property.

ProductName

ProductName(index As Long) As String

This property sets name of the product—for example, "Qualimatic's Talk-O-Matic."

Speaker

Speaker(index As Long) As String

This property sets name of the voice, or NULL if the name is not important. If set to NULL, the default TV speaker American English non-generic voice is loaded.

Speed

Speed As Long

This property sets the current average talking speed for a Voice Text engine, in words per minute. An application can specify TTSATTR_MINSPEED or TTSATTR_MAXSPEED for the minimum or maximum allowable value.

Style

Style(index As Long) As String

This property sets personality of the voice—for example:

"Business"

"Casual"

"Computer"

"Excited"

"Singsong"

There are actually many other available personalities, or you can modify to create your own by referencing the MSDN webengine.

SuppressExceptions

SuppressExceptions As Short

This property can intercept exceptions. When set to 1, exceptions will never occur. You must then check **LastError** to get the error code of the last method or property invocation.

TeethLowerVisible

TeethLowerVisible As Short

This property sets extent to which the lower teeth are visible. This is a linear range from 0xFF for the maximum extent, so the lower teeth and gums are completely exposed, to 0x00 for the minimum, so the lower teeth are completely hidden. If this member is 0x80, only the teeth are visible.

TeethUpperVisible

TeethUpperVisible As Short

This property sets extent to which the upper teeth are visible. This is a linear range from 0xFF for the maximum extent, so that upper teeth and gums are completely exposed, to 0x00 for the minimum, so the upper teeth are completely hidden. If this member is 0x80, only the teeth are visible.

TonguePosn

TonguePosn As Short

This property sets tongue position. This is a linear range from 0xFF if the tongue is against the upper teeth, to 0x00 if it is relaxed. If this member is 0x80, the tongue is visible.

TTSMode

TTSMode As String

This property sets the GUID of the current text-to-speech mode for a Voice Text engine. A text-to-speech engine typically provides an assortment of text-to-speech modes that can be used to play speech in different voices.

A.3.2   Methods

The Windows SAPI ActiveX Visual Basic **Voice Text** control has the following methods:

- AboutDlg
- FastForward
- GeneralDlg
- LexiconDlg
- Pause
- Resume
- Rewind
- Select
- Speak
- StopSpeaking
- TranslateDlg

AboutDlg

AboutDlg(hWnd As Long, title As String)

This method displays an About dialog box that identifies the text-to-speech engine and contains the copyright notice.

FastForward

FastForward()

This method advances audio playback by approximately one sentence or phrase. Voice text determines the beginning of a sentence or phrase by checking for terminal punctuation, such as a period or comma, at the end of the preceding sentence or phrase. **AudioFastForward** works better for some kinds of text than others—for example, prose with conventional punctuation rather than spreadsheet data. If less than a sentence remains in the playback queue, **AudioFastForward** jumps to the end of the playback queue and stops playing.

GeneralDlg

GeneralDlg(hWnd As Long, title As String)

This method displays a General dialog box that gives the user general control of the text-to-speech engine. The dialog box may also include controls that allow the user to open other dialog boxes provided by the engine.

LexiconDlg

LexiconDlg(hWnd As Long, title As String)

This method displays a Lexicon dialog box that allows the user to view and edit the pronunciation lexicon. For example, the user can edit the phonetics of mispronounced words so that the engine pronounces them properly.

Pause

Pause()

This method pauses text-to-speech output for a Voice Text command. **AudioPause** affects all applications using the engine, so the application should resume audio as soon as possible. When a Voice Text object is first created, text-to-speech output is not paused. Because pausing text-to-speech output affects all applications that use voice text on the engine, an application should resume text-to-speech output as soon as possible by calling the **Resume** method. When output has been paused, the **IsSpeaking** property is FALSE (0), even though the Voice Text object still has data available in its queue and has not yet sent a **SpeakingDone** event. No notifications are sent when audio is paused or resumed.

Resume

Resume()

This method resumes text-to-speech output after it has been paused by the **Pause** method. **Resume** affects all applications using the engine.

Rewind

Rewind()

This method backs up audio playback by approximately one sentence or phrase. Depending on the length of a passage of text, it may not be possible to rewind to the beginning of the passage. The Voice Text object caches only a few paragraphs of text, and **Rewind** cannot back up past the beginning of the cache. If **Rewind** is called at the beginning of the cache, audio begins playing at the first sentence in the cache. If **Rewind** is called after the end of a text stream has been reached, the audio begins playing again at approximately the last sentence in the stream. If no text is playing, **Rewind** returns NOERROR, but does nothing. To determine whether text is playing, an application can use the **IsSpeaking** property.

Select

Select(index As Long)

This method selects text-to-speech engine which **Speak** will use.

Speak

Speak(text As String)

This method starts playing the specified text, using the globally selected voice. If an application calls **Speak** when other text is being played, the specified text is added to the end of the playback queue. Calling **Speak** affects all applications using voice text on the engine, because all applications share the same playback queue.

StopSpeaking

StopSpeaking()

This method halts text that is currently being spoken and flushes all pending text from the playback queue. Calling **StopSpeaking** affects all applications using voice text on the engine, because all applications share the same playback queue.

TranslateDlg

TranslateDlg(hWnd As Long, title As String)

This method displays a Translation dialog box that allows the user to control symbols, currencies, abbreviations, and number-translation techniques, such as whether to speak "34" as "thirty-four," "three four," or the old English "four and thirty." This dialog box also allows the user to control the translation of abbreviations and case sensitivity, and to manage how both affect the prosody of spoken text.

A.3.3   Events

The Windows SAPI ActiveX Visual Basic **Voice Text** control can receive the following events:

- **AttribChanged**
- **ClickIn**
- **Speak**
- **SpeakingDone**
- **SpeakingStarted**
- **Visual**

AttribChanged

AttribChanged(attrib As Long)

This event occurs when a process has changed an attribute of the engine.

ClickIn

ClickIn(x As Long, y As Long)

This event occurs when the user clicks on a speech object icon.

Speak

Speak(Text As String, App As String, thetype As Long)

This event occurs when an application has added text to the playback queue for the speech engine. Return value is ignored.

SpeakingDone

SpeakingDone()

This event occurs when speaking is finished and no text remains in the playback queue.

SpeakingStarted

> *SpeakingStarted()*

This event occurs when the speaking has actually started.

Visual

> *Visual(Phoneme As Short, EnginePhoneme As Short, hints As Long, MouthHeight As Short, bMouthWidth As Short, bMouthUpturn As Short, bJawOpen As Short, TeethUpperVisible As Short, TeethLowerVisible As Short, TonguePosn As Short, LipTension As Short)*

This event notifies all applications on a Voice Text engine about the phoneme that is currently being spoken. Called whenever the shape of the mouth should change. This allows users to implement their own mouths. This event may or may not be supported by an engine. An application can use the information returned by **Visual** to synchronize character animation with spoken text.

A.4   Voice Telephony Control

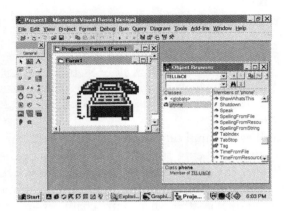

A.4.1   Properties

The Windows SAPI ActiveX Visual Basic **Voice Telephony** control has the following properties:

- AnswerAfterRings
- Initialized
- MaxLines

AnswerAfterRings

AnswerAfterRings As Long

This property sets the number of rings before the server picks up the phone.

Initialized

Initialized As Long

This property equals 1 if the control has been initialized, 0 if not. The user can force the control to initialize by setting this to 1. Use of most other Windows SAPI ActiveX methods and properties will automatically cause the control to initialize, if it hasn't been initialized already.

MaxLines

MaxLines As Long

This property sets maximum number of telephone lines that can be connected to the speech application server at one time.

A.4.2   Methods

The Windows SAPI ActiveX Visual Basic **Voice Telephony** control provides the following methods:

- CallDialog
- ChooseEngineDialog
- DateFromFile
- DateFromResource
- DateFromString
- DWORDGet
- DWORDSet
- ExtensionFromFile
- ExtensionFromResource
- ExtensionFromString
- FreeWave
- GrammarFromFile
- GrammarFromResource
- GrammarFromString
- PhoneFromFile
- PhoneFromResource
- PhoneFromString
- RecordFromFile
- RecordFromResource
- RecordFromString
- SendAbort
- SendDTMF
- SendDTMFToLine
- Speak
- TimeFromFile
- TimeFromResource
- TimeFromString
- WaveAddFromListFile

- WaveAddFromListResource
- WaveAddFromListString
- WaveAddFromMemory
- YesNoFromFile
- YesNoFromResource

CallDialog

CallDialog()

This method starts the server listening to all the phone lines. It also brings up a dialog box so an administrator can stop the application or monitor which lines are in use. **CallDialog** does not return until the administrator presses the "Stop Monitoring" button on the dialog.

ChooseEngineDialog

ChooseEngineDialog()

This method brings up a dialog box so an administrator can specify what speech recognition and text-to-speech engine to use.

DateFromFile

DateFromFile(lineID As Long, File As String, result As Long, parse As String)

This method loads a Date control from a file (erasing the old control) and starts the telephony control speaking and recognizing.

DateFromResource

DateFromResource(lineID As Long, instance As Long, resID As Long, result As Long, parse As String)

This method loads a Date control from a resource object, erasing the old control, and starts the telephony control speaking and recognizing.

DateFromString

DateFromString(lineID As Long, Grammar As String, result As Long, parse As String)

This method loads a Date control from a string, erasing the old control, and starts the telephony control speaking and recognizing.

DWORDGet

DWORDGet(lineID As Long, guid As String, data As Long)

This method gets a DWORD value. Before you can call **DWORDGet**, the DWORD value must be set with **DWORDSet**.

DWORDSet

DWORDSet(lineID As Long, guid As String, data As Long)

This method sets a DWORD value. If a value already exists, the old value is overwritten.

ExtensionFromFile

ExtensionFromFile(lineID As Long, File As String, result As Long, parse As String)

This method loads an Extension control from a file, erasing the old control, and starts the telephony control speaking and recognizing.

ExtensionFromResource

ExtensionFromResource(lineID As Long, instance As Long, resID As Long, result As Long, parse As String)

This method loads an Extension control from a resource and starts the telephony control speaking and recognizing.

ExtensionFromString

ExtensionFromString(lineID As Long, Grammar As String, result As Long, parse As String)

This method loads an Extension control from a string and starts the telephony control speaking and recognizing.

FreeWave

FreeWave(wave As Long)

This method frees memory containing data from a wave file.

GrammarFromFile

GrammarFromFile(lineID As Long, File As String, result As Long, parse As String)

This method loads an Application-Defined Grammar control from a file and starts the telephony control speaking and recognizing.

GrammarFromResource

GrammarFromResource(lineID As Long, instance As Long, resID As Long, result As Long, parse As String)

This method loads an Application-Defined Grammar control from a resourceand starts the telephony control engine speaking and recognizing.

GrammarFromString

GrammarFromString(lineID As Long, Grammar As String, result As Long, parse As String)

This method loads an Application-Defined Grammar control from a string and starts the telephony control engine speaking and recognizing.

PhoneFromFile

PhoneFromFile(lineID As Long, File As String, result As Long, parse As String)

This method loads a Phone Number control from a file and starts the telephony control speaking and recognizing. It returns the results in the *result* and *parse* parameters.

PhoneFromResource

PhoneFromResource(lineID As Long, instance As Long, resID As Long, result As Long, parse As String)

This method loads a Phone Number control from a resource and starts the telephony control speaking and recognizing. It returns the results in the *result* and *parse* parameters.

PhoneFromString

PhoneFromString(lineID As Long, Grammar As String, result As Long, parse As String)

This method loads a Phone Number control from a string and starts the telephony control speaking and recognizing. Returns the results in the *result* and *parse* parameters.

RecordFromFile

RecordFromFile(lineID As Long, File As String, result As Long, wave As Long, size As Long)

This method loads a Digital Audio control from a file and starts the telephony control speaking and recognizing.

RecordFromResource

RecordFromResource(lineID As Long, instance As Long, resID As Long, result As Long, wave As Long, size As Long)

This method loads a Digital Audio control from a resource and starts the telephony control speaking and recognizing.

RecordFromString

RecordFromString(lineID As Long, Grammar As String, result As Long, wave As Long, size As Long)

This method Loads a Digital Audio control from a string and starts the telephony control speaking and recognizing.

SendAbort

SendAbort(lineID As Long, val As Long)

This method sends an abort message to the currently running telephony control. An application should call **SendAbort** when the caller hangs up.

SendDTMF

SendDTMF(lineID As Long, DTMF As Long)

This method sends a DTMF to the currently running telephony control so the control can react to it.

SendDTMFToLine

SendDTMFToLine(lineID As Long, digits As String, duration As Long)

This method sends DTMF over a TAPI device. It does not work in the emulator.

Speak

Speak(lineID As Long, text As String)

This method adds text to be spoken onto the queue. It may start speaking right away. If the *text* parameter matches one of the strings already used for **WaveAddFromListFile, WaveAddFromListResource, WaveAddFromListString,** or **WaveAddFromMemory**, then a digital audio recording will be played/queued instead.

TimeFromFile

TimeFromFile(lineID As Long, File As String, result As Long, parse As String)

This method loads a Time control from a file and starts the telephony control speaking and recognizing. It returns the results in the *result* and *parse* parameters.

TimeFromResource

TimeFromResource(lineID As Long, instance As Long, resID As Long, result As Long, parse As String)

This method loads a Time control from a resource and starts the telephony control speaking and recognizing. It returns the results in the *result* and *parse* parameters.

TimeFromString

TimeFromString(lineID As Long, Grammar As String, result As Long, parse As String)

This method loads a Time control from a string and starts the telephony control speaking and recognizing. It returns the results in the *result* and *parse* parameters.

WaveAddFromListFile

WaveAddFromListFile(lineID As Long, filename As String)

This method adds one or more digital audio recordings to the list of recordings usable by the control. If the *text* string parameter in the **Speak** method matches a speak string in the file, then the recording will be played instead of text-to-speech. If the speak string is already in use, then the old recording is closed and replaced by the new one.

WaveAddFromListResource

WaveAddFromListResource(lineID As Long, hInstance As Long, resID As Long)

This method adds one or more digital audio recordings to the list of recordings usable by the control. If the *text* string parameter in the **Speak** method matches a speak string in the resource, then the recording will be played instead of text-to-speech. If the speak string is already in use, then the old recording is closed and replaced by the new one.

WaveAddFromListString

WaveAddFromListString(lineID As Long, liststring As String)

This method adds one or more digital audio recordings to the list of recordings usable by the control. If the *text* string parameter in the **Speak** method matches a speak string in the *liststring*, then the recording will be played instead of text-to-speech. If the speak string is already in use, then the old recording is closed and replaced by the new one.

WaveAddFromMemory

WaveAddFromMemory(lineID As Long, replace As String, wave As Long, wavesize As Long)

This method adds a digital audio recording to the list of recordings usable by the control. If the *text* string parameter in the **Speak** method matches the *replace* string parameter in the **WaveAddFromMemory** method, then the recording will be played instead of text-to-speech. If *replace* string is already in use, then the old recording is closed and replaced by the new one.

YesNoFromFile

YesNoFromFile(lineID As Long, File As String, result As Long, parse As String)

This method loads a Yes/No control from a file and starts the telephony control speaking and recognizing.

YesNoFromResource

YesNoFromResource(lineID As Long, instance as long, resID As Long, result As Long, parse As String)

This method loads a Yes/No control from a resource object and starts the telephony control speaking and recognizing.

YesNoFromString

YesNoFromString(lineID As Long, Grammar As String, result As Long, parse As String)

This method loads a Yes/No control from a string and starts the telephony control speaking and recognizing.

A.4.3   Events

The Windows SAPI ActiveX Visual Basic **Voice Telephony** control can receive the following events:

- ClickIn
- DoPhoneCall
- Initialize
- Shutdown

ClickIn

ClickIn(x As Long, y As Long)

This event occurs when the user clicks in the object's icon.

DoPhoneCall

DoPhoneCall(lineID As Long)

When a phone call comes into the line, the Voice Telephony control takes the line off hook and then sends a **DoPhoneCall** event. When the **DoPhoneCall** call-back returns, the Voice Telephony control hangs up the line and monitors to see if any new phone calls come in. The application must handle **DoPhoneCall** events. It needs to be a synchronous routine that lasts the duration of the phone call.

Initialize

Initialize(lineID As Long)

When an application sets the **Initialize** property, one thread will be created for each telephone line on the system. The **Initialize** event will be sent during thread initialization. An application should do its line initialization code in the **Initialize** event. The specifics will depend upon the application

*Note for Visual Basic 5 developers: The Visual Basic 5 debugger cannot debug multi-threaded applications, so while using the debugger, you will not be able to set a property or call a method during an **Initialize** event.*

Shutdown

Shutdown(lineID As Long)

A **Shutdown** event is sent just before a line-specific thread is destroyed. The application should free up all line-specific telephony speech server data here.

*Note for Visual Basic 5 developers: The Visual Basic 5 debugger cannot debug multi-threaded applications, so while using the debugger, you will not be able to set a property or call a method during a **Shutdown** event.*

A.5   Direct Speech Recognition Control

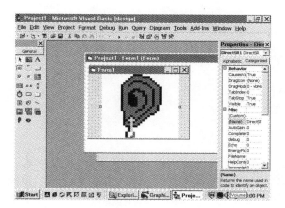

A.5.1   Properties

The Windows SAPI ActiveX Visual Basic **Direct Speech Recognition** control
provides the following properties:

- AutoGain
- CompleteTimeOut
- CountEngines
- CreateResultsObject
- Dialect
- Echo
- EnergyFloor
- EngineFeatures
- EngineID
- Features
- FileName
- Find
- FindEngine
- FlagsGet

- GetPhraseScore
- Grammars
- hWnd
- Identify
- IncompleteTimeOut
- Initialized
- Interfaces
- LanguageID
- LastError
- LastHeard
- MaxAutoGain
- MaxCompleteTimeOut
- MaxEnergyFloor
- MaxIncompleteTimeOut
- MaxRealTime
- MaxThreshold
- MaxWordsState
- MaxWordsVocab
- MfgName
- Microphone
- MinAutoGain
- MinCompleteTimeOut
- MinEnergyFloor
- MinIncompleteTimeOut
- MinRealTime
- MinThreshold
- ModeID
- ModeName
- Phrase
- ProductName
- RealTime

- ReEvaluate
- Sequencing
- Speaker
- SRMode
- SuppressExceptions
- Threshold
- Wave

AutoGain

AutoGain As Long

This property sets the state of the automatic gain for the incoming audio stream. A value of 0 indicates that automatic gain is disabled. A value of 100 indicates that the speech recognition engine always adjusts the gain, so that if the next utterance is spoken at the same level, the gain is set perfectly. A value between 0 and 100 moderates the automatic adjustments on a linear scale. For example, a **pdwAudioGain** value of 50 adjusts the gain to half the extent that the engine otherwise would. When automatic gain is enabled, the speech recognition engine may adjust the level at the end of an utterance and increase or decrease the gain.

CompleteTimeOut

CompleteTimeOut As Long

This property sets the number of milliseconds that the speech recognition engine waits before regarding a phrase as complete after the user has stopped speaking. For example, if **CompleteTimeOut** is 500, a user speaking "Send mail to Fred" would see results 0.5 seconds after finishing the phrase. An application can specify **MinCompleteTimeOut** or **MaxCompleteTimeOut** for minimum or maximum allowable values. **CompleteTimeOut** should be shorter than **TimeoutIncomplete**.

CountEngines

CountEngines As Long

This property sets number of recognition engines available. This is the highest number that can be used as an index to indexed properties and methods.

CreateResultsObject

CreateResultsObject(results As Long) As Long

This property sets substantiates the results value passed into **PhraseFinish** into a new referenced useable object. You must use this property to get a value to pass into functions which require results passed in.

Dialect

Dialect(index as integer) As String

This property sets dialect specific to the language—for example, "Texas" or "New York City." This member can be "Standard" for the standard dialect used by the television and radio news media.

Echo

Echo As Long

This property sets the state of echo canceling on the incoming audio stream. TRUE turns on echo canceling, FALSE turns it off. When **Echo** is TRUE, the engine typically ignores low-level audio signals. The state of echo canceling indicates whether the signal should be treated as though it has residual signal on it. In general, echo canceling causes the speech recognition engine to ignore low-level audio signals so that it doesn't attempt to recognize the residual signal of the echo cancellation.

EnergyFloor

EnergyFloor As Long

This property sets the value of the noise floor, in negative decibels. For example, a value of 30 indicates an energy floor of-30 dB. The noise floor is the noise value in the signal-to-noise ratio (SNR) for a particular environment. In general, the higher the noise value in the ratio, the more sensitive the speech recognition engine is to background noise. For example, a quiet office would have a high SNR (low floor), whereas a noisy factory would have a low SNR (high floor). An application might send this value to a speech recognition engine if it has information about the SNR to expect from the audio stream. The engine can use the value internally to adjust its calculated noise floor in expectation of the audio stream's SNR.

EngineFeatures

EngineFeatures(index as integer) As Long

This property sets features that are specific to the engine. These values are normally defined by the speech engine author.

EngineID

EngineID(index as integer) As String

GUID that identifies the engine.

This property sets GUID for the speech engine. It is possible for more than one mode to have the same engine identifier. In this case, the engine is capable of recognizing the different languages or voices of the modes.

Features

Features(index as integer) As Long

This property sets features that are available with the current active speech engine.

FileName

FileName As String

This property sets initializes using the default file-input audio source object, where the input file has the name set to **FileName.** Set to "" to go back to the default wave device.

Find

Find(RankList As String) As Long

This property sets returns the index of an engine which most closely matches the input parameter list, ranked in order.

FindEngine

FindEngine(EngineId As String, MfgName As String, ProductName As String, ModeID As String, ModeName As String, LanguageID As Long, dialect As String, Sequencing As Long, MaxWordsVocab As Long, MaxWordsState As Long, Grammars As Long, Features As Long, Interfaces As Long, EngineFeatures As Long, RankEngineID As Long, RankMfgName As Long, RankProductName As Long, RankModeID As Long, RankModeName As Long, RankLanguage As Long, RankDialect As Long, RankSequencing As Long, RankMaxWordsVocab As Long, RankMaxWordsState As Long, RankGrammars As Long, RankFeatures As Long, RankInterfaces As Long, RankEngineFeatures As Long) As Long

This property sets returns the index of an engine which most closely matches the input parameters and rankings. To ignore a field, set it to zero. Rank numbers are integers, 1 means lowest priority, 2 means next and so on.

FlagsGet

FlagsGet(results As Long, rank As Long) As Long

This property gets results flags on the results object created with **CreateResultsObject**.

GetPhraseScore

GetPhraseScore(results As Long, rank As Long) As Long

This property returns the score (from-100 to 100) of the recognized phrase or alternative phrases.

Grammars

Grammars(index as integer) As Long

This property sets types of grammar supported by the engine.

hWnd

hWnd As Long

This property sets Window handle.

Identify

Identify(results As Long) As String

This property sets a unique identifier for the results object so that an application can identify the results object at a later point. Each engine provides its own mechanism for generating a results identifier, probably incorporating the timestamps returned by the **TimeGet** method and some other differentiator, such as the time as specified in a Win32 FILETIME structure when the results object was generated.

IncompleteTimeOut

IncompleteTimeOut As Long

This property sets the number of milliseconds that the speech recognition engine waits before discarding an incomplete phrase because the user has stopped speaking.

Initialized

Initialized As Short

This property sets equals 1 if the control has been initialized, 0 if not. Use of most other Windows SAPI ActiveX methods and properties will automatically cause the control to initialize, if it hasn't been initialized already.

Interfaces

Interfaces(index as integer) As Long

This property sets the **Interfaces** that are supported.

LanguageID

LanguageID(index as integer) As Long

This property sets the language identifier as specified for the Win32 API. Bits 0 through 9 identify the primary language, such as English, French, Spanish, and so on. Bits 10 through 15 indicate the sublanguage, which is essentially a locale setting. For example, Portuguese has two sublanguages, Brazilian and Standard. For a list of primary and sublanguage identifiers, see the documentation for the MAKELANGID macro in the Win32 SDK. Language ID codes are limited to the Windows 32 definition of LANGID. Dialect strings can be anything.

LastError

LastError As Long

This property sets result code from the last method or property invocation.

LastHeard

LastHeard As String

This property is only semi-reliable because of lack of synchronization, this property stores the value of the last phrase heard. This property exists solely to enable limited recognition to containers that do not support the method syntax.

MaxAutoGain

MaxAutoGain As Long

This property sets maximum legal value for **AutoGain**.

MaxCompleteTimeOut

MaxCompleteTimeOut As Long

This property sets maximum legal value for **CompleteTimeOut**.

MaxEnergyFloor

MaxEnergyFloor As Long

This property sets maximum value for **EnergyFloor**.

MaxIncompleteTimeOut

MaxIncompleteTimeOut As Long

This property sets maximum legal value for **IncompleteTimeOut.**

MaxRealTime

MaxRealTime As Long

This property sets maximum value for **RealTime.**

MaxThreshold

MaxThreshold As Long

This property sets maximum legal value for **Threshold.**

MaxWordsState

MaxWordsState(index as integer) As Long

This property sets maximum number of words in any state of a grammar.

MaxWordsVocab

MaxWordsVocab(index as integer) As Long

This property sets maximum number of words allowed in an active vocabulary at any time.

MfgName

MfgName(index as integer) As String

This property sets name of the manufacturer—for example, "Qualimatic Software Corp."

Microphone

Microphone As String

This property sets the name of the current microphone for this audio source. If the property is an empty string, the current microphone is unknown.

MinAutoGain

MinAutoGain As Long

This property sets minimum legal value for **AutoGain.**

MinCompleteTimeOut

MinCompleteTimeOut As Long

This property sets minimum legal value for **CompleteTimeOut.**

MinEnergyFloor

MinEnergyFloor As Long

This property sets minimum value for **EnergyFloor**.

MinIncompleteTimeOut

MinIncompleteTimeOut As Long

This property sets minimum legal value for **IncompleteTimeOut**.

MinRealTime

MinRealTime As Long

This property sets minimum value for **RealTime**.

MinThreshold

MinThreshold As Long

This property sets minimum legal value for **Threshold**.

ModeID

ModeID(index as integer) As String

This property sets GUID that identifies the mode. These numbers are guaranteed to be unique by the Windows operating system, so it is not necessary for the application to monitor and record them. In addition, because GUID is not stored or used directly by OLE, it is not necessary to load it into the registry.

ModeName

ModeName(index as integer) As String

This property sets name of the recognition mode—for example, "Very Noisy Classroom."

Phrase

Phrase(result As Long, rank As Long) As String

This property returns the n'th ranked best match for a results object created with **CreateResultsObject**. This allows the application to examine alternatives for each recognition. An error is returned if the rank is out of bounds.

ProductName

ProductName(index as integer) As String

This property sets name of the product—for example, "US Dept. of Education's Multi-Lingual Classroom (MLC)."

RealTime

RealTime As Long

This property sets the real-time setting for the engine. The real-time setting is the percentage of processor time that the engine expects to use during constant speech. This value can be more than 100 for non-real-time applications, for example, transcribing prerecorded speech. For most engines, the amount of processor time required diminishes markedly during periods of silence. For example, if *RealTime* is 100, the engine takes one full minute of processor time to process one minute of speech. If *RealTime* is 50, the engine takes 30 seconds of processor time to process the same minute of speech. This value is difficult to compute precisely, so it should be regarded as an estimate.

ReEvaluate

ReEvaluate(results As Long) As Boolean

This property causes a speech recognition engine to reevaluate the recognition result represented by the results object created by **CreateResultsObject**. Reevaluating a recognition allows the engine to take advantage of new knowledge that it has recently acquired. Typically, **ReEvaluate** is used for dictation in which the application has the speaker do a speaking pass followed by a correction pass.

Sequencing

Sequencing(index as integer) As Long

This property sets recognition scheme.

Speaker

Speaker As String

This property sets the name of the current speaker for an audio source. If it is a new name, the engine creates a new speaker profile. If the speaker is unknown, **Speaker** can be an empty string. The string is case insensitive.

SRMode

SRMode As Long

This property sets the current speech recognition mode. An engine typically provides an assortment of modes that can be used to recognize speech in different languages, dialects, and audio-sampling rates. If two (or more) Direct Speech Recognition objects select the same engine, each object will load its own copy of the engine into memory. To share an engine, set the **SRMode** property of one object to **SRMode** property of the other.

SuppressExceptions

SuppressExceptions As Short

With this property, when set to 1, exceptions will never occur. You must check the **LastError** property to get the error code of the last method or property invocation.

Threshold

Threshold As Long

This property sets the threshold level for a speech recognition engine. The higher the value, the more certain the recognizer must be before passing down a recognized phase rather than unrecognized. If the value is out of range for the engine, an error is returned and the attribute is not changed.

Wave

Wave(result As Long) As Long

This property returns a handle to the audio for a results object that was created with **CreateResultsObject**.

A.5.2 Methods

The Windows SAPI ActiveX Visual Basic **Direct Speech Recognition** control supports the following methods:

- **AboutDlg**
- **Activate**
- **ActivateAndAssignWindow**
- **Archive**
- **Correction**
- **Deactivate**
- **DeleteArchive**
- **DestroyResultsObject**
- **GeneralDlg**
- **GrammarDataSet**
- **GrammarFromFile**
- **GrammarFromMemory**
- **GrammarFromResource**

- GrammarFromStream
- GrammarFromString
- GrammarToMemory
- InitAudioSourceDirect
- InitAudioSourceObject
- LexiconDlg
- Listen
- Pause
- PosnGet
- Resume
- Select
- SelectEngine
- TimeGet
- TrainGeneralDlg
- TrainMicDlg
- Validate

AboutDlg

AboutDlg(hWnd As Long, title As String)

This method displays an About dialog box that identifies the speech recognition engine and contains the copyright notice.

Activate

Activate

This method tells the recognizer to start listening, causing the sound card/microphone to be claimed. The recognizer must be initialized and a grammar must be loaded before calling **Activate**. Many engines restrict the number and type of grammars that can be active at the same time. Typically, an engine allows many context-free grammars but only one dictation or limited-domain grammar to be active at a time. Because speaking is asynchronous, changes to the active grammar must be made before the speaker begins to speak. Changing the active grammar during speech may not have any effect until after the utterance ends. In addition, the engine may respond as if it has activated a grammar and postpone its real activation until an opportune time, such as when an utterance stops. If any rule in a grammar has the auto-pause flag set, and the grammar has at least one rule active, the pause count is increased by 1 after a **PhraseFinish** event. If multiple rules have the auto-pause flag set, the pause count is still increased only by 1. Likewise, only one **Paused** event is sent, even if more than one rule has the auto-pause flag set.

ActivateAndAssignWindow

ActivateAndAssignWindow(hWnd As Long)

Because speaking is asynchronous, changes to the active grammar must be made before the speaker begins to speak. Changing the active grammar during speech may not have any effect until after the utterance ends. In addition, the engine may respond as if it has activated a grammar and postpone its real activation until an opportune time, such as when an utterance stops. If any rule in a grammar has the auto-pause flag set, and the grammar has at least one rule active, the pause count is increased by 1 after a **PhraseFinish** event. If multiple rules have the auto-pause flag set, the pause count is still increased only by 1. Likewise, only one **Paused** event is sent, even if more than one rule has the auto-pause flag set.

Archive

Archive(keepresults As Boolean, size As Long, pval As Long)

This method serializes a grammar object into memory, using a memory format that is native to the engine. The native format for the engine is stored in a data buffer. If the engine does not support a grammar standard format, **Archive** returns an error.

Correction

Correction(results As Long, phrase As String, confidence As short)

This method indicates to a speech recognition engine what the speaker actually said to cause a particular recognition result.

Deactivate

Deactivate(Menu As Long)

This method tells recognizer to stop listening and release the microphone/sound card resource. If you call this and the recognizer has not yet been activated, an error is generated.

DeleteArchive

DeleteArchive(Archive As Long)

This method frees the archive from memory.

DestroyResultsObject

DestroyResultsObject(long resobj)

This method frees up all resources and unreferences a results object substantiated with **CreateResultsObject**.

GeneralDlg

GeneralDlg(hWnd As Long, title As String)

This method displays a dialog box that gives the user general control of the speech recognition engine. The dialog box may also include controls that allow the user to invoke other dialog boxes provided by the engine.

GrammarDataSet

GrammarDataSet(Data As Long, size As Long)

This method archives the speech recognition grammar by calling **Archive**. An application can then use **GrammarToMemory** to save all of the grammar data, including the archive of the speech recognition grammar.

GrammarFromFile

GrammarFromFile(FileName As String)

This method Loads a grammar from a file. It automatically initializes the speech engine if not done already.

GrammarFromMemory

GrammarFromMemory(grammar As Long, size As Long)

This method is same as **GrammarFromString**, except *grammar* is a handle to raw memory rather than an object.

GrammarFromResource

GrammarFromResource(Instance As Long, ResID As Long)

This method loads a grammar from a resource. *Instance* is the instance handle for the application with the resource, and *ResID* is the resource identifier of the SRG resource. Note that grammar resources must be UNICODE. It also automatically initializes the speech engine if not already done.

GrammarFromStream

GrammarFromStream(Stream As Long)

This method loads a grammar from a stream. It also automatically initializes a speech engine if not already done.

GrammarFromString

GrammarFromString(grammar As String)

This method loads a grammar from a string. Note that line breaks have semantic meaning in the voice recognition grammars, so you will need to use vbNewLine to add line-breaks to your grammar string. It also automatically initializes the speech engine if not already done.

GrammarToMemory

GrammarToMemory(grammar As Long, size As Long)

This method writes the grammar data to memory. If the grammar has been compiled it also writes out the compiled data, saving the application from compiling the next time. The method will write out the engine-specific grammar if that exists.

InitAudioSourceDirect

InitAudioSourceDirect(direct As Long)

This method initializes recognition with Direct sound. Direct can either be an existing direct interface, or you can pass in NULL to create a new one.

InitAudioSourceObject

InitAudioSourceObject(object As Long)

This method initializes using the input audio source object. See advanced documentation for information on Audio source objects.

LexiconDlg

LexiconDlg(hWnd As Long, title As String)

This method displays a dialog box that allows the user to view and edit his or her pronunciation lexicon. For example, the user can edit the phonetics of mispronounced words so that the engine pronounces them properly.

Listen

Listen()

This method is a synonym for Activate.

Pause

Pause()

This method pauses the speech recognition engine, incrementing the pause count. The application must call the **Resume** method after each call to the

Pause method. Pausing an engine prevents it from processing future phrases but not from identifying the beginning and ending of utterances.

PosnGet

PosnGet(hi As Long lo As Long)

This method gets the Quad Word timing for current audio stream.

Resume

Resume()

This method reduces the pause count of a paused speech recognition engine by 1. When the engine's pause count reaches 0, the engine resumes processing incoming phrases.

Select

Select(index As Long)

This method selects an engine to use and loads it into memory.

SelectEngine

SelectEngine(index As integer)

This method is a synonym for **Select**.

TimeGet

TimeGet(results As Long, beginhi As Long, beginlo As Long, endhi As Long, endlo As Long)

This method retrieves the timestamps that mark the beginning and ending of the phrase.

TrainGeneralDlg

TrainGeneralDlg(hWnd As Long, title As String)

This method displays a dialog box that allows the user to provide phonetic training, which trains the engine for a preselected set of words.

TrainMicDlg

TrainMicDlg(hWnd As Long, title As String)

This method displays a dialog box that allows the user to train the engine for a particular microphone. This dialog box should be displayed at the request of the engine or whenever the speaker wants to display it.

Validate

Validate(results As Long, confidence As Short)

This method tells the engine that the current results object created by **CreateResultsObject** is valid, and correct.

A.5.3 Events

The Windows SAPI ActiveX Visual Basic **Direct Speech Recognition** control can receive the following events:

- AttribChanged
- BookMark
- ClickIn
- Interference
- Paused
- PhraseFinish
- PhraseHypothesis
- PhraseStart
- ReEvaluate
- Sound
- Training
- UnArchive
- UtteranceBegin
- UtteranceEnd
- VUMeter

AttribChanged

AttribChanged(Attribute As Long)

This event notifies an application that an engine attribute has changed. This notification is necessary because multiple processes or applications may be using the same speech recognition engine through the speech recognition sharing object, so another application may have changed the attribute.

BookMark

BookMark(MarkID As Long)

This event occurs when the engine encounters a bookmark in the incoming audio stream.

ClickIn

ClickIn(x As Long, y As Long)

This event occurs when the user clicks in the object's icon.

Interference

Interference(beginhi As Long, beginlo As Long, endhi As Long, endlo As Long, type As Long)

This event notifies the application that the engine cannot recognize speech properly for a known reason.

Paused

Paused()

This event occurs when the recognizer is paused.

PhraseFinish

PhraseFinish(flags As Long, beginhi As Long, beginlo As Long, endhi As Long, endlo As Long, Phrase As String, parsed As String, results As Long)

This event occurs when the speaker has finished a phrase and the speech recognition engine is certain about the words that were spoken. Beginhi/lo and Endhi/lo form quadwords which denote the start and end times of the utterance.

PhraseHypothesis

PhraseHypothesis(flags As Long, beginhi As Long, beginlo As Long, endhi As Long, endlo As Long, Phrase As String, Results As Long)

This event occurs when the engine has a hypothesis about what was said over the past few seconds but will not commit to a recognition.

PhraseStart

PhraseStart(hi As Long, lo As Long)

This event occurs when the engine has started processing audio data for a recognition result. *Hi* and *lo* form a quadword for the time it started.

ReEvaluate

ReEvaluate(Result As Long)

This event occurs when the engine changes a speech recognition results object as a consequence of the engine's background processing, rather than an explicit **ReEvaluate** call by the application. The application can use the information returned by the results object to determine the text to which it applies. The application does not have to use the **ReEvaluate** property to obtain the new information.

Sound

Sound(beginhi As Long, beginlo As Long, endhi As Long, endlo As Long)

This event notifies the application that the engine detected an unrecognizable sound or a very garbled word. The engine determines how long to wait before sending this event.

Training

Training(train As Long)

This event occurs when the engine requires training for the current speaker, the current grammar, or the current microphone. The application must then call the appropriate training dialog box for the engine.

UnArchive

UnArchive(result As Long)

This event occurs when a speech recognition results object that was archived with a grammar has been loaded along with the grammar. The application receives an **UnArchive** event for each speech recognition results object in existence when the grammar was archived. The unique identifier of the results object is maintained, so the application can tell which results object belongs to which text. An application can keep a results object for later reference, although the object can consume large amounts of memory.

UtteranceBegin

UtteranceBegin(beginhi As Long, beginlo As Long)

This event notifies the application that the engine has detected the beginning of an utterance or sound. Detecting the beginning of an utterance doesn't necessarily have any bearing on the recognition of words or the completion of a phrase. Because a call to **UtteranceBegin** implicitly signals the end of the silence, an application can use this function to detect long periods of silence and react accordingly.

UtteranceEnd

UtteranceEnd(beginhi As Long, beginlo As Long, endhi As Long, endlo As Long)

This event notifies the application that an utterance has ended. The engine sends this event 0.25 to 0.5 seconds after speech stops. Because a call to **UtteranceEnd** implicitly signals the beginning of silence, an application can use this function to detect long periods of silence and react accordingly.

VUMeter

VUMeter(beginhi As Long, beginlo As Long, level As Long)

This event notifies the application of the current VU level, which indicates the loudness of the digital-audio stream. The VU level returned by this function is only a rough estimate used to display a visual indicator on the screen. Depending on availability of resources, the engine usually sends this event about eight times per second.

A.6 Direct Speech Synthesis Control

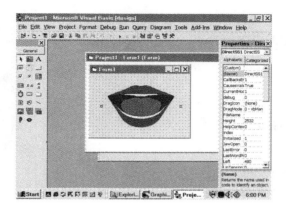

A.6.1 Properties

The Windows SAPI ActiveX Visual Basic **Direct Speech Synthesis** control provides the following properties:

- Age
- CallBacksEnabled
- CountEngines
- CurrentMode
- Dialect
- EngineFeatures
- EngineID
- Features
- FileName
- Find
- FindEngine
- Gender
- hWnd
- Initialized

- Interfaces
- JawOpen
- LanguageID
- LastError
- LastWordPosition
- LipTension
- LipType
- MaxPitch
- MaxRealTime
- MaxSpeed
- MaxVolumeLeft
- MaxVolumeRight
- MfgName
- MinPitch
- MinRealTime
- MinSpeed
- MinVolumeLeft
- MinVolumeRight
- ModeID
- ModeName
- MouthEnabled
- MouthHeight
- MouthUpturn
- MouthWidth
- Phonemes
- Pitch
- ProductName
- RealTime
- Sayit
- Speaker
- Speaking

- Speed
- Style
- SuppressExceptions
- Tagged
- TeethLowerVisible
- TeethUpperVisible
- TonguePosn
- VolumeLeft
- VolumeRight

Age

Age(index As Long) As Long

This property sets age of the voice. This property can be one of any valid human age.

CallBacksEnabled

CallBacksEnabled As Short

When **CallBacksEnabled** is set to 0, the control is disabled.

CountEngines

CountEngines As Long

This property sets number of speech synthesis voices installed on this computer. This is the highest number that can be used as an index to indexed properties and methods.

CurrentMode

CurrentMode As Long

This property sets the index for the currently selected voice, as passed into the various engine information calls and properties.

Dialect

Dialect(index As Long) As String

This property sets the dialect specific to the language—for example, "Texas" or "New York City." This property can be "Standard" or its localized equivalent for the standard dialect used by the television and radio news media for any region.

EngineFeatures

EngineFeatures(index As Long) As Long

This property sets features specific to a particular engine. These values are defined by the engine author.

EngineID

EngineID(index As Long) As String

This property sets the Globally Unique IDentifier (GUID) that uniquely identifies the engine. The GUID can be generated randomly using GUID-GEN.EXE, which is provided with the OLE Software Development Kit (SDK). It is possible for more than one mode to have the same engine identifier. In this case, with this particular Windows SAPI ActiveX control, the engine is capable of speaking the different languages or voices of specific modes.

Features

Features(index As Long) As Long

This property sets Text-to-speech features that are available with the currently active speech engine.

FileName

FileName As String

This property assigns a filename, and subsequent text-to-speech is recorded in a file of this name instead of played to the wave device. To re-enable the speakers and disable recording to a file, set **FileName** to "".

Find

Find(RankList As String) As Long

This property returns the index of an engine which most closely matches the input parameter list, ranked in order.

FindEngine

FindEngine(EngineId As String, MfgName As String, ProductName As String, ModeID As String, ModeName As String, LanguageID As Long, dialect As String, Speaker As String, Style As String, Gender As Long, Age As Long, Features As Long, Interfaces As Long, EngineFeatures As Long, RankEngineID As Long, RankMfgName As Long, RankProductName As Long, RankModeID As Long, RankModeName As Long, RankLanguage As Long, RankDialect As Long, RankSpeaker As Long, RankStyle As Long, RankGender As Long, RankAge As Long, RankFeatures As Long, RankInterfaces As Long, RankEngineFeatures As Long) As Long

This property returns the index of an engine which most closely matches the input parameters and rankings.

Gender

Gender(index As Long) As Long

This property sets gender of the voice. The **Gender** property can be one of two values: 1 means female, 2 means male.

hWnd

hWnd As Long

This property sets the speech Window handle.

Initialized

Initialized As Short

This property equals 1 if the control has been initialized, 0 if not. The user can force the control to initialize by setting this to 1.

Interfaces

Interfaces(index As Long) As Long

This property defines Interfaces supported by the engine.

JawOpen

JawOpen As Short

This property sets angle to which the jaw is open. This is a linear range from 0xFF for completely open to 0x00 for completely closed.

LanguageID

LanguageID(index As Long) As Long

This property sets language identifier as specified for the Win32 API. Bits 0 through 9 identify the primary language, such as English, French, Spanish, and so on. Bits 10 through 15 indicate the sublanguage, which is essentially a locale setting. For example, Portuguese has two sublanguages, Brazilian and Standard. For a list of primary and sublanguage identifiers, see the documentation for the MAKELANGID macro in the Win32 SDK.

LastError

LastError As Long

This property sets result code from the last method or property invocation.

LastWordPosition

LastWordPosition As Long

This property sets offset, in bytes, from the beginning of the text-to-speech buffer to the word that is currently being played.

LipTension

LipTension As Short

This property sets lip tension. This is a linear range from 0xFF if the lips are very tense to 0x00 if they are completely relaxed.

LipType

LipType As Short

When set to 0, the red female lips are drawn. When set to 1, the male pink lips are drawn.

MaxPitch

MaxPitch As Long

This property sets maximum legal value for **Pitch**.

MaxRealTime

MaxRealTime As Long

This property sets maximum legal value for **RealTime**.

MaxSpeed

MaxSpeed As Long

This property sets maximum legal value for **Speed**.

MaxVolumeLeft

MaxVolumeLeft As Long

This property sets maximum legal value for **VolumeLeft**.

MaxVolumeRight

MaxVolumeRight As Long

This property sets maximum legal value for **VolumeRight**.

MfgName

MfgName(index As Long) As String

This property sets name of the manufacturer,for example, "Qualimatic Software Corp."

MinPitch

MinPitch As Long

This property sets minimum legal value for **Pitch**.

MinRealTime

MinRealTime As Long

This property sets minimum legal value for **RealTime**.

MinSpeed

MinSpeed As Long

This property sets minimum legal value for **Speed**.

MinVolumeLeft

MinVolumeLeft As Long

This property sets minimum legal value for **VolumeLeft**.

MinVolumeRight

MinVolumeRight As Long

This property sets minimum legal value for **VolumeRight**.

ModeID

ModeID(index As Long) As String

This property sets GUID that uniquely identifies the mode.

ModeName

ModeName(index As Long) As String

This property sets name of the text-to-speech mode—for example, "Qualimatic Talk-O-Matic" or "Betty Boop Voice."

MouthEnabled

MouthEnabled As Short

When **MouthEnabled** is set to 0, the mouth does not animate. To make the mouth not get drawn at all, set the visible property to False. Also, setting the control size to zero has same effect.

MouthHeight

MouthHeight As Short

This property sets height of the mouth or lips. This is a linear range from 0xFF for the maximum possible height for the mouth to 0x00 for the minimum height when the mouth or lips are closed.

MouthUpturn

MouthUpturn As Short

This property sets extent to which the mouth turns up at the corners, that is, how much it smiles. This is a linear range from 0xFF for the maximum upturn, that is, the mouth is fully smiling, to 0x00 if the corners of the mouth turn down. If this member is 0x80, the mouth is neutral.

MouthWidth

MouthWidth As Short

This property sets width of the mouth or lips. This is a linear range from 0xFF for the maximum possible width for the face to 0x00 for the minimum width when the mouth or lips are puckered.

Phonemes

Phonemes(charset As Long, flags As Long, input As String) As String

This property sets phonemic representation of the text using the specified character set. It converts text to a phonemic representation, which is an intermediate stage between Unicode text and digital-audio data.

Pitch

Pitch As Long

This property sets current baseline pitch, in hertz, for a text-to-speech mode. If the text being spoken contains text-to-speech control tags, the actual pitch of the speaking voice typically fluctuates above this baseline. The **Pit** tag changes the baseline pitch setting for the mode, the same as when the **Pitch** property is set.

ProductName

ProductName(index As Long) As String

This property sets name of the product—for example, "Qualimatic's Talk-O-Matic."

RealTime

RealTime As Long

This property sets real-time setting for the engine, which is the percentage of processor time that the engine expects to use during constant speech. The engine tries to meet the real-time expectation, but the engine will not be able to consume exactly **RealTime** percentage of the CPU.

Sayit

Sayit As String

This property sets alternative method for starting speaking. The text is spoken when Sayit is assigned to a string. This is present to support certain limited OLE containers that do not support methods, but do support properties. Generally, do not use this unless the OLE container does not support methods.

Speaker

Speaker(index As Long) As String

This property sets name of the voice, or NULL if the name is not important, in which case the speech engine default is used.

Speaking

Speaking As Short

When set to 1, the synthesizer voice is speaking. When set to 0, the synthesizer voice is not speaking.

Speed

Speed As Long

This property retrieves the current baseline average speed for a text-to-speech mode, in words per minute. When assigned to this property the new value must be between **MaxSpeed** and **MinSpeed**, otherwise an exception occurs. If the value is out of range for the engine, an error is returned and the speed is not changed.

Style

Style(index As Long) As String

This property sets personality of the voice.

SuppressExceptions

SuppressExceptions As Short

When set to 1, exceptions will never occur. You must check **LastError** to get the error code of the last method or property invocation.

Tagged

Tagged As Boolean

This property determines whether or not tags are interpreted when calls to Speak are made.

TeethLowerVisible

TeethLowerVisible As Short

This property sets extent to which the lower teeth are visible. This is a linear range from 0xFF for the maximum extent, that is, the lower teeth and gums are completely exposed, to 0x00 for the minimum, the lower teeth are completely hidden. If this member is 0x80, only the teeth are visible.

TeethUpperVisible

TeethUpperVisible As Short

This property sets extent to which the upper teeth are visible. This is a linear range from 0xFF for the maximum extent, that is, the upper teeth and gums are completely exposed, to 0x00 for the minimum, the upper teeth are completely hidden. If this member is 0x80, only the teeth are visible.

TonguePosn

TonguePosn As Short

This property sets tongue position. This a linear range from 0xFF if the tongue is against the upper teeth, to 0x00 if it is relaxed. If this member is 0x80, the tongue is visible.

VolumeLeft

VolumeLeft As Long

This property sets current baseline speaking volume for the left channel of text-to-speech mode. When assigned to this property, the new value must be between **MaxVolumeLeft** and **MinVolumeLeft**, otherwise an exception occurs and the speaking volume is not changed.

VolumeRight

VolumeRight As Long

This property sets current baseline speaking volume for the right channel of text-to-speech mode. When assigned to this property, the new value must be between **MaxVolumeRight** and **MinVolumeRight**, otherwise an exception occurs and the speaking volume is not changed.

A.6.2   Methods

The Windows SAPI ActiveX Visual Basic **Direct Speech Synthesis** control provides the following methods:

- **AboutDlg**
- **AudioPause**
- **AudioReset**
- **AudioResume**
- **GeneralDlg**
- **GetPronunciation**
- **InitAudioDestDirect**
- **InitAudioDestMM**
- **InitAudioDestObject**
- **Inject**
- **LexiconDlg**
- **PosnGet**

- **Select**
- **Speak**
- **TextData**
- **TranslateDlg**

AboutDlg

AboutDlg(hWnd As Long, title As String)

This method displays an About dialog box that identifies the text-to-speech engine and contains the copyright notice.

AudioPause

AudioPause

This method immediately pauses text-to-speech output for an engine object.When **AudioPause** is called, the engine should unclaim the device, making it available for other applications.

AudioReset

AudioReset

This method resets the digital-audio stream. It stops speech and cancels all queued requests for speech.

AudioResume

AudioResume

This method resumes text-to-speech output that has been paused. Calling **AudioResume** affects output for the current engine object only.

GeneralDlg

GeneralDlg(hWnd As Long, title As String)

This method displays a General dialog box that gives the user general control of the text-to-speech engine and gives the user full access to engine-specific controls.

GetPronunciation

GetPronunciation(CharSet As Long, Text As Long, Sense As Long, Pronounce As String, PartOfSpeech As Long, EngineInfo As String)

This method returns pronunciation information for *Text* in *Sense, Pronounce, PartOfSpeech* and *EngineInfo*.

InitAudioDestDirect

InitAudioDestDirect(direct As Long)

This method sets up a Direct Sound object As the output device. Input parameter is an index for an existing object. If null is passed in, a private one is created.

InitAudioDestMM

InitAudioDestMM(deviceid As Long)

This method sets wave device ID automatically during startup.

InitAudioDestObject

InitAudioDestObject(object As Long)

This method sets up an arbitrary object as the output device. Input parameter is an index for the object.

Inject

Inject(value As String)

This method inserts text-to-speech control tags into the text currently being spoken. If the engine understands a tag, it should act on the tag as soon as possible after receiving it.

LexiconDlg

LexiconDlg(hWnd As Long, title As String)

This method displays a Lexicon dialog box that allows the speaker to view and edit his or her pronunciation lexicon. For example, the speaker can edit the phonetics of mispronounced words and load or unload personal exception dictionaries.

PosnGet

PosnGet(hi As Long, lo As Long)

This method retrieves the exact byte in the audio stream that is currently being played as exact as possible given audio device. The **PosnGet** method works only for real-time audio destinations, such as audio speakers; it does not work for non-real-time destinations, such as files. An application can use **PosnGet** to synchronize actions with events. For example, if an action should occur a certain interval after a particular byte is played, the application can call **PosnGet** to get the time that byte was played, add the interval to the time, and synchronize the action with the result.

Select

Select(index As Long)

This method selects a text-to-speech engine which **Speak** will use. See the **FindEngine** and **CountEngines** properties for more info.

Speak

Speak(text As String)

This method causes text to speech to speak the text. By default, the Microsoft female voice is played on the wave device.

TextData

TextData(characterset As Long, flags As Long, text As String)

This method starts the process of converting text into audio data to be spoken. It is almost same As **Speak**, but lets you set more flags. An application can pass in single or multiple control tags without any real text. For best results, the *text* parameter should be a complete sentence or paragraph. If the structure contains the address of a complete sentence or paragraph, ttext-to-speech buffer that **TextData** passes to the engine for conversation to audio data will be aligned on a sentence or paragraph boundary. Initially, an engine object plays any text that is sent to it as soon as possible. To change state, you should call the **AudioPause** method. Once **AudioPause** is called, no audio is output until **AudioResume** method is called.

TranslateDlg

TranslateDlg(hWnd As Long, title As String)

This method displays a Translation dialog box that lets the user control symbols, currencies, abbreviations, and number-translation techniques, such as whether to speak "34" as "thirty-four," "three four," or the old English "four and thirty." This dialog box also allows the user to control the translation of abbreviations and case sensitivity and how both affect the prosody of spoken text.

A.6.3   Events

The Windows SAPI ActiveX Visual Basic **Direct Speech Synthesis** control can receive the following events:

- **AttribChanged**
- **AudioStart**
- **AudioStop**

- **BookMark**
- **ClickIn**
- **TextDataDone**
- **TextDataStarted**
- **Visual**
- **WordPosition**

AttribChanged

AttribChanged (which attribute As Long)

This event occurs when an engine attribute has changed. This event is sent because in future versions, multiple processes or applications may be using the same text-to-speech engine through a text-to-speech sharing object,similar to the speech recognition sharing object.

AudioStart

AudioStart(hi As Long, lo As Long)

This event occurs when audio data starts playing. Audio may not start playing until several milliseconds after a buffer is placed while the engine computes the first fraction of a second of audio. If the engine does not actually send out audio information, **AudioStart** and **AudioStop** events are still called.

AudioStop

AudioStop(hi As Long, lo As Long)

This event occurs when audio data stops playing. If the engine does not actually send out audio information the **AudioStart** and **AudioStop** events are still called.

BookMark

BookMark(hi As Long, lo As Long, MarkNum As Long)

This event occurs when the engine has encountered a bookmark in the text being played. Bookmarks come from tags in tagged text and can be placed in text by embedding the **Mrk** tag before playing the text or by using the **Inject** method to insert the tag on the fly. BookMark events are not sent if the **AudioReset** method is called.

ClickIn

ClickIn(x As Long, y As Long)

This event occurs when the user clicks in the object's icon.

TextDataDone

TextDataDone (hi As Long, lo As Long, Flags As Long)

This event occurs when the text in a particular text-to-speech buffer has been sent to the audio-destination object or the application called the **AudioReset** method. **TextDataDone** is called once per **TextData** call. If there are two consecutive buffers, such as "I am" followed by "a girl", then **TextDataDone** is called after "I am" and then another one is called after "a girl." This event is sent when the text-to-speech buffer is emptied, either by sending its data to the audio-destination object or by the application calling the **AudioReset** member function to stop sending the text and empty the buffer. The **ITTSBufNotifySink** interface is released by the engine after an pending **BookMark** or **WordPosition** events are sent. Because the event is sent after the audio finishes processing, the application may receive the event before the audio in the buffer actually finishes playing.

TextDataStarted

TextDataStarted(hi As Long, lo As Long)

This event occurs when a particular text-to-speech buffer has reached the beginning of the text-to-speech buffer queue.

Visual

Visual(timehi As Long, timelo As Long, Phoneme As Short, EnginePhoneme As Short, hints As Long, MouthHeight As Short, bMouthWidth As Short, bMouthUpturn As Short, bJawOpen As Short, TeethUpperVisible As Short, TeethLowerVisible As Short, TonguePosn As Short, LipTension As Short)

This event occurs whenever the shape of the mouth should change. It notifies an application which phoneme is being used in the current digital-audio stream. This allows users to implement and synchronize their own talking mouth animations. If an engine sends **Visual** events, it should at least send one event per phoneme transition. However, the engine may send more events if necessary. An application can also use information returned by **Visual** to synchronize character animation with spoken text.

WordPosition

WordPosition(hi As Long, low As Long, byteoffset As Long)

This event notifies the application with text of the word that is currently being played. It is also used for synchronizing of speaker animation with computer speech or trigger other events.

Appendix B

Windows Visual Basic Speech Class ID Registrations

B.1 Adding ActiveX Speech Control Registrations To Your Program

Each programming environment has a different way of accessing ActiveX controls. Each of these methods have been explained in detail earlier in this book for all of the major Windows speech recognition programming environments that are compatible with Microsoft Windows SAPI 4.0, but are summarized again briefly for quick reference.

Each of these methods are basically the same for all Visual Basic 6 versus all Internet Web page programming using Visual Basic Script or Java Script. Both require that all of the SAPI ActiveX or DirectX controls have been loaded to Visual Basic IDE platform creating or modifying your Windows speech applications.

It is also required that the controls be fully registered to the Windows installation for each user PC that will run the Windows speech applications software that you develop or modify using Visual Basic and Windows Speech API, and referenced per SAPI 4.0 standards.

B.2   Visual Basic SAPI ActiveX Speech Control Installation and Registration

The simplest technique is to always follow these simple steps:

1. 'Right-click' on toolbar in Visual Basic IDE and select 'Components…' from the popup menu.

2. Check the Visual Basic SAPI ActiveX controls you want to use, then press OK.

3. Add control to a form by clicks on SAPI ActiveX control you want, then drag and drop onto the form.

4. Pull the controls to any shape or size on the form that you desire, it will never be seen to the user.

5. Select the object by clicking on it and you will see its properties in the 'Properties' window.

6. Note the '(name)' property, as it will be name you use to reference control inside Visual Basic code.

You can change this name to any descriptive name that you want, but must reference it with that name from then on in all code objects that refer back to your new object as referenced on your Visual Basic speech program form.

For example, if you wanted to create a simple SAPI Visual Basic speech recognition programming application that just says "hello world" when the program first starts, simply create a new project and follow the steps above to add a 'Microsoft Voice Text' control to Form1.

Next, add the follow code, assuming the name of the control as you have defined it in the NAME property is defaulted to 'TextToSpeech1':

```
Private Sub Form_Load()
TextToSpeech1.Speak "hello world"
End Sub
```

B.3   Web Page Visual Basic Script and Java Script References

There are several tools that create web pages and allow you to insert ActiveX as well as DirectX controls, including Windows SAPI controls for VB Script and JavaScript enabled web pages.

Each of these works differently, so you will have to read your own web page creation documentation on how to insert ActiveX and DirectX controls. You can just as easily use MS Notepad to add a control however, or MS Front Page Editor.

All you have to do is add the following tag reference to your HTML or other web script mark-up language code:

```
<object NAME="DirectVoice" TYPE="application/x-oleobject"
    CLASSID="clsid:EEE78591-FE22-11D0-8BEF-0060081841DE">
</object>
```

This particular example creates an instance of the Direct Speech Synthesis control.

You can specify any of the 6 SAPI ActiveX 4.0 controls, or even one of 2 DirectX 8.0 speech controls as you wish.

The SAPI ActiveX control that you wish to use as it is appropriate for either speech synthesis or speech recognition can both be handled it you have the proper input microphone or output speaker controls, or both, as required by your application, and this always coded in the 'NAME=' object tag.

However, you must always code the 'TYPE=' tags to indicate that it is an 'application/x-oleobject'.

You must also code the right Class ID corresponding the specific 'CLASSID=' registration for each control. This is determined by the Class ID of the control, which in this example is:

```
"clsid:EEE78591-FE22-11D0-8BEF-0060081841DE".
```

This must be coded exactly as is shown. Each control has its own class ID for:

```
<clsid:[CLASS ID]:>
```

which are listed as follows:

Control	Class ID
Voice Command	clsid:66523042-35FE-11D1-8C4D-0060081841DE
Voice Dictation	clsid:582C2191-4016-11D1-8C55-0060081841DE
Voice Text	clsid:2398E32F-5C6E-11D1-8C65-0060081841DE
Voice Telephony	clsid:FC9E740F-6058-11D1-8C66-0060081841DE
Direct Speech Recognition	clsid:4E3D9D1F-0C63-11D1-8BFB-0060081841DE
Direct Speech Synthesis	clsid:EEE78591-FE22-11D0-8BEF-0060081841DE

The name you use in the 'NAME=' field is up to you, as long as it is consistent to the name that you use in the NAME properties field across all of your application speech objects.

So to create a web page that speaks when it is loaded, simply add the HTML or web mark-up language tag above to register the object and then appropriate VB Script or JavaScript references as follows:

```
<script>
DirectVoice.Speak("hello world")
</script>
```

B.4   Customizing Referenced Visual Basic or VB Script Speech Voices

Anything that is entered and stored on the web page HTML within the brackets and quotes will be spoken in default voice for that particular Windows SAPI speech to text engine anytime that your registered and referenced Visual Basic speech program is started.

This is the same anytime that anyone links to any particular web page that references a Windows SAPI speech enabled web page from their own Internet browser or a Visual Basic application run concurrently with active Internet browser and ISP or web network linkages.

If you want to change the default voices or speaker control tags for a particular text string that you wish to use to speak to greet users who visit your web page, you should refer to Appendix D and insert the appropriate SAPI speech Control

Appendix C

Windows Visual Basic Runtime Speech Constants

C.1   Windows Visual Basic Speech API Runtime Files

In order to run the sample programs from SAPI 4.0 for either Visual Basic 5 or Visual Basic 6, you must have all of the SAPI speech runtime files for Visual Basic installed into the same directory as your SAPI 4.0 SDK.

This is necessary in order to modify the sample SAPI 4.0 programs, and also necessary if you want to package your Windows Visual Basic speech programs for use on another PC for a specific user or customer, and must always be included in your routine install program or procedure.

Although these runtime files were listed earlier in this book, they are listed again in this Appendix for quick reference. Be sure that you have all of the required Visual Basic speech API runtime files before listing the code that you will need to also be sure is always installed and distributed with your Visual Basic speech application programs. These files are listed in detail on the following page:

File	Description
setup1.exe	Program that installs the Visual Basic runtime.
VB5StKit.dll	Part of program that installs Visual Basic runtime.
MSVBVM50.dll	Visual Basic runtime dll.
StdOle2.tlb	OLE file needed for Visual Basic on Windows 95.
OleAut32.dll	OLE file needed for Visual Basic on Windows 95.
OlePro32.dll	OLE file needed for Visual Basic on Windows 95.
AsycFilt.dll	OLE file needed for Visual Basic on Windows 95.
Ctl3d32.dll	OLE file needed for Visual Basic.
ComCat.dll	OLE file needed for Visual Basic.
MSMAPI32.OCX	Control needed for email sample application.
COMCT232.OCX	Common controls used in sample applications.
comctl32.ocx	Common control used in sample applications.
RICHTX32.OCX	Rich text control used by dictation sample.
RichEd32.dll	Rich text control component.
MCI32.OCX	Multimedia control used by the email sample.

C.2   Windows Visual Basic Speech API Runtime Constant File

Although you should never attempt to modify any of the Visual Basic Speech runtime files and objects needed by SAPI 4.0 that were listed on the previous page, you should always make sure that they are all included in any distribution disk or installation program or build file for your own Visual Basic speech application programs.

But you should also make sure that the Visual Basic Speech API runtime constant file is included with every distribution disk or installation program and build file that you provide to your users with your own Visual Basic speech programs that use SAPI controls.

The name of this file is VBSPEECH.BAS and it should be included in every make and build for your Visual Basic speech programs in order that they will work properly.

You should understand that all of the many public constants listed in this file are the results of parameter setting from the SAPI ActiveX speech control properties, methods and events, as well as error handling and control tags for your Visual Basic speech programs.

You should keep both a back-up copies of the most recent version of the VBSPEECH.BAS file for your Visual Basic speech program, as well as previous generation versions of your VBSPEECH.BAS files with the appropriate version control that you use according to your own Visual Basic developer platform standards.

But you should also keep back-up copies of the default VBSPEECH.BAS file with original default constant settings as listed in this section of Appendix B.

You can refer to this section if you have any problems where your Visual Basic software is suddenly behaving differently than in the past or more importantly if it does not seem to be functioning as the standard SAPI ActiveX control documentation leads you to believe it should, especially with regard to voices, or input or output sound.

Also you should be aware that some VBSPEECH.BAS constants can not only be reset by adjustments to your SAPI ActiveX control property or event parameters by your own speech program, but can also be reset or adjusted by other speech programs that are installed on either your own or your potential users PC. So you should become acquainted with each of the public constants and their default values as listed on the following pages.

You should be able to run conventional compare utilities to point out differences between a default version of the VBSPEECH.BAS file or the last previous working version to find anything that has changed.

But if you do not have that option, the default Visual Basic speech program constants are listed on the following pages.

All of the public constants in the default VBSPEECH.BAS file from the standard install of SAPI 4.0 are listed in the order exactly as they are coded in the original default file. In order to obtain detailed information about any specific Public Constant in this file, you should refer to SAPI 4.0 online documentation on MSDN website or CD.

```
Public Const SVFN_LEN = (262)
Public Const LANG_LEN = (64)
Public Const EI_TITLESIZE = (128)
Public Const EI_DESCSIZE = (512)
Public Const EI_FIXSIZE = (512)
Public Const SVPI_MFGLEN = (64)
Public Const SVPI_PRODLEN = (64)
```

```
Public Const SVPI_COMPLEN = (64)
Public Const SVPI_COPYRIGHTLEN = (128)
Public Const SVI_MFGLEN = (SVPI_MFGLEN)


Public Const AUDERR_NONE = &H0
Public Const AUDERR_BADDEVICEID = &H80040301
Public Const AUDERR_NEEDWAVEFORMAT = &H80040302
Public Const AUDERR_NOTSUPPORTED = &H80004001
Public Const AUDERR_NOTENOUGHDATA = &H80040201
Public Const AUDERR_NOTPLAYING = &H80040306
Public Const AUDERR_INVALIDPARAM = &H80070057
Public Const AUDERR_WAVEFORMATNOTSUPPORTED = &H80040202
Public Const AUDERR_WAVEDEVICEBUSY = &H80040203
Public Const AUDERR_WAVEDEVNOTSUPPORTED = &H80040312
Public Const AUDERR_NOTRECORDING = &H80040313
Public Const AUDERR_INVALIDFLAG = &H80040204
Public Const AUDERR_INVALIDHANDLE = &H80070006
Public Const AUDERR_NODRIVER = &H80040317
Public Const AUDERR_HANDLEBUSY = &H80040318
Public Const AUDERR_INVALIDNOTIFYSINK = &H80040319
Public Const AUDERR_WAVENOTENABLED = &H8004031A
Public Const AUDERR_ALREADYCLAIMED = &H8004031D
Public Const AUDERR_NOTCLAIMED = &H8004031E
Public Const AUDERR_STILLPLAYING = &H8004031F
Public Const AUDERR_ALREADYSTARTED = &H80040320
Public Const AUDERR_SYNCNOTALLOWED = &H80040321


Public Const SRERR_NONE = &H0
Public Const SRERR_OUTOFDISK = &H80040205
Public Const SRERR_NOTSUPPORTED = &H80004001
Public Const SRERR_NOTENOUGHDATA = &H80040201
Public Const SRERR_VALUEOUTOFRANGE = &H8000FFFF
Public Const SRERR_GRAMMARTOOCOMPLEX = &H80040406
Public Const SRERR_GRAMMARWRONGTYPE = &H80040407
Public Const SRERR_INVALIDWINDOW = &H8004000F
Public Const SRERR_INVALIDPARAM = &H80070057
Public Const SRERR_INVALIDMODE = &H80040206
Public Const SRERR_TOOMANYGRAMMARS = &H8004040B
Public Const SRERR_INVALIDLIST = &H80040207
Public Const SRERR_WAVEDEVICEBUSY = &H80040203
```

```
Public Const SRERR_WAVEFORMATNOTSUPPORTED = &H80040202
Public Const SRERR_INVALIDCHAR = &H80040208
Public Const SRERR_GRAMTOOCOMPLEX = &H80040406
Public Const SRERR_GRAMTOOLARGE = &H80040411
Public Const SRERR_INVALIDINTERFACE = &H80004002
Public Const SRERR_INVALIDKEY = &H80040209
Public Const SRERR_INVALIDFLAG = &H80040204
Public Const SRERR_GRAMMARERROR = &H80040416
Public Const SRERR_INVALIDRULE = &H80040417
Public Const SRERR_RULEALREADYACTIVE = &H80040418
Public Const SRERR_RULENOTACTIVE = &H80040419
Public Const SRERR_NOUSERSELECTED = &H8004041A
Public Const SRERR_BAD_PRONUNCIATION = &H8004041B
Public Const SRERR_DATAFILEERROR = &H8004041C
Public Const SRERR_GRAMMARALREADYACTIVE = &H8004041D
Public Const SRERR_GRAMMARNOTACTIVE = &H4041E
Public Const SRERR_GLOBALGRAMMARALREADYACTIVE = &H8004041F
Public Const SRERR_LANGUAGEMISMATCH = &H80040420
Public Const SRERR_MULTIPLELANG = &H80040421
Public Const SRERR_LDGRAMMARNOWORDS = &H80040422
Public Const SRERR_NOLEXICON = &H80040423
Public Const SRERR_SPEAKEREXISTS = &H80040424
Public Const SRERR_GRAMMARENGINEMISMATCH = &H80040425
Public Const SRERR_BOOKMARKEXISTS = &H80040426
Public Const SRERR_BOOKMARKDOESNOTEXIST = &H80040427
Public Const SRERR_MICWIZARDCANCELED = &H80040428
Public Const SRERR_WORDTOOLONG = &H80040429
Public Const SRERR_BAD_WORD = &H8004042A

Public Const E_WRONGTYPE = &H8004020C
Public Const E_BUFFERTOOSMALL = &H8004020D

Public Const TTSERR_NONE = &H0
Public Const TTSERR_INVALIDINTERFACE = &H80004002
Public Const TTSERR_OUTOFDISK = &H80040205
Public Const TTSERR_NOTSUPPORTED = &H80004001
Public Const TTSERR_VALUEOUTOFRANGE = &H8000FFFF
Public Const TTSERR_INVALIDWINDOW = &H8004000F
Public Const TTSERR_INVALIDPARAM = &H80070057
Public Const TTSERR_INVALIDMODE = &H80040206
```

```
Public Const TTSERR_INVALIDKEY = &H80040209
Public Const TTSERR_WAVEFORMATNOTSUPPORTED = &H80040202
Public Const TTSERR_INVALIDCHAR = &H80040208
Public Const TTSERR_QUEUEFULL = &H8004020A
Public Const TTSERR_WAVEDEVICEBUSY = &H80040203
Public Const TTSERR_NOTPAUSED = &H80040501
Public Const TTSERR_ALREADYPAUSED = &H80040502

Public Const VCMDERR_NONE = &H0
Public Const VCMDERR_OUTOFMEM = &H8007000E
Public Const VCMDERR_OUTOFDISK = &H80040205
Public Const VCMDERR_NOTSUPPORTED = &H80004001
Public Const VCMDERR_VALUEOUTOFRANGE = &H8000FFFF
Public Const VCMDERR_MENUTOOCOMPLEX = &H80040606
Public Const VCMDERR_MENUWRONGLANGUAGE = &H80040607
Public Const VCMDERR_INVALIDWINDOW = &H8004000F
Public Const VCMDERR_INVALIDPARAM = &H80070057
Public Const VCMDERR_INVALIDMODE = &H80040206
Public Const VCMDERR_TOOMANYMENUS = &H8004060
Public Const VCMDERR_INVALIDLIST = &H80040207
Public Const VCMDERR_MENUDOESNOTEXIST = &H8004060D
Public Const VCMDERR_MENUACTIVE = &H8004060E
Public Const VCMDERR_NOENGINE = &H8004060F
Public Const VCMDERR_NOGRAMMARINTERFACE = &H80040610
Public Const VCMDERR_NOFINDINTERFACE = &H80040611
Public Const VCMDERR_CANTCREATESRENUM = &H80040612
Public Const VCMDERR_NOSITEINFO = &H80040613
Public Const VCMDERR_SRFINDFAILED = &H80040614
Public Const VCMDERR_CANTCREATEAUDIODEVICE = &H80040615
Public Const VCMDERR_CANTSETDEVICE = &H80040616
Public Const VCMDERR_CANTSELECTENGINE = &H80040617
Public Const VCMDERR_CANTCREATENOTIFY = &H80040618
Public Const VCMDERR_CANTCREATEDATASTRUCTURES = &H80040619
Public Const VCMDERR_CANTINITDATASTRUCTURES = &H8004061A
Public Const VCMDERR_NOCACHEDATA = &H8004061B
Public Const VCMDERR_NOCOMMANDS = &H8004061C
Public Const VCMDERR_CANTXTRACTWORDS = &H8004061D
Public Const VCMDERR_CANTGETDBNAME = &H8004061E
Public Const VCMDERR_CANTCREATEKEY = &H8004061F
Public Const VCMDERR_CANTCREATEDBNAME = &H80040620
```

```
Public Const VCMDERR_CANTUPDATEREGISTRY = &H80040621
Public Const VCMDERR_CANTOPENREGISTRY = &H80040622
Public Const VCMDERR_CANTOPENDATABASE = &H80040623
Public Const VCMDERR_CANTCREATESTORAGE = &H80040624
Public Const VCMDERR_CANNOTMIMIC = &H80040625
Public Const VCMDERR_MENUEXIST = &H80040626
Public Const VCMDERR_MENUOPEN = &H80040627


Public Const VTXTERR_NONE = &H0
Public Const VTXTERR_OUTOFMEM = &H8007000E
Public Const VTXTERR_EMPTYSPEAKSTRING = &H8004020B
Public Const VTXTERR_INVALIDPARAM = &H80070057
Public Const VTXTERR_INVALIDMODE = &H80040206
Public Const VTXTERR_NOENGINE = &H8004070F
Public Const VTXTERR_NOFINDINTERFACE = &H80040711
Public Const VTXTERR_CANTCREATETTSENUM = &H80040712
Public Const VTXTERR_NOSITEINFO = &H80040713
Public Const VTXTERR_TTSFINDFAILED = &H80040714
Public Const VTXTERR_CANTCREATEAUDIODEVICE = &H80040715
Public Const VTXTERR_CANTSETDEVICE = &H80040716
Public Const VTXTERR_CANTSELECTENGINE = &H80040717
Public Const VTXTERR_CANTCREATENOTIFY = &H80040718
Public Const VTXTERR_NOTENABLED = &H80040719
Public Const VTXTERR_OUTOFDISK = &H80040205
Public Const VTXTERR_NOTSUPPORTED = &H80004001
Public Const VTXTERR_NOTENOUGHDATA = &H80040201
Public Const VTXTERR_QUEUEFULL = &H8004020A
Public Const VTXTERR_VALUEOUTOFRANGE = &H8000FFFF
Public Const VTXTERR_INVALIDWINDOW = &H8004000F
Public Const VTXTERR_WAVEDEVICEBUSY = &H80040203
Public Const VTXTERR_WAVEFORMATNOTSUPPORTED = &H80040202
Public Const VTXTERR_INVALIDCHAR = &H80040208


Public Const LEXERR_INVALIDTEXTCHAR = &H80040801
Public Const LEXERR_INVALIDSENSE = &H80040802
Public Const LEXERR_NOTINLEX = &H80040803
Public Const LEXERR_OUTOFDISK = &H80040804
Public Const LEXERR_INVALIDPRONCHAR = &H80040805
Public Const LEXERR_ALREADYINLEX = &H40806
Public Const LEXERR_PRNBUFTOOSMALL = &H80040807
```

```
Public Const LEXERR_ENGBUFTOOSMALL = &H80040808
Public Const LEXERR_INVALIDLEX = &H80040809

Public Const CHARSET_TEXT = 0
Public Const CHARSET_IPAPHONETIC = 1
Public Const CHARSET_ENGINEPHONETIC = 2

Public Const VPS_UNKNOWN = 0
Public Const VPS_NOUN = 1
Public Const VPS_VERB = 2
Public Const VPS_ADVERB = 3
Public Const VPS_ADJECTIVE = 4
Public Const VPS_PROPERNOUN = 5
Public Const VPS_PRONOUN = 6
Public Const VPS_CONJUNCTION = 7
Public Const VPS_CARDINAL = 8
Public Const VPS_ORDINAL = 9
Public Const VPS_DETERMINER = 10
Public Const VPS_QUANTIFIER = 11
Public Const VPS_PUNCTUATION = 12
Public Const VPS_CONTRACTION = 13
Public Const VPS_INTERJECTION = 14
Public Const VPS_ABBREVIATION = 15
Public Const VPS_PREPOSITION = 16

Public Const TTSBASEATTR = &H1000
Public Const SRBASEATTR = &H2000
Public Const VDCTBASEATTR = &H3000
Public Const VCMDBASEATTR = &H4000
Public Const VTXTBASEATTR = &H5000
Public Const AUDBASEATTR = &H6000
Public Const TTSATTR_PITCH = (1)
Public Const TTSATTR_REALTIME = (0)
Public Const TTSATTR_SPEED = (2)
Public Const TTSATTR_VOLUME = (3)
Public Const TTSATTR_PITCHRANGE = (TTSBASEATTR + 5)
Public Const TTSATTR_PITCHRANGEDEFAULT = (TTSBASEATTR + 6)
Public Const TTSATTR_PITCHRANGEMAX = (TTSBASEATTR + 7)
Public Const TTSATTR_PITCHRANGEMIN = (TTSBASEATTR + 8)
Public Const TTSATTR_PITCHRANGERELATIVE = (TTSBASEATTR + 9)
```

```
Public Const TTSATTR_PITCHRANGERELATIVEMAX = (TTSBASEATTR + 10)
Public Const TTSATTR_PITCHRANGERELATIVEMIN = (TTSBASEATTR + 11)
Public Const TTSATTR_PITCHRELATIVE = (TTSBASEATTR + 12)
Public Const TTSATTR_PITCHRELATIVEMAX = (TTSBASEATTR + 13)
Public Const TTSATTR_PITCHRELATIVEMIN = (TTSBASEATTR + 14)
Public Const TTSATTR_PITCHDEFAULT = (TTSBASEATTR + 15)
Public Const TTSATTR_PITCHMAX = (TTSBASEATTR + 16)
Public Const TTSATTR_PITCHMIN = (TTSBASEATTR + 17)
Public Const TTSATTR_SPEEDRELATIVE = (TTSBASEATTR + 18)
Public Const TTSATTR_SPEEDRELATIVEMAX = (TTSBASEATTR + 19)
Public Const TTSATTR_SPEEDRELATIVEMIN = (TTSBASEATTR + 20)
Public Const TTSATTR_SPEEDDEFAULT = (TTSBASEATTR + 21)
Public Const TTSATTR_SPEEDMAX = (TTSBASEATTR + 22)
Public Const TTSATTR_SPEEDMIN = (TTSBASEATTR + 23)
Public Const TTSATTR_THREADPRIORITY = (TTSBASEATTR + 24)
Public Const TTSATTR_SINKFLAGS = (TTSBASEATTR + 25)
Public Const TTSATTR_VOLUMEDEFAULT = (TTSBASEATTR + 26)

Public Const SRATTR_AUTOGAIN = (1)
Public Const SRATTR_ECHO = (3)
Public Const SRATTR_ENERGYFLOOR = (4)
Public Const SRATTR_MICROPHONE = (5)
Public Const SRATTR_REALTIME = (6)
Public Const SRATTR_SPEAKER = (7)
Public Const SRATTR_TIMEOUT_COMPLETE = (8)
Public Const SRATTR_TIMEOUT_INCOMPLETE = (SRBASEATTR + 8)
Public Const SRATTR_THRESHOLD = (2)
Public Const SRATTR_ACCURACYSLIDER = (SRBASEATTR + 10)
Public Const SRATTR_LEVEL = (SRBASEATTR + 11)
Public Const SRATTR_LISTENINGSTATE = (SRBASEATTR + 12)
Public Const SRATTR_RESULTSINFO = (SRBASEATTR + 13)
Public Const SRATTR_RESULTSINFO_POSSIBLE = (SRBASEATTR + 14)
Public Const SRATTR_SINKFLAGS = (SRBASEATTR + 15)
Public Const SRATTR_THREADPRIORITY = (SRBASEATTR + 16)

Public Const VDCTATTR_AWAKESTATE = (VDCTBASEATTR + 1)
Public Const VDCTATTR_MODE = (VDCTBASEATTR + 2)
Public Const VDCTATTR_MEMORY = (VDCTBASEATTR + 3)
Public Const VDCTATTR_CORRECTIONRECT = (VDCTBASEATTR + 4)
Public Const VCMDATTR_AWAKESTATE = (VCMDBASEATTR + 1)
```

```
Public Const VCMDATTR_DEVICE = (VCMDBASEATTR + 2)
Public Const VCMDATTR_ENABLED = (VCMDBASEATTR + 3)
Public Const VCMDATTR_SRMODE = (VCMDBASEATTR + 4)

Public Const AUDATTR_USELOWPRIORITY = (AUDBASEATTR + 1)
Public Const AUDATTR_AUTORETRY = (AUDBASEATTR + 2)

Public Const SRRI_AUDIO = 1
Public Const SRRI_AUDIO_UNCOMPRESSED = 2
Public Const SRRI_ALTERNATIVES = 4
Public Const SRRI_WORDGRAPH = 8
Public Const SRRI_PHONEMEGRAPH = 16
Public Const SRASF_ATTRIBUTES = 1
Public Const SRASF_INTERFERENCE = 2
Public Const SRASF_SOUND = 4
Public Const SRASF_UTTERANCEBEGIN = 8
Public Const SRASF_UTTERANCEEND = 16
Public Const SRASF_VUMETER = 32
Public Const SRASF_PHRASEHYPOTHESIS = 64
Public Const SRASF_TRAINING = 128
Public Const SRASF_ERRORWARNING = 256

Public Const ILP2_ACTIVE = 1
Public Const ILP2_USER = 2
Public Const ILP2_BACKUP = 4
Public Const ILP2_LTS = 8

Public Const STMWU_CNC = 0
Public Const STMWU_DICTATION = 1
Public Const STMWU_LOWERGAIN = &H10000
Public Const STMWU_NOAUTOGAIN = &H20000
Public Const STMWF_CANSKIP = 1
Public Const STMWI_UNKNOWN = 0
Public Const STMWI_CLOSETALK = 1
Public Const STMWI_EARPIECE = 2
Public Const STMWI_HANDSET = 3
Public Const STMWI_CLIPON = 4
Public Const STMWI_DESKTOP = 5
Public Const STMWI_HANDHELD = 6
Public Const STMWI_TOPMONITOR = 7
```

```
Public Const STMWI_INMONITOR = 8
Public Const STMWI_KEYBOARD = 9
Public Const STMWI_REMOTE = 10
Public Const STMWIS_UNKNOWN = 0
Public Const STMWIS_SPEAKERS = 1
Public Const STMWIS_HEADPHONES = 2
Public Const STMWIS_BOTH = 3
Public Const STLD_DISABLEREMOVE = 1
Public Const STLD_DISABLEADD = 2
Public Const STLD_FORCEEDIT = 4
Public Const STLD_DISABLEPRONADDREMOVE = 8
Public Const STLD_TEST = 16
Public Const STLD_DISABLERENAME = 32
Public Const STLD_CHANGEPRONADDS = 64

Public Const IANSRSN_NODATA = 0
Public Const IANSRSN_PRIORITY = 1
Public Const IANSRSN_INACTIVE = 2
Public Const IANSRSN_EOF = 3
Public Const IASISTATE_PASSTHROUGH = 0
Public Const IASISTATE_PASSNOTHING = 1
Public Const IASISTATE_PASSREADFROMWAVE = 2
Public Const IASISTATE_PASSWRITETOWAVE = 3

Public Const SRMI_NAMELEN = SVFN_LEN
Public Const SRSEQUENCE_DISCRETE = (0)
Public Const SRSEQUENCE_CONTINUOUS = (1)
Public Const SRSEQUENCE_WORDSPOT = (2)
Public Const SRSEQUENCE_CONTCFGDISCDICT = (3)
Public Const SRGRAM_CFG = 1
Public Const SRGRAM_DICTATION = 2
Public Const SRGRAM_LIMITEDDOMAIN = 4
Public Const SRFEATURE_INDEPSPEAKER = 1
Public Const SRFEATURE_INDEPMICROPHONE = 2
Public Const SRFEATURE_TRAINWORD = 4
Public Const SRFEATURE_TRAINPHONETIC = 8
Public Const SRFEATURE_WILDCARD = 16
Public Const SRFEATURE_ANYWORD = 32
Public Const SRFEATURE_PCOPTIMIZED = 64
Public Const SRFEATURE_PHONEOPTIMIZED = 128
```

```
Public Const SRFEATURE_GRAMLIST = 256
Public Const SRFEATURE_GRAMLINK = 512
Public Const SRFEATURE_MULTILINGUAL = 1024
Public Const SRFEATURE_GRAMRECURSIVE = 2048
Public Const SRFEATURE_IPAUNICODE = 4096
Public Const SRFEATURE_SINGLEINSTANCE = 8192
Public Const SRFEATURE_THREADSAFE = 16384
Public Const SRFEATURE_FIXEDAUDIO = 32768
Public Const SRFEATURE_IPAWORD = 65536
Public Const SRFEATURE_SAPI4 = 131072


Public Const SRI_ILEXPRONOUNCE = 1
Public Const SRI_ISRATTRIBUTES = 2
Public Const SRI_ISRCENTRAL = 4
Public Const SRI_ISRDIALOGS = 8
Public Const SRI_ISRGRAMCOMMON = 16
Public Const SRI_ISRGRAMCFG = 32
Public Const SRI_ISRGRAMDICTATION = 64
Public Const SRI_ISRGRAMINSERTIONGUI = 128
Public Const SRI_ISRESBASIC = 256
Public Const SRI_ISRESMERGE = 512
Public Const SRI_ISRESAUDIO = 1024
Public Const SRI_ISRESCORRECTION = 2048
Public Const SRI_ISRESEVAL = 4096
Public Const SRI_ISRESGRAPH = 8192
Public Const SRI_ISRESMEMORY = 16384
Public Const SRI_ISRESMODIFYGUI = 32768
Public Const SRI_ISRESSPEAKER = 65536
Public Const SRI_ISRSPEAKER = 131072
Public Const SRI_ISRESSCORES = 262144
Public Const SRI_ISRESAUDIOEX = 524288
Public Const SRI_ISRGRAMLEXPRON = 1048576
Public Const SRI_ISRRESGRAPHEX = 2097152
Public Const SRI_ILEXPRONOUNCE2 = 4194304
Public Const SRI_IATTRIBUTES = 8388608


Public Const SRGRAMQ_NONE = 0
Public Const SRGRAMQ_GENERALTRAIN = 1
Public Const SRGRAMQ_PHRASE = 2
Public Const SRGRAMQ_DIALOG = 3
```

```
Public Const ISRNOTEFIN_RECOGNIZED = 1
Public Const ISRNOTEFIN_THISGRAMMAR = 2
Public Const ISRNOTEFIN_FROMTHISGRAMMAR = 4
Public Const SRGNSTRAIN_GENERAL = 1
Public Const SRGNSTRAIN_GRAMMAR = 2
Public Const SRGNSTRAIN_MICROPHONE = 4
Public Const ISRNSAC_AUTOGAINENABLE = 1
Public Const ISRNSAC_THRESHOLD = 2
Public Const ISRNSAC_ECHO = 3
Public Const ISRNSAC_ENERGYFLOOR = 4
Public Const ISRNSAC_MICROPHONE = 5
Public Const ISRNSAC_REALTIME = 6
Public Const ISRNSAC_SPEAKER = 7
Public Const ISRNSAC_TIMEOUT = 8
Public Const ISRNSAC_STARTLISTENING = 9
Public Const ISRNSAC_STOPLISTENING = 10

Public Const SRMSGINT_NOISE = (&H1)
Public Const SRMSGINT_NOSIGNAL = (&H2)
Public Const SRMSGINT_TOOLOUD = (&H3)
Public Const SRMSGINT_TOOQUIET = (&H4)
Public Const SRMSGINT_AUDIODATA_STOPPED = (&H5)
Public Const SRMSGINT_AUDIODATA_STARTED = (&H6)
Public Const SRMSGINT_IAUDIO_STARTED = (&H7)
Public Const SRMSGINT_IAUDIO_STOPPED = (&H8)
Public Const SRHDRTYPE_CFG = 0
Public Const SRHDRTYPE_LIMITEDDOMAIN = 1
Public Const SRHDRTYPE_DICTATION = 2
Public Const SRHDRFLAG_UNICODE = 1
Public Const SRRESCUE_COMMA = 1
Public Const SRRESCUE_DECLARATIVEBEGIN = 2
Public Const SRRESCUE_DECLARATIVEEND = 3
Public Const SRRESCUE_IMPERATIVEBEGIN = 4
Public Const SRRESCUE_IMPERATIVEEND = 5
Public Const SRRESCUE_INTERROGATIVEBEGIN = 6
Public Const SRRESCUE_INTERROGATIVEEND = 7
Public Const SRRESCUE_NOISE = 8
Public Const SRRESCUE_PAUSE = 9
Public Const SRRESCUE_SENTENCEBEGIN = 10
Public Const SRRESCUE_SENTENCEEND = 11
```

```
Public Const SRRESCUE_UM = 12
Public Const SRRESCUE_WILDCARD = 13
Public Const SRRESCUE_WORD = 14
Public Const SRCFG_STARTOPERATION = (1)
Public Const SRCFG_ENDOPERATION = (2)
Public Const SRCFG_WORD = (3)
Public Const SRCFG_RULE = (4)
Public Const SRCFG_WILDCARD = (5)
Public Const SRCFG_LIST = (6)
Public Const SRCFGO_SEQUENCE = (1)
Public Const SRCFGO_ALTERNATIVE = (2)
Public Const SRCFGO_REPEAT = (3)
Public Const SRCFGO_OPTIONAL = (4)

Public Const SRCK_LANGUAGE = 1
Public Const SRCKCFG_WORDS = 2
Public Const SRCKCFG_RULES = 3
Public Const SRCKCFG_EXPORTRULES = 4
Public Const SRCKCFG_IMPORTRULES = 5
Public Const SRCKCFG_LISTS = 6
Public Const SRCKD_TOPIC = 7
Public Const SRCKD_COMMON = 8
Public Const SRCKD_GROUP = 9
Public Const SRCKD_SAMPLE = 10
Public Const SRCKLD_WORDS = 11
Public Const SRCKLD_GROUP = 12
Public Const SRCKLD_SAMPLE = 13
Public Const SRCKD_WORDCOUNT = 14
Public Const SRCKD_NGRAM = 15
Public Const SRTQEX_REQUIRED = (&H0)
Public Const SRTQEX_RECOMMENDED = (&H1)
Public Const SRAUDIOTIMESTAMP_DEFAULT =-1
Public Const SRCORCONFIDENCE_SOME = 1
Public Const SRCORCONFIDENCE_VERY = 2
Public Const SRGEX_ACOUSTICONLY = 1
Public Const SRGEX_LMONLY = 2
Public Const SRGEX_ACOUSTICANDLM = 4

Public Const SRRESMEMKIND_AUDIO = 1
Public Const SRRESMEMKIND_CORRECTION = 2
```

```
Public Const SRRESMEMKIND_EVAL = 4
Public Const SRRESMEMKIND_PHONEMEGRAPH = 8
Public Const SRRESMEMKIND_WORDGRAPH = 16


Public Const SRATTR_MINAUTOGAIN = 0
Public Const SRATTR_MAXAUTOGAIN = 100
Public Const SRATTR_MINENERGYFLOOR = 0
Public Const SRATTR_MAXENERGYFLOOR = &HFFFF
Public Const SRATTR_MINREALTIME = 0
Public Const SRATTR_MAXREALTIME = &HFFFFFFFF
Public Const SRATTR_MINTHRESHOLD = 0
Public Const SRATTR_MAXTHRESHOLD = 100
Public Const SRATTR_MINTOINCOMPLETE = 0
Public Const SRATTR_MAXTOINCOMPLETE = &HFFFFFFFF
Public Const SRATTR_MINTOCOMPLETE = 0
Public Const SRATTR_MAXTOCOMPLETE = &HFFFFFFFF


Public Const SRGRMFMT_CFG = &H0
Public Const SRGRMFMT_LIMITEDDOMAIN = &H1
Public Const SRGRMFMT_DICTATION = &H2
Public Const SRGRMFMT_CFGNATIVE = &H8000
Public Const SRGRMFMT_LIMITEDDOMAINNATIVE = &H8001
Public Const SRGRMFMT_DICTATIONNATIVE = &H8002


Public Const TTSI_NAMELEN = SVFN_LEN
Public Const TTSI_STYLELEN = SVFN_LEN


Public Const GENDER_NEUTRAL = (0)
Public Const GENDER_FEMALE = (1)
Public Const GENDER_MALE = (2)


Public Const TTSFEATURE_ANYWORD = 1
Public Const TTSFEATURE_VOLUME = 2
Public Const TTSFEATURE_SPEED = 4
Public Const TTSFEATURE_PITCH = 8
Public Const TTSFEATURE_TAGGED = 16
Public Const TTSFEATURE_IPAUNICODE = 32
Public Const TTSFEATURE_VISUAL = 64
Public Const TTSFEATURE_WORDPOSITION = 128
Public Const TTSFEATURE_PCOPTIMIZED = 256
```

```
Public Const TTSFEATURE_PHONEOPTIMIZED = 512
Public Const TTSFEATURE_FIXEDAUDIO = 1024
Public Const TTSFEATURE_SINGLEINSTANCE = 2048
Public Const TTSFEATURE_THREADSAFE = 4096
Public Const TTSFEATURE_IPATEXTDATA = 8192
Public Const TTSFEATURE_PREFERRED = 16384
Public Const TTSFEATURE_TRANSPLANTED = 32768
Public Const TTSFEATURE_SAPI4 = 65536

Public Const TTSI_ILEXPRONOUNCE = 1
Public Const TTSI_ITTSATTRIBUTES = 2
Public Const TTSI_ITTSCENTRAL = 4
Public Const TTSI_ITTSDIALOGS = 8
Public Const TTSI_ATTRIBUTES = 16

Public Const TTSDATAFLAG_TAGGED = 1
Public Const TTSBNS_ABORTED = 1
Public Const TTSNSAC_REALTIME = 0
Public Const TTSNSAC_PITCH = 1
Public Const TTSNSAC_SPEED = 2
Public Const TTSNSAC_VOLUME = 3

Public Const TTSNSHINT_QUESTION = 1
Public Const TTSNSHINT_STATEMENT = 2
Public Const TTSNSHINT_COMMAND = 4
Public Const TTSNSHINT_EXCLAMATION = 8
Public Const TTSNSHINT_EMPHASIS = 16

Public Const TTSAGE_BABY = 1
Public Const TTSAGE_TODDLER = 3
Public Const TTSAGE_CHILD = 6
Public Const TTSAGE_ADOLESCENT = 14
Public Const TTSAGE_ADULT = 30
Public Const TTSAGE_ELDERLY = 70

Public Const TTSATTR_MINPITCH = 0
Public Const TTSATTR_MAXPITCH = &HFFFF
Public Const TTSATTR_MINREALTIME = 0
Public Const TTSATTR_MAXREALTIME = &HFFFFFFFF
Public Const TTSATTR_MINSPEED = 0
```

```
Public Const TTSATTR_MAXSPEED = &HFFFFFFFF
Public Const TTSATTR_MINVOLUME = 0
Public Const TTSATTR_MAXVOLUME = &HFFFFFFFF

Public Const VCMD_APPLEN = 32
Public Const VCMD_STATELEN = VCMD_APPLEN
Public Const VCMD_MICLEN = VCMD_APPLEN
Public Const VCMD_SPEAKERLEN = VCMD_APPLEN

Public Const VCMDMC_CREATE_TEMP = &H1
Public Const VCMDMC_CREATE_NEW = &H2
Public Const VCMDMC_CREATE_ALWAYS = &H4
Public Const VCMDMC_OPEN_ALWAYS = &H8
Public Const VCMDMC_OPEN_EXISTING = &H10

Public Const VCMDRF_NOMESSAGES = &H0
Public Const VCMDRF_ALLBUTVUMETER = &H1
Public Const VCMDRF_VUMETER = &H2
Public Const VCMDRF_ALLMESSAGES = (VCMDRF_ALLBUTVUMETER +
VCMDRF_VUMETER)

Public Const VCMDEF_DATABASE = &H0
Public Const VCMDEF_ACTIVE = &H1
Public Const VCMDEF_SELECTED = &H2
Public Const VCMDEF_PERMANENT = &H4
Public Const VCMDEF_TEMPORARY = &H8
Public Const VWGFLAG_ASLEEP = &H1

Public Const VCMDACT_NORMAL = (&H8000)
Public Const VCMDACT_LOW = (&H4000)
Public Const VCMDACT_HIGH = (&HC000)

Public Const VCMDCMD_VERIFY = &H1
Public Const VCMDCMD_DISABLED_TEMP = &H2
Public Const VCMDCMD_DISABLED_PERM = &H4
Public Const VCMDCMD_CANTRENAME = &H8

Public Const VCMD_BY_POSITION = &H1
Public Const VCMD_BY_IDENTIFIER = &H2
```

```
Public Const IVCNSAC_AUTOGAINENABLE = &H1
Public Const IVCNSAC_ENABLED = &H2
Public Const IVCNSAC_AWAKE = &H4
Public Const IVCNSAC_DEVICE = &H8
Public Const IVCNSAC_MICROPHONE = &H10
Public Const IVCNSAC_SPEAKER = &H20
Public Const IVCNSAC_SRMODE = &H40
Public Const IVCNSAC_THRESHOLD = &H80
Public Const IVCNSAC_ORIGINAPP = &H10000

Public Const IVTNSAC_DEVICE = &H1
Public Const IVTNSAC_ENABLED = &H2
Public Const IVTNSAC_SPEED = &H4
Public Const IVTNSAC_VOLUME = &H8
Public Const IVTNSAC_TTSMODE = &H10

Public Const VSRMODE_OFF = &H2
Public Const VSRMODE_DISABLED = &H1
Public Const VSRMODE_CMDPAUSED = &H4
Public Const VSRMODE_CMDONLY = &H10
Public Const VSRMODE_DCTONLY = &H20
Public Const VSRMODE_CMDANDDCT = &H40

Public Const VDCT_TOPICNAMELEN = 32
Public Const VDCT_TEXTADDED = &H1
Public Const VDCT_TEXTREMOVED = &H2
Public Const VDCT_TEXTREPLACED = &H4
Public Const VDCT_TEXTCLEAN = &H10000
Public Const VDCT_TEXTKEEPRESULTS = &H20000

Public Const VDCTGUIF_VISIBLE = &H1
Public Const VDCTGUIF_DONTMOVE = &H2
Public Const VDCTGUIF_ADDWORD = &H4

Public Const VDCTFX_CAPFIRST = &H1
Public Const VDCTFX_LOWERFIRST = &H2
Public Const VDCTFX_TOGGLEFIRST = &H3
Public Const VDCTFX_CAPALL = &H4
Public Const VDCTFX_LOWERALL = &H5
Public Const VDCTFX_REMOVESPACES = &H6
```

```
Public Const VDCTFX_KEEPONLYFIRSTLETTER = &H7

Public Const VTXTST_STATEMENT = &H1
Public Const VTXTST_QUESTION = &H2
Public Const VTXTST_COMMAND = &H4
Public Const VTXTST_WARNING = &H8
Public Const VTXTST_READING = &H10
Public Const VTXTST_NUMBERS = &H20
Public Const VTXTST_SPREADSHEET = &H40

Public Const VTXTSP_VERYHIGH = &H80
Public Const VTXTSP_HIGH = &H100
Public Const VTXTSP_NORMAL = &H200

Public Const TTS_LANGUAGE = 1
Public Const TTS_VOICE = 2
Public Const TTS_GENDER = 4
Public Const TTS_VOLUME = 8
Public Const TTS_PITCH = 16
Public Const TTS_SPEED = 32
Public Const TTS_ABBREVIATION = 64
Public Const TTS_PUNCTUATION = 128
Public Const TTS_PAUSEWORD = 256
Public Const TTS_PAUSEPHRASE = 512
Public Const TTS_PAUSESENTENCE = 1024
Public Const TTS_SPELLING = 2048
Public Const TTS_QUALITY = 4096
Public Const TTS_FRICATION = 8192
Public Const TTS_ASPIRATION = 16384
Public Const TTS_INTONATION = 32768

Public Const TTSATTR_MINPAUSEWORD = &H0
Public Const TTSATTR_MAXPAUSEWORD = &HFFFFFFFF
Public Const TTSATTR_MINPAUSEPHRASE = &H0
Public Const TTSATTR_MAXPAUSEPHRASE = &HFFFFFFFF
Public Const TTSATTR_MINPAUSESENTENCE = &H0
Public Const TTSATTR_MAXPAUSESENTENCE = &HFFFFFFFF
Public Const TTSATTR_MINASPIRATION = &H0
Public Const TTSATTR_MAXASPIRATION = &HFFFFFFFF
Public Const TTSATTR_MINFRICATION = &H0
```

```
Public Const TTSATTR_MAXFRICATION = &HFFFFFFFF
Public Const TTSATTR_MININTONATION = &H0
Public Const TTSATTR_MAXINTONATION = &HFFFFFFFF

Public Const TTSNSAC_LANGUAGE = 100
Public Const TTSNSAC_VOICE = 101
Public Const TTSNSAC_GENDER = 102
Public Const TTSNSAC_ABBREVIATION = 103
Public Const TTSNSAC_PUNCTUATION = 104
Public Const TTSNSAC_PAUSEWORD = 105
Public Const TTSNSAC_PAUSEPHRASE = 106
Public Const TTSNSAC_PAUSESENTENCE = 107
Public Const TTSNSAC_SPELLING = 108
Public Const TTSNSAC_QUALITY = 109
Public Const TTSNSAC_FRICATION = 110
Public Const TTSNSAC_ASPIRATION = 111
Public Const TTSNSAC_INTONATION = 112
Public Const TTSI_ITTSEXTERNALSYNTHESIZER = 16

Public Const TTSERR_SYNTHESIZERBUSY = &H80004100
Public Const TTSERR_ALREADYDISPLAYED = &H80004101
Public Const TTSERR_INVALIDATTRIB = &H80004102
Public Const TTSERR_SYNTHESIZERACCESSERROR = &H80004103
Public Const TTSERR_DRIVERERROR = &H80004104
Public Const TTSERR_UNRECOVERABLEERROR = &H80004105
Public Const TTSERR_DRIVERACCESSERROR = &H80004106
Public Const TTSERR_BUFFERTOOSMALL = &H80004107
Public Const TTSERR_DRIVERNOTFOUND = &H80004108
Public Const TTSERR_CANNOTREGISTER = &H80004109
Public Const TTSERR_LANGUAGENOTSUPPORTED = &H80004110
```

Appendix D

SAPI International Phonetic Alphabet Unicode Values

The International Phonetic Alphabet (IPA) is a standardized universal computer linguistics system for mark-up tags of specific human voice language sounds, or phonemes.

If a Windows SAPI engine supports IPA, one way your Visual Basic speech application program can adjust the pronunciation of words by passing to IPA phonemes that represent the correct pronunciation, expressed as Unicode values.

This appendix lists the Unicode values for common IPA phonemes. Every Windows Visual Basic speech application programming developer can use the information in this section to adjust pronunciations used by any Microsoft SAPI compliant speech recognition or text-to-speech engine that supports the IPA.

D.1 Origins of the International Phonetic Alphabet for SAPI Unicode

Every text-to-speech and speech recognition engine that is compatible with the Microsoft Windows SAPI speech specification uses its own phonetic character set. But the standardized character sets are usually not as complete as necessary for third-party vendor's purposes, with regard to both English speaking vertical professional localizations, as well as non-English speaker foreign language or dialects.

Each vendor must define how engine-specific phonemes map to standardized character sets. If you want to develop your own speech engine for any non-English or special vertical professional Visual Basic speech applications. You must use IPA unicodes. This includes American English professional speech engines, especially speech engines for medical doctors or lawyers, because these two professions include heavy emphasis on Latin phonemes that are not always part of conventional American English vernacular in standard SAPI engines.

The International Phonetic Alphabet (IPA) is a standard phonetic character set that is already supported in Unicode. Although the IPA is not developed just for SAPI, it is the international speech notation standard of all linguists, so SAPI converts IPA to Unicodes.

There are no known human language vocalizations that are not included in the expansive IPA character sets. All known sounds that have been demonstrated to have any language as well as emotional and guttural or non-language human vocalizations can be coded according to some combination of IPA phonetic characters sets.

This is possible due to over 100 years of analysis by linguists, anthropologists, and physicians who have systematically studied all of the possible sounds that can be created by normal human vocal anatomy. All vocal anatomy referenced by IPA can be mapped by SAPI.

All of the known linguistic parameters including all of the anthropometric and biometric ranges that reflect age, gender and emotional states which are effected by subtle variations in the parameters to simulate the anatomy of the throat, tongue and mouth have been extensively analyzed over the last 100 years. Consequently, all of that data is reflected in both the design of SAPI 4.0 and the public constant defaults in VBSPEECH.BAS files, and SAPI ActiveX controls.

This results in the capability to computer generate speech for any gender or age, as well as various categories of robot or alien voices as well as voices for various emotions. This include anthropomorphic humanization of voices that can represent animals, cartoon characters, or even to approximate qualities of known living people's voices, such as actors or political figures. This is done by simply by tweaking IPA and Unicode values in combination with Control Tags, as listed for specific SAPI Visual Basic ActiveX controls in Appendix D.

The IPA character set is fully defined as the default SAPI Unicode standard. It normally occupies an address range from '0x0250' through '0x02AF' for human sounds and some Latin characters, and '0x02B0' through '0x02FF' for the modifier characters, including emotion and alien or robot as well as animal anthropomorphic distortion attributes.

Because of the size of the IPA character set, the only way to send IPA characters to or receive them from any Windows SAPI compliant engine is via Microsoft SAPI speech recognition programming IPA Unicodes.

There is no 8-bit method of using the SAPI standard phonetic Unicode IPA compliant sounds. You can use the Phoneme Conversion object in Speech

Tools to display an 8-bit phoneme set that is language specific. But if you must support 8-bit platforms the results must be hard-coded into your Visual Basic program after appropriate event handlers that detect and confirm that 8-bit conversion is really needed. You should be prepared that if it is required to support such 8-bit conversion your Windows speech application will very likely slow considerably.

The IPA standard considers its characters to be a separate alphabet that includes the lowercase Latin characters "a" through "z" and other symbols as they are commonly written and spoken in English.

IPA Latin characters are not all included in American English SAPI Unicode, so many IPA characters are found outside the standard Windows phonetic frame modifier blocks. This is why Latin words or phrases such as they are often used in medical and legal professional English need special codings, and some U+ values must be redefined.

Because the IPA is primarily used by linguists to capture spoken language in print, IPA characters in the standard phonetic block are listed below in their order of their resemblance to the Latin characters "a" through "z" as they are most commonly written and spoken in American English, rather than their actual linguistic phonetic similarity. You have probably already been exposed to IPA phonemes without knowing it, since they are always used in all American English unabridged dictionaries to show pronunciation along with the definitions of common words.

As a result, adjacent Unicode values may bear no relation to each other phonetically, and are not really 'alphabetized'. So Visual Basic speech programmers should acquaint themselves with the entire listing of standard IPA Unicodes that are available as phonemes in SAPI compliant applications before choosing too quickly to use the first available IPA phoneme Unicode value that appears to be applicable.

Also, if the results are not entirely to your satisfaction, or always understandable by your Visual Basic speech recognition programming application users, you should not hesitate to try several alternative IPA phoneme Unicode combinations until you find the best fit for the series of computer speech synthesis sounds that work best for your application.

D.2   *Microsoft Windows Speech API Unicode Blocks IPA Addresses*

The following table lists groups of IPA characters and the Microsoft Windows Visual Basic Unicode address blocks in which they can commonly be found or referenced. The U+ prefix is the same convention that identifies all Microsoft Windows conventional Unicode values, but in this case they are all listed as 16-bit hex values.

IPA Characters	Unicode block
Standard Latin	U+0041 -- U+00FF
European and Extended Latin	U+0010 -- U+01F0
Standard phonetic characters	U+0250 -- U+02AF
Modifier letters (spacing)	U+02B0 -- U+02FF
Diacritical marks (nonspacing)	U+0300 -- U+036F

D.3   Microsoft Windows SAPI Unicode Character Set Symbols for IPA

The symbols used for American English phonemes in Windows SAPI for Visual Basic speech recognition programming are listed on the following pages.

Each phoneme symbol is accompanied by an example, as well as the IPA description, the Unicode name for the IPA standard phonetics, and the Unicode value as it must be coded to the Visual Basic speech program.

Some phonemic labels are described as phoneme combination clusters. For these, it may be preferable to rely on the MS labels, rather than the actual values of each Unicode component phoneme values, since some non-MS after-vendor TTS engines only handle single combined data points for phonemes, rather than synthesize them as combinations of separately modeled phonemes.

Always remember that some vendors many need to substitute U+ values for codings other than American English. You may need to refer to the individual vendor documentation on their U+ coding values, or their list of MS labels for the Unicode names, even in some professional American English or special vertical speech engines just to be sure.

Also, in reference to standard IPA phonemes as they are implemented in the Microsoft SAPI Unicode names for Visual Basic, 'LATIN' means 'LATIN SMALL LETTER' and 'GREEK' means 'GREEK SMALL LETTER'.

MS	Example	IPA Description	Unicode name	Unicode
iy	Feel, eve, me	front close unrounded	LATIN I	U+0069
ih	Fill, hit, lid	front close unrounded (lax)	LATIN CAPITAL I	U+026A
ae	at, carry, gas	front open unrounded (tense)	LATIN AE	U+00E6
aa	Father, ah, car	back open unrounded	LATIN ALPHA	U+0251
ah	cut, bud, up	open-mid back unrounded	LATIN TURNED V	U+028C
ao	dog, lawn, caught	open-mid back round	LATIN OPEN O	U+0254
ay	Tie, ice, bite	diphthong with quality: aa + ih		
ax	ago, comply	central close mid (schwa)	LATIN SCHWA	U+0259
ey	ate, day, tape	front close-mid unrounded (tense)	LATIN E	U+0065
eh	pet, berry, ten	front open-mid unrounded	LATIN OPEN E	U+025B
er	Turn, fur, meter	central open-mid unrounded rhotis	LATIN SCHWA W/HOOK	U+025A
ow	go, own, tone	back close-mid rounded	LATIN O	U+006F
aw	Foul, how, our	diphthong with quality: aa + uh		
oy	Toy, coin, oil	diphthong with quality: ao + ih		
uh	book, pull, good	back close-mid unrounded (lax)	LATIN UPSILON	U+028A
uw	Tool, crew, moo	back close round	LATIN U	U+0075
b	big, able, tab	voiced bilabial plosive	LATIN B	U+0062
p	put, open, tap	voiceless bilabial plosive	LATIN P	U+0070
d	dig, idea, wad	voiced alveolar plosive	LATIN D	U+0064
t	Talk, sat	voiceless alveolar plosive &	LATIN T	U+0074
	meter	alveolar flap	LATIN R W/FISHHOOK	U+027E
g	gut, angle, tag	voiced velar plosive	LATIN SCRIPT G	U+0067
k	cut, oaken, take	voiceless velar plosive	LATIN K	U+006B
f	Fork, after, if	voiceless labiodental fricative	LATIN F	U+0066
v	vat, over, have	voiced labiodental fricative	LATIN V	U+0076
s	sit, cast, toss	voiceless alveolar fricative	LATIN S	U+0073
z	zap, lazy, haze	voiced alveolar fricative	LATIN Z	U+007A
th	Thin, nothing, truth	voiceless dental fricative	GREEK THETA	U+03B8
dh	Then, father, scythe	voiced dental fricative	LATIN ETH	U+00F0
sh	she, cushion, wash	voiceless postalveolar fricative	LATIN ESH	U+0283
zh	genre, azure	voiced postalveolar fricative	LATIN EZH	U+0292
l	Lid	alveolar lateral approximant	LATIN L	U+006C
	elbow, sail	velar lateral approximant	LATIN L W/MIDDLE TILDE	U+026B
r	Red, part, far	retroflex approximant	LATIN R	U+0279
y	yacht, onion, yard	palatal sonorant glide	LATIN J	U+006A
w	with, away	labiovelar sonorant glide	LATIN W	U+0077
hh	help, ahead, hotel	voiceless glottal fricative	LATIN H	U+0068
m	mat, amid, aim	bilabial nasal	LATIN M	U+006D
n	no, end, pan	alveolar nasal	LATIN N	U+006E
nx	sing, anger, drink	velar nasal	LATIN ENG	U+014B
ch	chin, archer, march	voiceless alveolar affricate: t + sh		U+02A7
jh	Joy, agile, edge	voiced alveolar affricate: d + zh		U+02a4

D.4   Microsoft Windows SAPI Unicode Phrase Grammar Symbols for IPA

The following symbols can be used to construct phoneme strings and phonetic input to a TTS engine to support SAPI Visual Basic encoded phrase grammar objects. These are based on high order Microsoft Windows Unicode and assume ability to handle 16-bit addresses with some performance decrement depending on the complexity of the TTS engine that is used as well as the complexity of the Visual Basic speech project. So the precise effects may vary in different TTS engines as well as each individual Visual Basic speech recognition programming application.

MS	Description	Unicode name	Unicode	Usage/Effect
-	syllable boundary	HYPHEN-MINUS	U+002D	separates syllables
#	word boundary	NUMBER SIGN	U+0023	separates words
(space)	word boundary	SPACE	U+0020	separates words
_	silence	UNDERLINE	U+005f	indicates silent period
1	primary stress	MODIFIER LETTER LINE	U+02C8	precedes affected vowel
2	secondary stress	MODIFIER LETTER LOW LINE	U+02CC	precedes affected vowel
(blank)	word boundary	SPACE	U+0020	separates words
.	period	FULL STOP	U+002E	pitch fall, pause
?	question mark	QUESTION MARK	U+003F	pitch rise, pause
!	exclamation	EXCLAMATION MARK	U+0021	raised pitch range, pause
,	comma	COMMA	U+002C	continuation rise, pause

You can always use the **PRN** control tag to indicate how to pronounce text by passing the phonetic equivalent to the engine. For information about **PRN** control tag, refer to Appendix D. Also note these general rules for using IPA Unicode in Visual Basic:

- Stress marks must *precede* the affected vowel.
- Any phoneme lacking a preceding stress mark is interpreted as unstressed.
- Blank should be used as a word-separator only.

For more information about IPA characters and speech recognition programming Unicode standards used in SAPI, see the following publications:

- *The Unicode Standard*, Volumes 1 and 2 (Addison-Wesley).
- *Phonetic Symbol Guide* (Pullum, G.K., Univ. of Chicago Press).
- *The Unicode Standard, Version 1.1* (The Unicode Consortium).

NOTE: This document can be found on CD # 2 for Microsoft Developer Network (MSDN) and website.

Appendix E

SAPI ActiveX Control Tags for Visual Basic Text to Speech

This appendix describes the SAPI text-to-speech control tags that can be embedded into your Visual Basic code to improve the prosody as well as application appropriateness of your own Visual Basic speech recognition programming computer synthesis text-to-speech translations.

E.1 SAPI Control Tags for Visual Basic DirectTextToSpeech API

Both the IPA phoneme character sets and corresponding Microsoft Speech API Unicodes are usually required in order to develop your own SAPI compliant speech engines. This also holds true for both vertical language dialect localization and horizontal professional lexicon and vocabulary file objects, both normally beyond expected skillsets of Visual Basic speech programming application software developers.

You should become well acquainted with all of the IPA phoneme Unicodes in Appendix C. Although you will not normally need them, just in case you have a very special or complicated speech recognition problem or need to create a very unique voice that can not be easily customized by simply adjusting VBSPEECH public constant defaults or SAPI ActiveX property settings.

However, for the majority of Visual Basic speech applications, and for most Visual Basic speech programmers, it is more important to be aware of the many SAPI Visual Basic voice customization control tags that are provided with SAPI 4.0 for use with SAPI ActiveX and DirectX speech controls.

In most cases, it is much easier and more efficient to use standard Microsoft speech engines and voices, and to simply apply conditional logic within your own Visual Basic code that loads the standard SAPI speech engines and voices, and then make very systematic discrete and specialized modifications to adjust SAPI Control Tags. These settings can dramatically alter such characteristics as gender, age, body type, or even behavioral attitude and demeanor of computer speech.

Some of the many SAPI control tags that can be used with Visual Basic speech programs in order to alter Microsoft SAPI standard voices used with standard SAPI speech engines, as well as most SAPI compliant vendor speech engines that fully support the SAPI 4.0 specification include the following, which are described in slightly more detail following this list within this Appendix.

However, in order to obtain more detailed information on usage of these available SAPI speech synthesis control tags for customizing voice properties you should refer to MSDN online documentation.

The following control tag specifications relate specifically to the most commonly used and adaptable SAPI computer speech synthesis for text to speech applications, the DirectTextToSpeech ActiveX control, however, it also applies in most cases to the properties that are available with all other Microsoft SAPI ActiveX and DirectX speech.

- **CHR** : Voice Character Specifications
- **COM** : Unspoken Control Tag Code Comments
- **CTX** : Set Conditional Control Tag Context Rule Source
- **DEM** : De-Emphasize Next Word (speak quiet)
- **EMP** : Emphasize Next Word (speak LOUD)
- **ENG** : Reference Different Local Speech Engine
- **MRK** : Book-Mark Point in Text (to select special engine)
- **PAU** : Pause X Number of Seconds Between Words
- **PIT** : Adjust Pitch Higher or Lower Per Hertz Parameter
- **PRA** : Set Max and Min Pitch Range
- **PRN** : Override Speech Engine to Accept a IPA Unicode String
- **PRO** : Override Default Speech Engine Prosody Until Reset Back
- **PRT** : Set Punctuation Rule Text Rules for Default Pause Delay
- **RMS** : Read Mode Standard Time Delay For Phonemes (sound out)
- **RMW** : Read Mode Standard Time Delay For Words (list out)
- **RPIT** : Relative Pitch Reset to Gender Age Speech Neutral
- **RPRN** : Relative Pitch Range Range to Gender Age Neutral
- **RSPD** : Relative Speech Speech Reset to Engine Speech Default
- **RST** : Reset to All Initial Speech Engine and Voice Defaults
- **SPD** : Reset Speech of Speech to Specified Words Per Minute
- **VCE** : Reset Voice to Other Chr Supported by a Speech Engine
- **VOL** : Reset SAPI Speech Volume Going to PC Output Speaker

E.2 SAPI Control Tag Usage for Visual Basic DirectTextToSpeech API

Any SAPI compliant vendor text-to-speech engine can usually translate individual words to speech successfully in your Visual Basic speech applications software, for SAPI DirectTextToSpeech or other controls.

However, as soon as any speech engine begins to speak a sentence, the perceived quality of its translation decreases because the engine cannot correctly synthesize human prosody for every PC sound system and speakers. This involves the voice inflection, accent, and timing of human speech as we humans commonly perceive characteristics such as gender, age, body type and emotional demeanor.

As a general rule, you should try to fit your applications within the most common ranges for whatever gender, age, body type and emotional demeanor that your are seeking to emulate for the optimum response of most users for your Visual Basic speech application. This should generically encompass any PC hardware or other software they are running within the range of common hardware and software you can expect your potential users to be running your Visual Basic speech software application with.

This section describes some critical control tags and their parameters that you can use to alter the nature of the computer generated synthetic speech that results from text file object input to your own Visual Basic speech programs.

You should be aware that all tags are optional except the bookmark (**MRK**) tag, which must be specified as the beginning and ending of a SAPI control tag section in your code.

Otherwise, unless you provide additional control tag specifications in the following lines of code the defaults for your current active speech engine and voice will not be changed unless you specifically request a change via control tags.

You must also be aware of the following rules for SAPI control tags:

1. Tags are case-insensitive. *For example, \vce\ is the same as \VCE\.*

2. Tags are white-space—dependent. *For example, \Rst\ is not the same as \ Rst \.*

3. To include a backslash character in tagged text, but outside a tag, use a double backslash (\\).

4. If the application has tagged text bit on and wishes to speak a filename, such as *"c:\windows\system\test.txt"*, then it can double backslashes (e.g., *"c:\\windows\\system\\test.txt"*).

E.3 Common SAPI Control Tag Usage Parameters for Visual Basic Speech

<u>CHR</u>

Chr=*string*[[,*string*...]]\

Sets the character of the voice.

Example: **Chr**="Angry"\

The default characteristic is "Normal," which produces a normal tone of voice.

Although the **CHR** tag is less specific than setting the inflection, stress, attack, and whispering qualities individually, it is easier to use and allows the SAPI speech engine more flexibility and potentially more conditional logic intelligence in its response.

Several characteristics can be specified in the same tag, separated by commas. Depending on its capabilities, an engine may not support all of the characteristics listed here, or it may support additional characteristics. Some common characteristics are the following:

"Angry"

"Business"

"Calm"

"Depressed"

"Excited"

"Falsetto"

"Happy"

"Loud"

"Monotone"

"Perky"

"Quiet"

"Sarcastic"

"Scared"

"Shout"

"Tense"

"Whisper"

COM

\COM=*string*\

Embeds a comment in the text. Comments are not translated into speech. They provide valuable documentation and annotations, just as with any other coding language comments.

But usual Visual Basic comments do not work, remember that you are within a special speech engine API localization not just VB alone.

Example: \COM="This is a comment."\

CTX

\CTX=*string*\

Sets the context for the text that follows, which determines how symbols are spoken.

Example: \Ctx="Unknown"\

This parameter passed to **CTX** can be one of these strings:

Context string	Description
"Address"	Addresses and/or phone numbers
"C"	Code in the C or C++ programming language
"Document"	Text document
"E-Mail"	Electronic mail
"Numbers"	Numbers, dates, times, and so on
"Spreadsheet"	Spreadsheet document
"Unknown"	Context is unknown (default)
"Normal"	Normal/default speech mode.

DEM

\Dem\

De-emphasizes the next word.

EMP

\Emp\

Emphasizes the next word to be spoken.

Example: the \Emp\truth, the \Emp\whole truth, and nothing \Emp\but the truth.

ENG

\Eng;*GUID*:*command*\

Embeds an engine-specific command that affects only the engine with the specified globally unique identifier (GUID). Subsequent engine-specific tags for that engine can omit the GUID until an engine-specific tag for a different Windows SAPI compliant engine is used.

MRK

\Mrk=*number*\

Example: Mrk=7500

When the text-to-speech engine encounters this tag, it notifies the application by calling the **ITTSBufNotifySink::BookMark** member function. Bookmarks have a DWORD range (specified in the dwMarkNum parameter of the **ITTSBufNotifySink::BookMark** member function), and the Mrk tag accepts a decimal representation. Bookmark number zero (\Mrk=0\) is reserved; a **ITTSBufNotifySink::BookMark** member function is not sent for bookmark number zero. Bookmark tags are inserted directly into the text sent to the engine when calling the **ITTSCentral::TextData** member function.

PAU

\Pau=*number*\

Pauses speech for the specified number of milliseconds.

Example: \Pau=1000\

PIT

\Pit=*number*\

Sets the baseline pitch of the text-to-speech mode to the specified value in hertz frequency.

Example: \Pit=90\

The actual pitch fluctuates above and below this baseline. Embedding a Pit tag in text is the same as calling the **ITTSAttributes::PitchSet** member function.

PRA

\Pra=*value*\

Sets the pitch range.

PRN

\Prn=*text*=*pronunciation*\

Indicates how to pronounce text by passing the phonetic equivalent to the engine.

Example: \Prn=tomato=tomaato\

NOTE: Cary Grant and Audrey Hepburn would have loved this one.

Using the **Prn** tag without specifying the word pronunciation (\Prn=text\) will undo the changes to the pronunciation; that is, it will return the word to the original pronunciation.

This tag is valid only for engines that support the Microsoft Windows SAPI compliant International Phonetic Alphabet and IPA Unicodes.

The engine should continue to use this pronunciation for the current text-to-speech mode and should store the pronunciation in its lexicon for later use.

If a lexicon entry already exists for a particular word, the **Prn** tag should be ignored for that word, so use carefully.

PRO

Pro=*number*\Activates and deactivates prosodic rules, which affect pitch, speaking rate, and volume of words independently of control tags embedded in the text. Prosodic rules are applied by the engine.

Example: **Pro**=0\

Prosody does not have a corresponding **ITTSAttributes** interface as speed and pitch do. If the engine supports control of prosody, use the Pro tag instead for more direct speech speed control.

PRT

Prt=*string*\

Indicates the part of speech of the next word.

Example: **prt**="Abbr"\

This PRT parameter can be one of these strings:

String	Description
"Abbr"	Abbreviation
"Adj"	Adjective
"Adv"	Adverb
"Card"	Cardinal number
"Conj"	Conjunction
"Cont"	Contraction
"Det"	Determiner
"Interj"	Interjection
"N"	Noun
"Ord"	Ordinal number
"Prep"	Preposition
"Pron"	Pronoun
"Prop"	Proper noun
"Punct"	Punctuation
"Quant"	Quantifier
"V"	Verb

For more information about the parts of speech, see VOICEPARTOFSPEECH on the MSDN online documentation or CD.

RMS

\RmS=*number*\

This control tag sets SAPI text input reading mode to spelling out each letter of each word, or turns it off. Not all engines support this tag, so an application can get more consistent results by normalizing the text itself and putting spaces between letters.

RMW

\RmW=*number*\

This tag sets reading mode to leaving audible pauses between each word, or turns it off.

Not all SAPI speech engines support this tag, so an application can get more consistent results by normalizing the text itself and putting periods between words.

RPIT

\RPit=*value*\

This SAPI speech control tag sets the relative pitch. The value for relative pitch is always 100 for original default pitch for a voice.

RPRN

\RPrn=*value*\

This SAPI speech control tags sets the relative pitch range. The value for relative pitch is always 100 for original default pitch range for any given SAPI voice.

RSPD

\RSpd=*value*\

This SAPI control tag sets the relative speed. The value for relative speech speed is always 100 for original default pitch range for any given SAPI voice.

RST

\Rst\

This control tag resets the engine to the default settings for the current mode, as though the mode had just been re-created or started.

SPD

\Spd=*number*\

This SAPI control tage sets the baseline average talking speed of the text-to-speech engine mode to the specified number of words per minute.

Example: \Spd=120\

NOTE: Embedding an **SPD** tag in text is the same as calling the **ITTSAttributes::SpeedSet** member function.

VCE

\Vce=*charact*=*value*[[,*charact*=*value*]]\ This SAPI control tag instructs the engine to change its speaking voice to one that has the specified characteristics.

The a SAPI speech engine voice characteristics change as though a new mode object were created (using that voice) and used.

The SAPI speech engine pitch, speed, volume, all revert to the defaults for the new voice.

If **ITTSCentral::ModeGet** is called, it will reflect the new mode. Characteristics are specified in the order of importance. The active SAPI speech engine selects a voice that most closely matches the characteristics specified at the beginning of the list.

The *charact=value* argument can be any of the following:

Language=*language*. Requests the engine speak in the specified language

Accent=*accent*. Requests the engine speak in the specified accent. For example, if language="English" and Accent="French" the engine will speak English with a French accent.

Dialect=*dialect*. Requests the engine speak in the specified dialect

Gender=*gender*. Specifies the gender of the voice: "Male", "Female", or "Neutral".

Speaker=*speakername*. Specifies the name of the voice, or NULL if the name is unimportant

Age=*age*. Specifies the age of the voice, which can be one of the values shown below

Style=*style*. The personality of the voice—for example: "Business", "Casual", "Computer", "Excited", or "Singsong".

The Description Parameter can be specified to any of the following:

Age string	Description
"Baby"	About 1 year old
"Toddler"	About 3 years old
"Child"	About 6 years old
"Adolescent"	About 14 years old
"Adult"	Between 20 and 60 years old
"Elderly"	Over 60 years old

NOTE: You should easily understand that along with **CHR**, the **VCE** Control Tag is one of the most critical to establishing a personality or age compatible reference with any special voice you want to emulate, especially such extremes as very young or old voices.

VOL

Vol=*number*\

This SAPI Control Tag sets the baseline speaking volume for the text-to-speech mode for your Visual Basic speech program.

Example: **Vol**=32768\

The volume level is a linear range from 0 for absolute silence to 65535 for the maximum monaural volume. The default is 65535. If you specify a value greater than 65535, the engine assumes that you want to set the left and right channels separately and converts the value to a double word, using the low word for the left channel and the high word for the right channel. For example, a value of 65536 sets the left channel to the maximum baseline speaking volume and the right channel to the minimum. Embedding a Vol tag in text is similar to calling the ITTSAttributes

Appendix F

Common Error Codes for SAPI ActiveX Controls

The reference error code information provided for each control in the Microsoft Windows Speech API in this Appendix includes a list of error values as well as the reserved name references that each of the categories of SAP speech ActiveX controls can generate if it fails.

These error reference names correspond to Public Constant names and values that have been listed earlier within the Visual Basic code that must be included in all of your Visual Basic speech program builds from the VBSPEECH.BAS file.

Although you can easily change default parameters via Visual Basic SAPI ActiveX control settings for any other type of setting in the VBSPEECH.BAS file, if any value differs from the default settings in the original VBSPEECH.BAS file for the settings that relate to errors they will be regarded as exceptions and not errors. This should be subject to either specific local error handlers within your Visual Basic speech program as appropriate or else will revert to general fail error handling.

In addition to these values, the higher level controls can generate error values that were actually generated by a lower level component.

You should be aware of this in case lower level Windows foundation class error handlers take an exception that was not anticipated by you own Visual Basic high level speech services program. If you were not anticipating errors or exceptions that did not occur on the PC platform that you had originally developed and tested your Visual Basic code on, if in fact your Windows Visual Basic speech software was not tested on a wide variety of PC hardware and software that it might actually be run on, it can result in a GPF crash.

In most cases, Windows SAPI 4.0 is rigorous enough that it can run on almost any platform past Pentium class microprocessors using minimum of Win95 with at least 32 meg and Soundblaster compatible sound board. But anything less than this could result in a variety of problems that may need to be diagnosed on an individual PC and user basis.

So one of the most important things for you to remember is that the error codes that you get back may not always equate precisely to error codes that you expect. So you must first of all confirm that the error codes you receive actually came from your high level SAPI and Visual Basic service requests rather than anything that may have conflicted with lower level Windows foundation architecture services according to the common error handling rules on MSDN online and CD.

For example, a low level Windows hardware driver audio-source object can generate error values that can be passed to a speech recognition object, and then to a Voice Command control. This passing of error values applies to all objects in the Speech API except for those provided by the audio objects, which are the lowest level of the API.

Just because you get an error value back with a corresponding name for a high level SAPI constant does not necessarily mean that was where the failure actually happened. It may have been a low level hardware error that happened and sent a value back to the last most recent active high level service before the failure.

So the critical first diagnostic is to look at any error value that is returned. You must decide if it looks reasonable compared to the values that you have loaded from the default VBSPEECH.BAS file or initialized by your own Visual Basic speech program error handler code then you can fix accordingly.

But if the values returned are outside normal ranges, or garbage, then you have a very good indication that there is probably no software compatibility problem, it is more likely to be a hardware problem instead.

In addition, due to the fact SAPI Visual Basic AcitiveX speech components are processed as local servers clients instead of as true in-process servers, it is possible for a speech object to generate an error value that does not map to any of the hexadecimal error values that appear in the header files.

This is because a system component has mapped the error value to an HRE-SULT by using the HRESULT_FROM_WIN32 macro. So if you receive a value that does not correspond to any of the documentation that you have from SAPI manuals or MSDN, it may be a hardware shut-down value or it may also be a value that you may need to translate accordingly.

If a speech object generates error values that do not seem to be in the OLE range, you should first of all try to strip off the bits added by the HRESULT_FROM_WIN32 macro, convert the error value to decimal, and then check for a non-OLE error value that matches the generated error value.

F.1   Most Common Valid Error Codes for SAPI Visual Basic Speech

The following potentially valid common error values may be generated by a speech program that is coded in Visual Basic:

Error value (hex)	Description
&h80070057	One or more arguments are invalid.
&h80004002	The interface is not supported by the object.
&h8007000E	There is no more memory.
&h8000FFFF	An unexpected error occurred.
&h00040806	The lexicon already contains information for the given word.
&h80040808	The buffer that is to receive the additional information about the given word is too small.
&h80040805	The string that contains the phonetic or phonemic transcription of the given word contains an invalid character.
&h80040802	The value that indicates the alternate pronunciation or meaning of the word is invalid.
&h80040801	The string that contains the word to pronounce contains an invalid character.
&h80040803	The given word is not in the lexicon.
&h80040804	The disk does not contain enough space to save the information to be added to the lexicon.
&h80040807	The buffer that is to receive the phonetic or phonemic transcription for the given word is too small.

In addition to the error values described in the preceding list, controls can pass error values generated by lower-level objects or calls to the Win32 API. For example, the Direct Speech Recognition control might pass an error value generated by the audio-destination object.

Most programmers will find it easier to learn how to use these controls by examining the sample programs that come with the Microsoft Speech API and Speech SDK.

It is a good learning experience to try to generate each of the types of errors by modifying the Visual Basic code in ways that you expect to get errors according to a test script and see what the results are for your own programs. It is also a good practice to define range filters in your Visual Basic error handler code that can allow you to selectively ignore, recover, or shut-down as you deem appropriate.

It is strongly advised that you start with existing samples that are somewhat similar to what you want to learn, rather than attempting to understand every method and property possible.

Many methods and properties are only used in very special or advanced circumstances that you may never encounter, so save time and start with examples from SAPI sample programs error handler code as models.

F.2   Error Codes for SAPI Visual Basic ActiveX Voice Command Control

The following errors may be generated by the Microsoft SAPI Voice Command ActiveX control for Visual Basic. These errors are very common to all SAPI speech recognition programming:

Error	Description
VCMDERR_CANNOTMIMIC	No command was found to match the input string.
VCMDERR_CANTCREATEAUDIODEVICE	An audio source object cannot be created for speech recognition.
VCMDERR_CANTCREATEDATASTRUCTURES	The internal data structures needed to build a grammar cannot be created.
VCMDERR_CANTCREATESRENUM	A speech recognition enumerator object cannot be created.
VCMDERR_CANTCREATESTORAGE	Space cannot be created in the database for the menu.
VCMDERR_CANTINITDATASTRUCTURES	The internal data structures needed to build a grammar cannot be initialized.
VCMDERR_CANTSELECTENGINE	A speech recognition engine cannot be selected.
VCMDERR_CANTSETDEVICE	The device identifier cannot be set into the audio source object.
VCMDERR_CANTXTRACTWORDS	The unique words needed by the engine grammar object cannot be extracted.
VCMDERR_INVALIDCHAR	There is an invalid character in the voice menu.
VCMDERR_INVALIDLIST	There was an invalid list passed to ListSet or ListGet.
VCMDERR_INVALIDMODE	No site exists, the site does not support this attribute, or the voice command object is already registered with a site.
VCMDERR_INVALIDWINDOW	The window is invalid.
VCMDERR_MENUACTIVE	The menu is currently active and cannot be deleted.
VCMDERR_MENUDOESNOTEXIST	The requested menu does not exist in the database.
VCMDERR_MENUEXIST	The requested new or temporary menu already exists in the database.
VCMDERR_MENUOPEN	The menu exists but has not been released, so it cannot be deleted.
VCMDERR_MENUTOOCOMPLEX	The menu is too complex to use.
VCMDERR_MENUWRONGLANGUAGE	The language is not supported by the speech recognition engine.
VCMDERR_NOCACHEDATA	There is no internal cache entry for this menu.
VCMDERR_NOENGINE	No speech recognition engine is active.
VCMDERR_NOFINDINTERFACE	The speech recognition enumerator interface does not have a Find interface.
VCMDERR_NOGRAMMARINTERFACE	No engine grammar object is available.
VCMDERR_NOSITEINFO	Site information to open this site is not available.
VCMDERR_NOTSUPPORTED	The function is not supported by the engine.
VCMDERR_OUTOFDISK	No disk space is left to write information.
VCMDERR_OUTOFMEM	There is no more memory.
VCMDERR_SRFINDFAILED	The speech recognition object could not find an appropriate mode.
VCMDERR_TOOMANYMENUS	There are too many active menus.
VCMDERR_VALUEOUTOFRANGE	The value is out of range.

As always, in addition to the error values described in the preceding list, controls can pass error values generated by lower-level objects or calls to the Win32 API.

For example, the Direct Speech Recognition control might pass an error value generated by the audio input object.

This can include both microphones and .WAV file inputs that echo back recorded speech. This is a particularly common problem for speech recognition error handling and error code diagnostics analysis.

F.3 Error Codes for SAPI Visual Basic ActiveX Voice Text Control

The following errors may be generated by the Microsoft SAPI Voice Text ActiveX control for Visual Basic. These errors are very common to SAPI computer speech synthesis and text to speech programming:

Error	Description
VTXTERR_INVALIDMODE	The text-to-speech mode is invalid, or the application has not been registered to use the voice text on the site.
VTXTERR_INVALIDPARAM	A parameter is invalid.
VTXTERR_INVALIDWINDOW	A window is invalid.
VTXTERR_NOTENABLED	Voice text is not enabled.
VTXTERR_NOTENOUGHDATA	The text stream has been rewound beyond the beginning or fast-forwarded past the end of the stream.
VTXTERR_NOTSUPPORTED	The dialog box is not supported by the engine.
VTXTERR_OUTOFMEM	There is not enough memory.
VTXTERR_QUEUEFULL	The playback queue is full.
VTXTERR_WAVEDEVICEBUSY	The wave device is busy.

In addition to the error values described in the preceding list, controls can pass error values generated by lower-level objects or calls to the Win32 API. For example, the Direct Text To Speech control might pass an error value generated by audio-destination object such as in the case of a speaker not ready or bad driver.

F.4 Error Codes for SAPI Visual Basic ActiveX Direct Speech Control

The following errors may be generated by the Microsoft SAPI Direct Speech Recognition SAPI ActiveX control for Visual Basic.

These errors are very common to SAPI computer speech synthesis and text for two-way speech and recognition integrated interactive response programming as is common for multimedia and game software.

The following errors may typically be generated by the Microsoft Windows SAPI ActiveX Direct Speech Recognition control:

Error	Description
SRERR_BAD_PRONUNCIATION	The pronunciation passed in is invalid. To be valid, a pronunciation has to be 1 to 100 characters long and should have valid IPA characters.
SRERR_GRAMMARERROR	Error in the grammar.
SRERR_GRAMMARTOOCOMPLEX	Grammar is too complex to load or to be activated.
SRERR_GRAMMARWRONGTYPE	This grammar type is not supported.
SRERR_GRAMTOOLARGE	Grammar is too large to load.
SRERR_INVALIDCHAR	Invalid character in a grammar or in a list.
SRERR_INVALIDFLAG	One of the flags is invalid.
SRERR_INVALIDINTERFACE	Invalid interface for notification.
SRERR_INVALIDKEY	Invalid key value.
SRERR_INVALIDLIST	Invalid list.
SRERR_INVALIDMODE	Invalid speech mode.
SRERR_INVALIDPARAM	Invalid parameter.
SRERR_INVALIDRULE	Invalid rule is activated.
SRERR_INVALIDWINDOW	Window is invalid.
SRERR_NOUSERSELECTED	No speaker was specified.
SRERR_NOTENOUGHDATA	Not as much data as anticipated; or, no longer has any digital-audio data because the object has deteriorated or the memory has been freed.
SRERR_NOTSUPPORTED	A function, link, archive, or something in a grammar is not supported by this engine.
SRERR_OUTOFDISK	Out of disk space.
SRERR_RULEALREADYACTIVE	The rule is already active.
SRERR_RULENOTACTIVE	The rule is not active.
SRERR_SPEAKEREXISTS	Speaker already exists on the current system.
SRERR_SPEAKERNOTFOUND	Speaker information not found in the current system.
SRERR_TOOMANYGRAMMARS	Cannot load the grammar because too many are already loaded.
SRERR_VALUEOUTOFRANGE	A value is out of range.
SRERR_WAVEFORMATNOTSUPPORTED	No wave formats supported.

In addition to the error values described in the preceding list, controls can pass error values generated by lower-level objects or calls to the Win32 API.

For example, the Direct Speech Recognition control might pass an error value generated by the audio-destination object, which may include the case not only of the PC speaker not being ready and enabled or a bad driver, or there is a conflict with another resource, including multimedia sound boards or .WAV files.

NOTE: For much more detailed error name labels and recommended values and usage for each individual SAPI ActiveX speech control, you should refer to the MSDN online documentation.

Appendix G

Windows Speech Recognition Software Vendor Web Links

This appendix section lists some of the most useful web address links for Windows speech vendors that should be helpful to every Windows speech application programmer. The categories of speech vendors are grouped as follows:

- Official Microsoft Speech Websites
- Major MS Windows Third-Party Vendor Websites
- Other Operating System Vendor Speech Websites
- Speech Developer Kit Vendor Toolset Websites
- Important Speech Industry Forum Websites

G.1   Official Microsoft Speech Websites

Microsoft Downloads Search Page

   www.microsoft.com/downloads

This is the best place to start to find the most current version of the free Windows Speech API (SAPI).

Microsoft Speech Technology Research Page

   www.microsoft.com/us/dev

This is the official site for the Microsoft Developer Network (MSDN) to get detailed SAPI online documentation.

Microsoft Speech Developers Network Page

> *www.microsoft.com/speech*

This is not MSDN but is the best site to find the latest about the Speech Application Language Tag (SALT) special working group, and other forum links and press releases for SAPI.

Microsoft Compatible XP Speech Headset Page

> *www.plt.getofficexpheadsets.com*

This is the official site for obtaining specs and ordering recommended audio voice input microphone headsets for the latest Microsoft XP speech user functions for MS Office 2002.

Microsoft Speech Technology Research Page

> *www.microsoft.com/iit/research/srg*
> *www.microsoft.com/research/srg*

These are the official sites for the IIT (Intelligent Interface Technologies) Microsoft Speech Recognition Group developing latest MS speech tools. This is the place to watch to find out more about upcoming new MS speech technology code-named their "whisper engine" (and about as secret as the sleath bomber was).

G.2   *Major MS Windows Third-Party Vendor Websites (Historical & Current)*

ScanSoft/Lernout&Hauspie/Dragon NaturallySpeaking™ Page

> *www.lhsl.com/naturallyspeaking*

This was the official site for obtaining specs and ordering both vertical speech software products and speech software development kits based on the popular Dragon NaturallySpeaking™ SDK and shrink-wrap. Notably, this popular product has had 3 owners in 3 years: Dragon Systems developed it, then sold out to competitor Lernout & Hauspie, then L&H sold out to scanner add-on vendor ScanSoft in late 2001 (so if you link to this site you may be taken directly to the new ScanSoft home page). The other thing to be aware of is that although ScanSoft acquired both Dragon and L&H, their big seller to date has been NatSpeak. Yet, L&H has its own very powerful and advanced third-party SAPI compliant SDK, named "RealSpeak", which is in fact one of the best of the litter if you may want to bolt SAPI to language translation tools.

The Original Dragon NaturallySpeaking™ Page

www.dragonsys.com

This is the original official site that started the Window speech revolution, and may not be around long after L&H sells to ScanSoft, but hopefully it will still have a pass-thru link for old-time's sake. Aat the time when this book was first published there was still a pass-thru page with some historical Dragon NatSpeak info, but it may be totally rolled up into the ScanSoft website same as L&H by the time this book is on the shelves. However, if in fact it disappears, you can check out the author's website for historical info about Dr. Baker and other founders of Dragon Systems, whose NaturallySpeaking naturally shook up the speech industry.

The Omnibus ScanSoft/L&H/Dragon NatSpeak OmniScan™ Page

www.scansoft.com

This is the site where most major speech software players ended up in their various mature embodiments.

The Original IBM ViaVoice™ Page

www.software.ibm.com/speech

This should be another walk down memory lane for pioneer speech recognition programmers, and knowing IBM they will not miss a trick to continue using the same address as a way to catch new programmers interested in adapting related IBM speech technology for use with SAPI 4.0 to 5.1 (+?). It is also interesting to note this is where to find the remnants of SRAPI, which are now called "SMAPI" (which is the Microsoft Windows compatible version of SRAPI).

The Omnipresent Kurzweil Technology Speech and OCR Page

www.kurzweiltech.com

Although both Microsoft and ScanSoft would be reticent to admit it, many speech technology historians as well as computer industry analysts regard Ray Kurzweil as the original inventor of both omni-font Optical Character Reader scanning as well as speech recognition programming. Ray was in fact a major contributor to both SRAPI and SAPI standard, and though not currently a leader, he could be again one day.

The Original Open Systems Speech Programmer's Page

www.att.com/aspg

Although AT&T is not really an MS/OEM, in the 'old days' they still had an OS competitive to IBM/OS2 and MS/DOS, but did not survive early Windows shakeout. Yet R&D at Bell Labs (now Lucent) preceded SAPI and in 2002 they introduced WATSON, a SAPI 4 based competitor to SAPI 5.

The Original Speech Programmer's Page

> *www.speech.be.philips.com*

This is not only the oldest website for pre-SAPI Open Speech Recognition API programmers, but has kept up with all the latest developments in speech technology thanks to Philips Electronics and their partners, and in 2002 they introduced a new line of multi-lingual Speech Recognition vertical software products for the new Euro Commonwealth, that automatically cross-translate English to French to German to Dutch.

The Current Leader in IVR Speech Programming's Page

> *www.intervoice.com*

Last but far from least, the up and coming leader in Interactive Voice Response (IVR) systems for speech enabled telephone menu technology is Intervoice, which has acquired nearly as many early speech technology start-ups as ScanSoft, including the well-respected Brite Systems. Intervoice has very strong strategic partnerships with both Microsoft and Intel, and is an early leader to accommodate MS Speech Server. Intervoice is also the leading Microsoft-certified speech technology training company and has several excellent courses that are recommended by Microsoft as preparation to apply for SAPI-certification. There is actually close strategic relationship between ScanSoft and Intervoice, under the watchful eye of Microsoft, and it will be interesting to see if they all remain independent, or a future merger is in the works.

G.3   Other Operating System Vendor Speech Websites

The Original "Other Windows" Open Speech Programmer's Page

> *www-speech.sri.com*

SRI is a highly experimental and cutting edge research oriented organization newly into the competitive vendor marketplace, but they are developing a UNIX and LINUX speech API comparable to SAPI 5 that also works on top of SAPI 4, and could make SGI and all Unix platforms truly open speech platforms.

The Original "Other Windows" Speech Programmer's Page

> www.apple.com/macos/speech

Although Apple definitely has their own OS, and it preceded both SAPI or SRAPI to get into speech recognition programming, it was experimental (and still is); and it is really not open systems OS speech.

The "Really Original Other Windows" Speech Programmer's Page

> www.fife.speech.cc.cmu.edu/sphinx

This is the Carnegie Mellon University speech lab (which is in fact actually the remnants of the old DARPA military speech recognition laboratory that developed all the "really original" computer speech software most of which ran on Crays. Now everything runs on Sun and SDI with Java implementations, and the U.S. military is slowly turning everything over the public domain with documentation and testing by CMU and Sun Microsystems. Nothing really classified or top secret in this anymore, but it is interesting historically for its impact on commercial public speech software development by IBM and eventually Microsoft SAPI, and there are rumors Microsoft is watching this site to get more creative ideas for the MS "whisper engine".

G.4 Speech Developer Kit Vendor Toolset Websites

Natural Speech Toolsuite Page

> www.naturalspeak.com

This is "NaturalSpeak" (not "NatSpeak", though it is a technology vendor that was originally a strategic partner of Dragon, and in fact is now a big reseller and OEM of NaturallySpeaking marketed by ScanSoft). It markets and customizes NatSpeak, Aurora and other SDK's for handicapped and disability access systems, and also integrates with "TAP", to convert speech (and attempted speech) to mouse or key entries.

Speech Studio Toolsuite Page

> www.speechstudio.com

The leading speech programming platform SDK toolset for SAPI and Visual Basic ActiveX controls.

Speech Solutions Toolsuite Page

www.speechsolutions.com

Another leading speech programming platform SDK toolset for SAPI and Visual Basic ActiveX controls.

Speech Wave Solutions Toolsuite Page

www.voicenet.ca

A cross-platform open systems SDK toolset for SAPI or SRAPI with its own controls for web speech.

SpeechActs Toolsuite Page

www.sun.com/research/speech

A true state-of-the-art open systems SDK for SAPI or SRAPI with Java standard for Unix Sun Solaris.

True Windows Open Systems Cross-Platform Speech Toolsuite Page

www.chant.com

CHANT is the leading speech programming platform SDK toolset that can support both SAPI and SRAPI for MS, as well as IBM Open Systems extensions for Microsoft Windows (a.k.a. "SMAPI") using Visual Basic ActiveX speech control with VB, C++, or Java.

Small Footprint Speech Toolsuite Page

www.fonix.com

If you are interested in using SAPI and TAPI in PDA or subminiature laptops using Windows CE, this is the vendor that can provide you all the value-added third-party SAPI tools that you need. Their FAAST toolkit can support embedded speech development for both TTS and IVR, from a variety of telephony platforms.

WAV ActiveX Extensions Toolsuite Page

www.research-lab.com

Dictation 2002, a WAVToText and TextToWAV SDK toolset with SAPI extensions which provides Visual Basic ActiveX controls that generate transcription text from downloaded or recorded .WAV files, or can generate .WAV files from text, which can be used to quickly create apps like VB Answer Machine.

G.5 Important Speech Industry Forum and Speech Research Update Websites

The Official Web Speech Standard Working Group Page

www.saltforum.org

This site is funded and sponsored by Microsoft, and there has been some criticism that it is independently duplicating the working group efforts of the following two sites combined. However, this is the official SALT (Speech Applications Language Tag) standard working group for Windows. One way or another you should expect as a Microsoft Windows speech programmer, you are going to need to be aware of SALT, and more than likely be using it to more than just spice up your speech apps in the future.

The Official Open Standards Speech Web HTML Tags Working Group Page

www.speecHTML.com

This is the "official" open systems alternative to Microsoft SALT working group to establish standards for speech HTML tags that are not dependent on Microsoft technology, and notably funded and sponsored by some of Microsofts OS business competitors, which explains why the.COM versus an.ORG domain.

The Official Open Standards Speech Web XML Dynamic Tags Working Group Page

www.voicexml.org

This is the "official" open systems alternative to Microsoft SALT working group to establish standards for speech dynamic XML tags that are not dependent on Microsoft technology. But it has a more austere and academic sponsorship that may enable it to more completely approach open systems as true.ORG domain.

A Website to Find the Latest Speech Technology News, Research and Industry Updates

www.speechtek.com

SpeechTek has an online magazine, hardcopy technical materials, and also sponsors some of the top speech industry conferences outside of COMDEX (and CTExpo, for that matter). Almost everyone who "speaks" SAPI stays abreast by watching (and "listening" to) SpeechTek.

A Website to Find the Latest Speech Technology News, Research and Industry Updates in Euro

www.voice-world.com

No, not misrecognized from "in utero", though the European speech technology industry is regarded by the American and Asian speech technology industry as still in its relative infancy (except for Russia and East Germany, but that is another book and not much related to SAPI). The Language Technology Forum (based in London) is however moving very rapidly to adopt and apply SAPI technology (faster than the French, which may possibly help give U.K. a bit more of an upper hand with the broader Common Market).

A Website to Find Best Places to See Latest Automated Universal Language Translation Demos

www.lang-tech.org

The European Forum for Speech and Language Technology (based in Paris) is widely regarded as the premier organization in the world for organizing conferences and trade shows on universal translators, some of which use SAPI related technology for voice entry speech recognition or multi-lingual computer speech.

The Website to Find the Best Places to See the Latest Windows Speech Tools Demonstrated

www.CTExpo.com

You can probably see all of the latest speech software application tools and SDK's demonstrated for Microsoft Windows as well as all other operating system platforms at Communication Technology fair, "CTExpo". (Hope to see you there!)

The Website that is Hosted by the Author of this Book

www.qualimatic.com/speech

And finally, the home site of the author of this book, Dr. Keith A. Jones. This website contains a wealth of helpful speech tools, utilities, add-ons, links and coding samples, as well as FAQ and contact information for the author. He gives speech recognition programming and software training seminars and also provides expert consulting related to topics covered in this book, as well as design, development and project management for Windows speech systems. You are encouraged to visit and leave your comments or suggestions for this or related books in this series, and the author is especially interested in proposals for joint development projects or technology ventures and R&D from like-minded computer professionals.

About the Author

Dr. Keith A. Jones is the author of numerous books on topics related to speech applications technology and software development, including the *Official Dragon NaturallySpeaking Programming Guide, Teach Yourself Speech Programming with Visual Basic in 21 Days, Software Test Engineering and Quality Assurance, Automated Software Quality Measurement, Automated Software Performance Measurement*, and others. He has worked as a software developer and technical systems analyst for such leading companies as American Airlines, Dun & Bradstreet, Nielsen TV Ratings, Ford, 7-Eleven, J.C.Penney as well as project manager and principal research scientist for EPA, FDA, NASA and most recently US Dept. of Ed., where he used MS Visual Basic and SAPI to develop Multi-Lingual Classroom speech software. He is a frequent speaker at technology user groups and a university lecturer, and the founder and CEO of Qualimatic Software, a high technology consulting firm that specializes in statistical pattern recognition and data mining as well as artificial intelligence software agents for web or embedded speech applications.